Austa Malinda French

Slavery in South Carolina and the Ex-Slaves

Or, The Port Royal mission

Austa Malinda French

Slavery in South Carolina and the Ex-Slaves
Or, The Port Royal mission

ISBN/EAN: 9783744738583

Printed in Europe, USA, Canada, Australia, Japan

Cover: Foto ©Suzi / pixelio.de

More available books at **www.hansebooks.com**

SLAVERY IN SOUTH CAROLINA

AND

THE EX-SLAVES;

OR,

THE PORT ROYAL MISSION.

BY MRS. A. M. FRENCH,

EDITRESS OF THE "BEAUTY OF HOLINESS."

"Verily I say unto you, Inasmuch as ye have done it unto one of the least of these my brethren, ye have done it unto me."

NEW YORK:
WINCHELL M. FRENCH, 5 BEEKMAN STREET.
MDCCCLXII.

CONTENTS.

INTRODUCTION vii

CHAPTER I.—PORT ROYAL.

Medical Sea—Bay Point—Hilton Head—Coast—Africans—Guilt—Self-implicated—Country—Contrabands—Faces—Hawks—Sea Birds—Manhood—Excited stare.... 13

CHAPTER II.—THE FIRST CONTRABANDS.

Plantation Boat—Consciousness of ungainly self—Sly, keen Observation—Secrecy—First Congregation—Concealed Sorrow—Life drawn out......................... 17

CHAPTER III.—THE LAND OF TEARS.

The Ship Atlantic—Feelings—Government—Kidnap—All eager—Aground—Supper—Song—White trash—Shoe Blacks and Rag Pickers—Whittier's Poem—At Port Royal 19

CHAPTER IV.—MEETING ON BOARD.

Sketch of Addresses by E. L. Pierce and Rev. Mr. French—Shock of contact with Slavery—Drivers—Evils remedied—Independence—Freedmen—Lash prohibited—Setting upon a Barrel—Parents restrained—Military punishment—Untried mission—Idle, roaming—Sensitive—Patronizing and real Friends—One interest—Doubt, dignity—The Acres of humanity—Excitement—Not adapted—Crushed Child—Cruel failures—Experience... 25

CHAPTER V.—LANDING.

Beaufort—Mist—Sandy streets—Foundations—Fires—Spirits—Desolation—Dr. Peck's home—Servants—Breakfast—Dr. Edwards' descendant—Vegetation—Buildings—Thrift—Robin—Slavery's echoes—Ghosts—Cradle—Mistress—Wholesale dealer—Innocents—God silent—Watering place—Dress—Expenses—Wine................. 30

CHAPTER VI.—FIRST CONVERSE WITH EX-SLAVES.

Reverence—Servant—Religious state—Silver—Daughter's sorrow—Field-hand—Drudge—Desire to see Masters—Free—Trusting—God able—School—Sabbath-school—Patience—Liberating Power—Presentiments........................... 34

CHAPTER VII.—BEAUFORT.

Slaves and Souls of men—Merchants—Every ship-mast—City of two centuries—Buildings—Gardens—Streets—Parades—Tide—Walls—Buildings—Suburbs—Monuments—Churches—Aristocracy—Quarters—Saint—Rags—Table—Visitors—Architecture—Dark faces—Turbans—Curses—Nonsense 37

CHAPTER VIII.—VEGETATION OF THIS LATITUDE.

Spirit of Slavery—Trees—Weeds—Sand—Live oaks—Cactus—Fragrance—Forests—No union—Beauty—Over-topping—Maples—Locusts—Respect of the Colored—Child's answer.. 41

CHAPTER IX.—GOVERNMENT'S TIME AND CLAIMS.

Honesty—Government tables—Writing—Dignity—Chinking—Dishonor—Edifice—Inequalities—Hard pressure—Scheme—Ark—Miriams—Rewriting—Awful subject—Faithful pictures—Poverty... 44

CHAPTER X.—CRUELTY REIGNS.

Voice—Birds—Horses—Cows and dogs—Aged women—Neber had but one—Children—Babies—Field-hand women—The dying boy—Heavenly Father take dis, I praise him—White father—Tea—Rags—Clean—Lady of luxury—Dehumanizing—Birds—Theft—Honest table—Millennium and slavery—Woman and punishment—Spirit of Washington—The murder—Massah's power over life—Loss of property a preventive?.... 46

CONTENTS.

CHAPTER XI.—THE MISSION TO PORT ROYAL.
Discouragements—Elevated by oppressors—Lies—Sold by Christians—Obstacles immense—No God—The two angels—New trophies.. 52

CHAPTER XII.—THE VACANT HOMES.
Sacred by events—Words—Relics—Sorrows—Tears 'nough to wash dis flo'—Tender for the absent—Rebellion—Occupied sadly in their behalf—No personal hatred—Sin and suffering joined—Reports of burning alive—Slavery a forbidden topic.... 54

CHAPTER XIII.—SLAVERY A SEALED BOOK.
Sealed to many within its precincts—Aggravated cases—Inured to hide feelings—Must tell strangers—Strangers deceived—The Senator's lady's story—Soldiers—Dark places—Law at South Carolina—Deception—Visitors—The padlock—From sun to sun—Sabbath—Reports of De Vesey's rebellion—Reading character—Tact—Indescribable—Sympathizing talk—Deaths—Proofs—Live but five years—Writers deceived.. 56

CHAPTER XIV.—SLAVERY A VICE.
Holds victims—Passions—Power gained by dollars at slave pens—Love of domineering—Shows—Fights—Horrify—Picture of Congressman—Treat Negroes long whippings—Chance for artist—Contempt dreaded—Virtues shrivel into vices—Child torturer—Victims—Life as nothing—Nation murderers or no slavery—Robbery—Discomfort—Intermarriages of relatives—Forty innocents—Reason given......... 66

CHAPTER XV.—SLAVES HELD FROM NECESSITY.
Kind opposed—Propitiating their demon—Both twilights—Massah broken-hearted—Ministers protest—Oder people—Missus pray to die 'for de war—Die—Thomas Jefferson imploring—Daughters sold, Harem—Coerced to Africa—Dr. Nelson—Tears—Years—Trying support at the North—Periodicals—Music—Pleading—Bosom of God.. 74

CHAPTER XVI.—BOND AND FREE SERVANTS.
Prison—Drive on in minutiæ—Abortive efforts—Lash not effective power—Northern lady—Southern—Bride—Testimony—Murder no one's business—Shirking......... 79

CHAPTER XVII.—FREE LABOR.
Remedy—Military—Cloudy future—Stating the case—Sudden development—Effects—Colored and White laborers—Begins at creation.................................. 83

CHAPTER XVIII.—HEART SERVICE.
Sweetness of being freely served—Driving—Dignified to be ruled by slaves—Life-killing states of mind—Meanest services—Bind to the bar of God—Weary fellow-sinner pleading—Scriptures—All imprecations—Thankfully beg—Slaves or life—Sew? or chase Negroes?—Be their servants—Two cases—First blessings—Servants when free—Imbruted Mistress—Whippings—Dr. Howe's account—Publicity...... 85

CHAPTER XIX.—SOUTHERN CHIVALRY.
Curse glancing and falling—Heaven fuller—Woman—Barbaric nations—Challenge to the world—Girls must marry—Affectionate race—Look admiration—No censure—Married in matrimony—Farther South—Avarice—Facts—'Lowed to drop hoe—Bring mud up from riber—Basis of slaveholders' dignity—Awful suffering—K's hand—Government dash hopes 92

CHAPTER XX.—INCIDENTS IN SLAVE WOMAN'S LIFE.
Case of the slave woman—Buried alive—Case of young girl—Mother dies—Mistress—Charities—Other punishments for the crime of not being able to work—Born in fiel'... 99

CHAPTER XXI.—RESULTS TO POOR WOMAN.
Where?—Under clods of the valley—Few old women—Exceptions—Image of Jesus—Marks of death—Graves—Greenwood—Martyrs.. 103

CHAPTER XXII.—WOMAN AND CIVILIZATION.
Field labor in Women and Civilization impossible—Never seen—Show on Sunday—Deference—Ambition—Perseverance—God hath arisen 105

CONTENTS.

CHAPTER XXIII.—CRUSHED INTELLECTS.
Crushed by blow—Heavy terror, stupefied—Instance—Noble driver—Suffering to serve others—Brain—Resurrection 106

CHAPTER XXIV.—THE INNER LIFE OF THE PIOUS.
Transformed—Judges—Seal of God—Sanctified—Heart-breaking—Noble government—Not sex, or woman considered, but color—Women drivers—Work faster—Desire to suffer with them—The people blamed—Voters responsible. 111

CHAPTER XXV.—THE GENIUS OF SLAVEDOM.
Treachery in everything—Spell—Wierd, confused feelings—Examine—Confusion as to all ownership—Illustration—Travellers—Lost power—Dishonesty recognized—Arabs 115

CHAPTER XXVI.—AVARICE OR POVERTY.
Parsimoniousness—Poverty—Barbadoes—Jamaica—Account-books—Servants—Good days—Oaths—Ministers—Weighing 118

CHAPTER XXVII.—EMBITTERED SPRINGS.
Religion a torture—Manhood—Philosopher—Contempt—Hatred—Separations—Avenues 123

CHAPTER XXVIII.—THE APOSTLES OF SLAVERY.
Preachers 'lowed nothing but for Massah—Dr. Nelson's Testimony—Worse than none—Curse—The owner—Minister—Dignity—Common sense—Mr. May's testimony—Dragging slave to death—Minister and son—Colored ministers—God in the soul—Humility 126

CHAPTER XXIX.—PRAYERS OF THE EX-SLAVES.
Effort to gain them—Force—Failure—Not suffered to lie down when sick—Voice—Mus' pray—Fort 133

CHAPTER XXX.—AMALGAMATION.
Follower of slavery—Strangers—Oberlin—Races separate naturally—Col. Johnson—Fervor—No shadow of amalgamation—Incident—Purity—Fitness—Outrages—Bleaching ground 135

CHAPTER XXXI.—OUT OF LYING.
Satanic—Harness shape of men—Live patriot—Cannibals—Call on Devil—Soldier's liberties—Child killed—Lincoln's portrait—Laugh 140

CHAPTER XXXII.—MANLINESS.
Foundation—Shame—Principles—Covered with welts—Whip mother—Little girls—Crime of sleeping—Sees Jesus—Coming—Master—Listening—Nobility—Sale—Who the least?—Disgraced?—Nearer than angels 145

CHAPTER XXXIII.—ENERGY OF THE COLORED.
Developed early—Hide in mud—Travellers—Superhuman—Thinking dangerous—Poisonous lizard—'Spectable—Coat—Wits—Peter learning to read—Washington. 153

CHAPTER XXXIV.—NEGRO QUARTERS.
All works belie the Negro—False light—Contemptible falsehood—Apartments—Great effort—Home—Pro-slavery visitor—Awful huts—Martyrs to Chastity—Torture—Furniture—Filth—Villainous darkness—Cast out—F. R. Association—Improvements—Altar for lash 159

CHAPTER XXXV.—PREJUDICE AGAINST COLOR.
Epithets—Impressible—Dr. Philip—Thomas Pringle—Beauty—Grace—Create expectations—England—Victoria—Moral standing—Deacons in tow—Cruelty at Donelson 166

CHAPTER XXXVI.—THE SOUTHERNER.
Character—Hospitality—System—Job—Paul—Less money—Gains—Yale College—Body-guard—Gives up—Gains—Ashamed of ancestors 172

CHAPTER XXXVII.—INNER AND OUTER LIFE.
Anguish quivers—Real life—Corn burn up—Emotion—Life not regarded—Hedges—Unintentional reproof—Des' sojers 176

CHAPTER XXXVIII.—THE TRUE DEBASEMENT.

Not self-righteous—Miracle—Woman's Testimony—Unblushing calumnies—Why excitable—Adepts—Curse—Crazy—Not look sorry—True virtue 180

CHAPTER XXXIX.—HEART CHASTITY.

Enigma—All cities—Purity—Counterfeit—Amazed—Virtue and vice—A language—Jewels—Soul God's—Aunty—Docility—Broadway—Sweet letter—Weak—False Coloring—Carousal—Wine—Task and whip for chastity—Delicacy—Disgust...... 184

CHAPTER XL.—NORTHERN CHIVALRY.

Opinion of Southern ladies—Standard—Concealed wounds—Wretched families—Maulne—Broken-hearted—Praying for death—President Madison's sister—Devilish power—Delusions—Moral power—England's emancipating—Malignity—Pure homes—Foulest slander—Licentiousness North—Heart agonies—Washington's saying 192

CHAPTER XLI.—THE TASK-MASTERS.

God-defying D.D.'s delegated—Law of South Carolina—400 lashes—Wish for death—Will—Baptist minister—14 pounds—Work—My physician—Warning—Lawful killing—71 offences punished by death... 206

CHAPTER XLII.—TRUTHFULNESS OF THE COLORED.

Serene Congressman—Colored woman—Hope come to bury me—Leave all with Jesus—Boy's caution—New Yorkers—Bostonians—Deep, mysterious—Men or books?.. 214

CHAPTER XLIII.—KNOWLEDGE OF THE COLORED.

Case supposed—Toussa..t—The chaplain—Quarrels—Exceptions—Sewell—93 freemen doing the labor of 225 slaves—Britons—Resemblance of monkeys—Rosseau—Lawrence—Dr. Tiedeman—Blaumenbach—Watson—Oaths—Sabbath—Thieving. 218

CHAPTER XLIV.—SHALL THE BOND GO FREE?

Wrong question—Deacon Davis—Is you loose?—Apprenticeship—Self-reliant—Barbadoes—Notables 240

CHAPTER XLV.—APPRECIATION OF ALL MEN.

Fondness—Popular heart—Caterers South—Merit—Humboldt—Wesley—Wilberforce—Aunt Mary—Moffat—Park 246

CHAPTER XLVI.—THE WASTE OF LIFE.

Patrick Henry—Overseers—Life and labor—Death in basket—All dead—Womanhood. 255

CHAPTER XLVII.—INGRATITUDE.

Instances of—Amo—Princess of Brunswick—Drs. Madden and Chamberlaine—Catechims.. 260

CHAPTER XLVIII.—IS WOMAN WOMAN?

Depression—Duped—Thousand-fold better than sang—A case—Sacrificing hands—Economy—Dr. Reed 266

CHAPTER XLIX.—ABSENTEES.

True Tyrants—D.D.'s villainous course—Cotton—Virginian—Massah kill, torture—Suicides—Nation 272

CHAPTER L.—BITTERNESS OF SLAVERY.

Channing—Temptation—Defy—All drivers—Slavery doomed—Boys trained—Officer—White trash...... 277

CHAPTER LI.—UNSANCTIFIED INDIGNATION.

Government—Tyranny—Liberty—Pulpit—Blasted Manhood—Features of Times—Pharisees—John Brown—Colonization—Jay—Wilberforce—McAuley—Hayti..... 284

CHAPTER LII.—HUNTER'S PROCLAMATION.

Rejoicing—Aunt—A man—Blessings on Hunter—Choristers—Land Transformed—Economy 804

CHAPTER LIII.—CAPTURE AND PASSAGE.

Africa—Dance—Home—Gustavus Vassa—Literary—Ellsworth—Baker—Lyon—Winthrop—Harlans—Lovejoys—Whittier—Colored 809

INTRODUCTION

Surely, there is a line of right somewhere; surely, there are principles of right necessarily eternal, since God is; surely, these principles cannot change; surely, circumstances, cannot reach or affect them; surely, there must be laws enforcing those principles; surely, as the principles are eternal, the laws cannot change; surely, they must have the strength of the Administration, as a pledge of their execution; surely, they must respect all beings alike, must apply to the minutest action. Surely, then, every action must be with, or against those laws, must compel their eternal approval, or penalty, every action calling upon the laws of eternal justice for the "well done," or the penalty. Surely that award, must be as eternal, as the sin, and those laws. Surely a Mediator makes no escape from them. He is not the minister of sin. He only makes obedience possible to us. He establishes, the law, dies! that we be forgiven, cleared of its past records, cleansed, and compelled to break it no more, through the power that death provides. All this adds awful weight, and dignity, to that law, renders disobedience an eternal insult, not only to the law, but to that Mediator, that tenderest grace, that costliest sacrifice. So that disobedience is an insult, not only to the law, which cannot forgive, overlook, or fail in penalty, but to that grace, that death, that offering of soul for sin. Surely, then, God, his law, his sacrifice, cannot be slighted, without full penalty. Surely that penalty must be exacted alike of each rational being. Man must be left free to break that law, else no free obedience could he render, from his not being free, or able to disobey. Evidently, when he knows that there is grace provided for him, and offered freely, and available, he is alone responsible for having that grace.

Inevitably, then, he stands upon one, or the other side of this law, is this moment condemned or approved, and every action at once ranges itself on one or the other side of this law, and by it, he is this moment justified or condemned.

God's own image is the sacredest thing upon earth, and man was made in it. But man is free to show how he will treat that image, perfectly free, or he could not be perfectly guilty. As he treats that man, that image of God, he treats God. Mortal cannot sever the oneness that exists between God and his own. It is an indwelling but more, it is an actual oneness, in one vital, spiritual life. God is then driven forth, tasked, beaten, killed. God is sold, bought, defiled. There is no escape. God is in that man or that woman, and you cannot put him out. Mortal cannot sunder that one life. He says, "Inasmuch as ye did it unto them, ye did it unto me." You do that to-day. Slaveholder, with its light you began anew to despoil God, or give freedom and liberty to that one. If he say voluntarily, being entirely free, "I will labor for you, for so much," and you accord freedom to him in every way, you are free from the penalty, the sin of compelling God. If you hold him, and pay him a thousand, yea, a million fold more, still you enslave God. It is not how you treat him, or how he feels, but do you hold him? He may do very little, but do you compel him? or virtually, or by influence? For if, in addition to robbing the body, you rob the soul, or mind, how much worse. If you can so influence a human being as to lead him to say, "I will be a slave;" if you can infuse that influence, what robbery of God! If that one actually prefer your service, you can make him legally free, so that you can lift your hand to God, and say, "I compel, enslave, no man. I do not enslave God in man. I do not insult God in his image, in the worst, nor in his actual presence, in the best." Is it not well to know what those laws ACTUALLY REQUIRE? You and I must stand alone, face to face, with these great truths, and facts, and God, and ETERNITY! Is there not a safe side?

THIS WORK is a fruit of sorrow, of duty clear, of adverse temptations great, of responsibility eternal, of hope in self, or in man little, of faith in God, as a grain of mustard seed. It is put forth, in the prolonged absence in the service of his brother, country, Maker, of him who has been the dear staff of thirty years, whose concurring convictions urge us on, in the work, whose judgment in regard to publishing different articles has saved our literary life, from most worry, wear, and care. For witnesses of the truth of the facts, we refer to different members of the mission, of the military, and civilians. In but one case, have later developments thrown a shadow of doubt. That is of the Congressman, whose father, it seems it was, who feasted upon the Mondays' whippings. We could take you, gentle reader, to the spot where it, and nearly all these incidents, occurred. With pain and shame have we recorded these things which, were the cause only removed, were better—or more honorably to our nation—forgotten. But something must arouse the ladies of the North, for if we can get the strong influence at the fireside right, all will soon be done. The object in this writing, and in the cuts, is to make deep, vivid impressions. We regret that we have served the cause of the Colored, so poorly, but cannot dishonor our sense of duty, by saying we could have done better, under all the circumstances. Parts of the work, have been stereotyped two months, which is an age now, upon this question. Still, pro-slaveryism is rampant, and the balances unsettled. Upon which shall preponderate, depends the future of this nation. Agonizing, may be our future remorse, in dark days, or in the dying! of our nation, unless the sweet whisper of the spirit is "You did what you could."

INTRODUCTION.

THERE IS HUMANITY, to appreciate, a great wrong, and that can be moved to compassion by a great anguish, by brave endurance, by perfect Christian patience; there are, everywhere, hearts that revolt against tyranny, cruelty, oppression; there is in noble man feeling for innocent childhood; for tender woman; there is sense of justice, of manhood. How can these principles, be mightily moved in the masses? for the Colored? How can the minds of many who imagine they understand slavery, be disabused, and brought to protest against the crime? Well intentioned, but faultering measures will not answer, now; none but the strongest, sternest, unselfishest. How can the masses be brought up to the noble holy work? Ah let them see slavery not in confused masses, odious from being so colossal, but in individuals, in facts—so we write, where even Elliot, Cheever, Stowe, Goodell, Jay, Douglass, have nobly written—sent home, by the Author of light, and love. The character of the candid man is not settled, or stereotyped. Best, noblest, philanthropists, may yet arise from the Border States, or even farther South, to bless their country! and race.

WONDERFULLY did God provide helpers for this precious mission. Some of the ablest of men in New York, Boston, and Philadelphia, gave their best powers, energies, and time, to this work. Ministers plead for it, people wept, prayed, and gave, for it; Government spread the strong, and now, most honored and prized, military power over it. They were required to be protective: they have been chivalrous, generous, brotherly. Captain Eldridge, of the Atlantic, laid us under eternal tribute of gratitude for his gentlemanly care and kindness, seconded by Government officers. From our first introduction to the Military, we have received the utmost chivalric and gentlemanly attention from them. On our voyage, Lieut. West would come down, and, standing in the aisle between our state-rooms, would call out, "Ladies, ladies! it will never, never do! for you to give up to sea-sickness so. You must come on deck. Come, come! get ready, and come out, and I will help you on deck." After repeated efforts, all finally reached the deck, where most took tea, engaged in conversation, reading, singing of many patriotic and Christian songs, then closing with prayer, a pleasant evening, which had otherwise closed most sadly and unwholesomely in our rooms.

The presence of Mrs. Senator Harlan was providential. Though recent sore bereavement, and delicate health, much influenced her noble husband, in consenting to spare her, still, her deep interest in the mission, excellent manners, and good sense, made her presence and prestige, of great value in its feeble commencement.

Of other beloved members of this mission we had spoken individually, taking Paul for a sanction of commendation, but, by request, we leave the pure white page, upon which all may read their humility and worth.

The kindness and fostering care, since our arrival of that excellent and able man, General Stevens, could not be surpassed; also so far as requisite of Generals Sherman, Saxton, and Com. Dupont. General Stevens, in his highly valued calls, was frequently attended by his lovely and most excellent lady, who, like her husband, ever manifested a deep interest. Nothing that was required to be done for our honor, comfort, or success, that his Aids: Provost Marshal Belcher, or Commissary Gregory, and other noble officers, could do, has been omitted.. In our feeble and persecuted mission, this attention we feel far more than we can express, and can only return our most ardent prayers. To appreciate this kindness, one must know all.

The following list of the first company, who went out under the auspices of the "Freedman's Relief Association," we give, regretting we have not later arrivals:

E. L. Pierce, Special Agent of Treasury Department; Rev. M. French, Agent of "National Freedman's Relief Association;" David Mack, Rev. Nathan R. Johnson, Samuel D. Philips, Rev. Isaac W. Brinkerhoff, William T. Clarke, George B. Peck, Daniel Bowe, Edmund Price, Frederick A. Eustis, John D. Lathrop, James E. Taylor, Drury F. Cooper, William E. Park, Robert N. Smith, Edward W. Hooper, Edward S. Philbrick, Henry H. Cowdery, Wm. C. Gannett, George H. Blake, Dr. James P. Greves, Prof. John C. Zachas, John T. Ashley, Dr. A. Judson Wakefield, James F. Sisson, George C. Fox, Isaac W. Cole, James W. R. Hill, James H. Palmer, John H. Brown, Lyman Nolton, Albert Bellamy, David F. Thorpe, T. Edwin Ruggles, James M. F. Howard, Francis E. Barnard, Dr. James Waldock, Richard Soule, jr., Leonard Wesson, Dr. Chas. H. Brown, Ninian Nivin. LADIES.—Hon. Mrs. James Harlan, Mrs. Walter R. Johnson, Mrs. Elizabeth B. Hale, Mrs. Mary Nicholson, Miss Susan Walker, Miss Mary A. Donaldson, Miss Hannah Curtis, Miss Elizabeth Peck, Miss Mary A. Waldock, Miss E. H. Winsor, Miss M. Hale, Mrs. A. M. French. Thus far the mission is a PERFECT SUCCESS.

AS TO FUTURE WARFARE, in this holy cause, let us all say in the words of Rev. E. P. Lovejoy—whose AUTOGRAPH we here give—editor of the "Observer," Alton, Ill., in his LAST ADDRESS BEFORE MARTYRDOM! to the pro-slavery mobs, thirsting for his blood: "As I shall answer it, to my God, in the great day, I dare not abandon my sentiments, or cease in all right ways to propagate them."

SLAVERY IN SOUTH CAROLINA

AND THE

EX-SLAVES.

CHAPTER I.

PORT ROYAL.

Oh, for a world in principle as chaste
As this is gross and selfish; over which
Custom and prejudice shall bear no sway,
That governs all things here, shouldering aside
The meek and modest Truth, and forcing her
To seek a refuge from the tongue of Strife
In nooks obscure, far from the ways of men!
COWPER

AFTER four days of sea and sky, with the medical treatment of the former, and the varying moods—all ending in smiles—of the latter, we arrived off Bay Point, a seeming thin line of white sand, curving out into the sea and looking as if the next wave would erase it. Below, in the far distance, is Hilton Head, crowned with its fort, and looking in the distance like an immense brickyard, with awnings stretched over parts of it. But now, six weeks later, it has a long pier extending into the river, a fine large hospital crowns the shore, and with new buildings, and many more erecting, it looks quite freedom-like. Between these places is Port Royal Inlet, the mouth of Broad River.

The semicircular coast looks from the ship, to be of three terrace lines. First above the blue waves is a bank of snow-white sand of several feet; next, a grey belt, composed of the bare and even trunks of the standing pines, of twice the height of the sand-shore; and, above these, the green pine-tops, rising to twice the height of the trunks, in a clear feathery line, against the fine sky; an oppressive beauty, quiet, sameness, however, being the general effect of the whole. You look with strange feelings upon that coast. You think of the cargoes of poor Africans who have gazed upon it for the first time, as you now do, with not a hope, an aim, a friend, having already taken, in the awful hold of the slave-ship, their first lessons from the southern missionaries, stealing even a false Christianity. You think of those poor fugitives who have, in so many ways, dared those guilty waters—guilty waters, we say, for everything, even nature itself, seems becoming guilty. Why else have the sea and the earth swallowed out of sight their tears and blood, conniving against them with man? As you gaze, and gaze, and think, the weird Spirit of Slavery comes to greet you—a vitalized reality—and cooly takes possession of you, of mind, fancy, feeling, as if they were an old habitation, and haunts you, through every change, and every department of your residence. Just now, she is tauntingly singing in your ear, "Land of the free, and home of the brave," or "Hail Columbia, happy land." There steals over you the feeling that you are passing under a great cloud of accumulated wrongs, in which you seem mysteriously implicated, the vague feeling that you yourself have done something awful, somewhere in the dim past. You say, Who am I? and assure yourself that, for twenty years, you have been in the head and front of the offending against slavery. But who has done it? My country. And is not my country myself? But I could have done no more that I can see against it! could I? Let's see. You try to think of instances, once mountainous, in which you have suffered, in mind, estate, reputation, and more deeply in affections, in opposing this sin. But they are suddenly and strangely dim, in the dark overshadowing of the mighty wrong. You can scarcely recall them. "Yes," you admit, "I am a part of my country, and I in it, and with it, have done this. I! who had so long considered myself, with mine, almost martyrs to opposition to this awful wrong. We! at last, not innocent?" Yes, so it is. Every effort should have been far, far, more strenuous. Look at those poor "contrabands" in that boat! How plainly they show, that not an effort to crush the manhood, yea, the grace of God! out of them, has been spared. And the awful robbery of all, except what the soul grasps and holds, in spite of the Master, can never, never, be compensated for, with many of them life is waning. The garment of invisibility seems dropping from all forms of cruelty. Slavery is written upon the dark line between every ripple, into which the bright protesting wave, after a moment's resistance, subsides. Slavery is written upon the shore, the trees, the sky, the air. You see it in the faces of these men coming on board. Is it because you look so queer, and excited, and guilty, that they do? The enormous black hawks, with their screams, seem to be its very spirits. No wonder they caw, caw, over this land—mean vultures, waiting for blood.

You look for the beautiful white sea-birds, so constant in all your voyage; they are now far away in the distance, just skimming the open sea that looks toward freedom. You wonder that good and true men dared to alight upon these shores when slavery was in full bloom. You do not wonder that, seeing they came and remained, they usually parted with their fancied manhood here. You seem tempted to lose confidence in man, in yourself, in God. How could he by whom every violet is individually clad, suffer such evils so long? No wonder that the dwellers here could not speak anywhere upon any topic without babbling of slavery. The sprite would not let them, but threw, and threw, it into every cauldron, stained every thought, and fancy, and feeling with it, by a degree men cannot pass. We have found it inconvenient enough for twenty years to be possessed of an abolition zeal; but it was nothing to a slavery sprite, even under her broken reign. Our company, or the impressible, too, have an excited stare. Yes, they are all enduring those peculiar feelings of which we have since heard so much, yet which words cannot paint. It seemed like passing into a land of horrid dark dreams, or dim memories of the agonies of centuries. Now, from this moment, every one must be more or less, a man. It is inevitable. These are positive influences, you must rise or sink under them. Every one's sense of right and wrong must here, be vitalized, or blighted.

CHAPTER II.

THE FIRST CONTRABANDS.

"He shall judge the poor of the people. He shall save the children of the needy and shall break in pieces the oppressor."
—PSALM lxxii., 4.

THE first contrabands we saw, were six men, in a "plantation boat," alongside our good ship.

"How differently they do look from our Colored people!" said one.

Yes. Intense endurance, long gazing after something that never came, shame, gloom, and despair, have left upon those poor faces their distinct and iron impress, over which the veil of hope is now thinly drawn. Besides, a vivid consciousness of ungainly self, of deficiency in dress, manners, and respectability of appearance, the bitter doom of the slave is now upon them. They do not look up, or converse among themselves, except by stealth, though long in waiting. Yet one can see in them, a sly, keen observation of everything, and that they are inured to pain and patience, also to self-control and secrecy, the eye being habitually dropped to conceal thought.

Never, we may here premise, can we describe our feelings on seeing the first congregation of these poor ex-slaves. The deep lines of fatigue, and sternly concealed sorrow, the patient, compelled composure of face—the evidence of long, resolute efforts at pious resignation, still severely tested by the clouds hanging over their future—the loving, confiding, yet keenly scrutinizing gaze at the minister—the effort to look as if they did not wonder whether or not he would say anything about their liberty—the willingness to be comforted, yet the dire heaviness of soul—yet in some, deep trust and triumph in God, and dwelling in his pure love, was evident—all these, with the appearance in most that the very life of their bodies, minds, and souls, had been drawn out of them, by extreme, hopeless toil—the knowledge that I, or almost the same, my beloved country, had so, so! wronged them: all these things overwhelmed the heart; and when, at the close of an excellent sermon, we were asked to sing

"There is rest for the weary."

how did our soul praise God, that for them there is a heaven, not under the administration of man—a heaven of rest and bliss ineffable.

CHAPTER III.

THE LAND OF TEARS.

"Rob not the poor because he is poor; neither oppress the afflicted in the gate; for the Lord will plead their cause, and spoil the soul of those that spoil them."--PROVERBS xxii., 22, 23.

Our noble ship, the Atlantic, is now nearing South Carolina. With what throngs of mingled feelings and solicitudes do we approach it! To hear, see, feel, all new, with this poor people, so late in bondage, now free, but with the imperfect, political sense of right, standard of duty, or at best, the inefficiency of this national government, hanging over them, as a dark cloud of possible enslavement. But surely a government cannot commit a crime for which it executes citizens, namely, enslaving the free, and as slaveholders have not now power over these people, who has? Government? Who will say that government holds them, except to protect them as citizens, to require of them, as of all citizens, subjection to law, and to military law, when necessary for their and the general weal, and to receive from their labor a compensation for providing for them? Then, they are free, and must remain so, unless this government can kidnap, which cannot, of course, be thought of. Our Government will not defile itself with that villainous work. Never! Never!

But we are at last, having parted with our noble Atlantic, and nobler Captain Eldridge, on board a transport that plies Beaufort River, expecting to be in Beaufort in three hours, and thus have time to prepare for the holy Morrow. All are eager, anxious for the work, and now, to get the best views of the plantations we are to pass, and whose land in the distance looks scarcely higher than the waves. When, lo! "aground!" So we pocket with various degrees of patience and charity, the mistake, or treachery, as many think it, and pay a high price for a "secesh" supper, and leave the table with anything but dear remembrances, unless for the price.

But darkness comes on. The third or fourth table laid in the only cabin, is cleared away, the boat, and the situation is dis-cussed, at least, and in one knot sacred song commences. As we come to sing

"His soul is marching on,"

members of our company look on with various shades of approval; and sundry boat, and other officials, look daggers at us. But it is evident that the last believe, or at least fear, it is all true. Others hear with wonder, first among whom are "white trash," of whom we here see the first specimen, and compared with whom the shoeblacks and rag-pickers of New York are kings in manly bearing. They are listening, half scared, half gratified, half mystified; yet, seemingly for the first time, they wear a countenance that does not seem to ask pardon of every one for ever having been born, or even presuming to exist. Did slavery do nothing but so unman a large class of citizens, by crushing financial oppression, vigilant contempt, and blasting tyranny, that surely were reason enough, in every noble mind, for its being forever put away, at whatever cost. For what is money to manhood, in a republic? You never see such cringing Uriah Heeps, among the toilers of the North. Never! But of these again.

A minister, by request, read the following, from the nation's, yea, humanity's poet, Whittier, composed, perhaps, on these very waters:

AT PORT ROYAL.—1861.

BY J. G. WHITTIER.

The tent-lights glimmer on the land,
    The ship-lights on the sea;
The night-wind smooths with drifting sands
    Our track on lone Tybee.

At last our grating keels outslide,
    Our good boats forward swing;
And while we ride the land-locked tide,
    Our negroes row and sing.

For dear the bondman holds his gifts
    Of music and of song;
The gold that kindly nature sifts
    Among his sands of wrong;

The power to make his toiling days
    And poor home-comforts please;
The quaint relief of mirth that plays
    With sorrow's minor keys.

Another glow than sunset's fire
    Has filled the West with light,
Where field and garner, barn and byre
    Are blazing through the night.

The land is wild with fear and hate,
    The rout runs mad and fast
From hand to hand, from gate to gate,
    The flaming brand is passed.

The lurid glow falls strong across
   Dark faces broad with smiles;
Not theirs the terror, hate, and loss
   That fire yon blazing piles.

With oar-strokes timing to their song,
   They weave in simple lays
The pathos of remembered wrong,
   The hope of better days—

The triumph note that Miriam sung,
   The joy of uncaged birds;
Softening with Afric's mellow tongue,
   Their broken Saxon words.

SONG OF THE NEGRO BOATMAN.

Oh! praise an' tanks! De Lord he come
   To set de people free;
An' massa tink it day ob doom,
   And we ob jubilee.
De Lord dat heap de Red Sea waves,
   He jus' as 'trong as den;
He say de word: we las' night slaves,
   To-day, de Lord's free men.
      De yams will grow, de cotton blow,
         We'll hab de rice an' corn;
      Oh! nebber you fear, if nebber you hear
         De driver blow his horn!

Ole massa on he trabbles gone,
   He leeb de land behind;
De Lord's breff blow him furder on,
   Like corn-shuck in de wind,

DE PROMISE NEBER FAIL.

We own de hoe, we own de plow,
   We own de hands dat hold ;
We sell de pig, we sell de cow,
   But nebber chile be sold.
      De yam will grow, de cotton blow,
         We'll hab de rice an' corn ;
      Oh ! nebber you fear, if nebber you hear
         De driver blow his horn !

We pray de Lord he gib us signs
   Dat some day we be free ;
De Norf wind tell it to de pines,
   De wild duck to de sea ;
We tink it when de church-bell ring,
   We dream it in de dream ;
De rice-bird mean it when he sing,
   De eagle when he scream.
      De yam will grow, de cotton blow,
         We'll hab de rice an' corn ;
      Oh ! nebber you fear, if nebber you hear
         De driver blow his horn !

We know de promise nebber fail,
   An' nebber lie de word ;
So, like de 'postles in de jail,
   We waited for de Lord ;
An' now he open ebery door,
   An' trow away de key ;
He tink we lub him so before,
   We lub him better free.
      De yam will grow, de cotton blow,
         He'll gib de rice an' corn ;
      So nebber you fear, if nebber you hear,
         De driver blow his horn !

So sing our dusky gondoliers;
   And with a secret pain,
And smiles that seem akin to tears,
   We hear the wild refrain.

We dare not share the negro's trust,
   Nor yet his hope deny;
We only know that God is just,
   And every wrong shall die.

Rude seems the song; each swarthy face,
   Flame-lighted, ruder still:
We start to think that hapless race
   Must shape our good or ill;

That laws of changeless justice bind
   Oppressor with oppressed;
And, close as sin and suffering joined,
   We march to fate abreast.

Sing on, poor heart! your chant shall be
   Our sign of blight or bloom—
The Vala-song of Liberty,
   Or death-rune of our doom!

                        ATLANTIC MONTHLY.

CHAPTER IV.

MEETING ON BOARD.

" For the oppression of the poor, for the sighing of the needy, now will I arise, saith the Lord. I will set him in safety from him that puffeth at him."—PSALM vii., 5.

A LARGE meeting was held, wherein E. L. Pierce, Esq., Government Agent, and Rev. M. French, Agent of the Freedman's Relief Association, addressed the band of fifty-four persons, who go out upon a nobler errand than that of the Mayflower. A nobler errand, we say, not nobler messengers; for while they of the Mayflower went for themselves, their posterity, their principles, these, or some of them at least, came solely for others, and a despised, degraded, peeled race, too; a race which, under the benign and unrestrained influence and power of the morality, the virtue, and the religion of American slavery, has sunk as low as man can sink man. Then, because so degraded, so stultified, so dismantled, they are most heartily and implacably hated! All this we prove by facts in subsequent chapters.

But surely the more sunken they are, the more noble, God-like, is the work of serving them. To lose self in such a work and purpose, in a principle made dearer than self, or rather life, is surely true greatness. In such a work, no one who cannot stand alone for humanity, for principle, for God, can do anything. No one who must have the multitude with him, or a majority, or even companionship, out of God, can stand with him on this mount of transfiguration, or hear his voice in this Patmos.

But to the meeting. Our first shock of actual contact with slavery, was on hearing Mr. Pierce say to those who were going to plantations: "You will find on each a driver, or head Colored man, who measures out to each Negro a peck of corn a week. You will act your best judgment about increasing it, and adding other food. No marked change can be made at once, without probable injury to them. You will find they have no regular time for meals, each eating as he can. They will be found filthy, and some even vermined, and must have time given them, and be taught to take care of themselves. All these evils must be met and remedied in the most wise, kind, and quiet manner. New garments must be paid for in their labor, to cherish in them feelings of independence." He hoped they went from the broadest humanity—a humanity not to be quenched by any repulsiveness, untidiness, or stubbornness in those they came to benefit. "You go to freedmen," said he, "to elevate, to purify and fit them for all the duties of American citizens. You go to be their friends, counsellors and protectors. The government is to be parental. The lash is prohibited. Some cases of discipline must arise, but shutting up, or setting upon a barrel, has been found sufficient, in all cases. Parents are to be led to punish their children, when it is necessary, but in more cases to be restrained, as severity is all they know, or are used to. Any indignity to woman, by some few base soldiers, is to be zealously guarded against, and will meet, as we are assured, with the most condign punishment from military authorities here. Those who have been led astray, are not to be looked upon as those who have had more light and different influences." These, with a large number of economical regulations, were dwelt upon with great talent, precision, and sympathy of heart.

Rev. Mr. French, the next day, among other remarks, said, "Ours is, indeed, a new, untried mission, the final results of which may decide the fate of the poor slaves, and through them, of the nation. To do our work, and do it properly, requires such wisdom as God only can give. You will find the Negroes of the plantations, in some cases, idle, and roaming about—husbands searching for their wives, parents for their children, sold from them. All possible facilities must be afforded them in this sacred work. Order must be established, industry, tidiness in personal habits, as well as in their dark and miserable cabins, secured, and all, when age or health will allow it, must have immediate employment. They will receive you as friends, but they will not only carefully weigh your words and actions, but they will try your spirit. They are sensitive, acute observers, and readily distinguish between a patronizing friend and a real one. To have an influence over them, you must first convince them that yours is a brother's hand and heart. Under the old system, there was a constant strife between master and slave, each guarding jealously their own interests, productive of evil only to either party.

"First prove to them that their interests are yours, and you will acquire power to elevate and improve them. They are more or less in doubt as to their future condition, and will inquire earnestly your opinions. You may not feel assured of their liberty by any action of the government as yet, still I believe He who overruleth all things, has now decreed them FREE, and FREE FOREVER [applause], and that events will soon prove it. It is this conviction that gives warrant, dignity, as well as sacredness to our mission.

"Going, with this conviction, you can sow the good seed of knowledge and all improvement, in strong faith for a harvest. Obstacles, confusion and delays, or slowly manifesting signs of improvement, will not discourage such laborers. Some have desired a lease of the land, and wanted the Negroes to cultivate them. We desire a lease of the broad and long neglected acres of humanity, and the land thrown in, to develop this humanity.

"You ask me if it will be well to assure them of their freedom. We should do all things as wisely as possible. It may be best to tell them, that we believe they are free, and that now they have an opportunity to prove to the world whether they are capable of self-government and support, and general respect, or not—that we have come to render them all possible aid—that the government and the North, generally, desire the experiment to be successful, but still, much will depend on their own efforts.

"The former system led to involuntary overdraft upon the physical man. The excitement of free labor, if the people are what we believe they are, will require an increase of food, to avoid injury from overtasking. So peculiar and great is the work before us all, that a true fitness can be obtained for it only by divine grace, and in the field itself. Some of us may find that, though we have come with honest intent to do a good work, we nevertheless are not adapted to it, and had better retire and give place to others. To leave in such a case, should be regarded as honorable.

"Under the slave system, the people having the evil of their natures developed, every look and act of their Master tended to impress them with a sense of inferiority and degradation. Let any parent pursue a similar course with a lovely and promising child, and it would not be long before that child, in its little crushed heart, would assent to its own degradation, give way to the worst passions, and seek the worst company. We have known some such sad, cruel failures on the part of parents. Watch for good, and when the tender plant appears, cherish it. Approve judiciously of every good thing. Chide for evil, sparingly and sympathizingly. Lead them to be encouraged, even from failures. Experience of any kind may always be turned to good account in some direction.

"They have a religious experience deep in the heart, learned in the school of toil and sorrow, which possesses great value to them. Any lack of appreciation, or especially any contempt manifested toward their religious opinions or feelings, will wound very deeply. In some of the deep things of God, we may learn from some of them. We have come from different sections of the country, with differences, no doubt, in creeds, but it is hoped that we shall be so united in heart and effort, as to secure perfect unity in the mission, and the greatest possible good to these poor people."

CHAPTER V.

LANDING.

ARRIVING at last at Beaufort, at twelve, on Saturday evening, Dr. Peck, an excellent Baptist minister, and who was the first missionary on the ground after the desertion of Beaufort, was soon on board, and exchanging salutations through the ceiling; he kindly invited us to his house on the following morning. Accordingly we were stirring early, and in the mist which dimmed the outlines of encircling shores, and filled every space and corner of wharfs, streets, and porches, we commenced our wade through the sandy and narrow streets, like all in Beaufort, except a very few blocks, minus sidewalks. Truly, "the ways" of these arch-rebels "were movable," their foundations sandy and slippery. We plod up the bank—for the original features of mother earth are not impudently obliterated here by gradings, as in Northern cities—we pass by old dwelling-houses, bakeries, etc., till we emerge upon an open street, with Beaufort River upon one hand, and tolerable residences upon the other. We pass where years ago there must have been fires, whose spirits yet exult upon arches, chimneys, steps, walls, and eyeless windows. What desolation! Not a person have we met, or even seen, excepting two frizzly headed white boys, peeping out of a bakery window into the mist.

"Here is our home," said Dr. Peck, and we enter a house a century old, at least, with porches new, and one tier of rooms comparatively new, into the upper of which we are ushered. This, with modern windows on three sides, the never-failing large wardrobe, the piano, bookshelves, sofas, cheerful ancient fire upon the hearth, floor of snowy whiteness, and, far more, the genial Christian welcome, seems a refuge from dreariness. Soon the neat, turbanned, and low courtesied servants came in, and laid breakfast, of fine coffee, mackerel, potatoes, and butter and bread. Our host, Dr. P., is of the most dignified and gentlemanly bearing, his fine blue eyes, ample forehead and snowy locks, and earnest expression, all speaking the great, tender Christian minister. His daughter, the great-great-great-grandchild of Dr. Jonathan Edwards, and of Thomas Hooper, and seeming worthy of her noble lineage, and three fellow-travellers, complete the circle. Our windows, on this sixth of March, look down upon orange and lemon-trees in full leaf, and their pure white buds just bursting, a large rose geranium, whose leaf covers our hand, oleanders budding, roses in bloom, and much other shrubbery. Still, the aspect is that of sterility. Singular! such growths out of a bed of sand, where poor grass and sickly weeds strive vainly for eminence. The outbuildings here, as everywhere, struck us as most decrepit, dozing in all manner of queer attitudes; fences, poor at first, abused and aged. In short, all the never-failing signs of lack of thrift, and interest in slave laborers, everything askew and ill-placed. Dr. Peck, however, has been here some weeks, and given freshened appearances.

Hark! The scream of a bird smites our ear. "A robin," says one. "That can hardly be a robin, surely," said we, though aware of the fact that while the plumage of birds is finer, their notes are coarser, in these latitudes. "Yes. What an excited harsh note! Can it be from our position on the bay-looking river, or is it from the strange nervousness of our soul, or system, in this land of horrid visions of cruelty and sin? Yes; it is a robin, our favorite bird,—the second note proves it. But it seems screaming over the desolations here. Yes, it shrieks slavery, and the distant shores reëcho it—the rising tide whispers it—the morning breezes sigh it—yonder pines talk mournfully of it—the wind, now strengthening, roars it. The ghosts of cruelty seem gliding about the room, and perching upon the book-shelves, sofas, piano, wardrobe, cradle. Yes, cradle, for that sacred thing is here! It is high and elegant, and so provided that the stinging insects of slavedom should not reach one babe; while another, because darker, is thrown by the Christian mistress into the irresponsible hands of the worst of men, under the influence of the worst passions, intensified and licensed by drink, avarice, and licentiousness, almost invariably. The mistress, though she honors the worse wholesale dealer, scorns to speak to this man of all sin. But she throws these innocents, and helpless girls into his irresponsible power, and God is silent. It matters not that it is done by the hands of another; she, the cause, is responsible, and scorns not to live upon such gains. Slavery does not and cannot anywhere exist without this, for no family will, or does, keep the increase. The mistress, too, must go to a watering-place, take a journey, have new furniture, or new dress, and her faithful, trembling, agonized servant's child must be sold to pay expenses; and that, after she had voluntarily promised her, over and over, she would sell—"no mo'! no mo'!" Or, perhaps, mean appetite calls, and "they sell a boy for a harlot, and a girl for wine," as is proven by yards, toppling down houses, lanes, stables, and garrets, being almost literally paved with wine bottles, which led an officer to remark, "These Southerners loved three things. Negroes, wine, and religious magazines." But all the magazines we saw, built them up in the sin of slavery, by silence, and by conveying thereby the assurance, that they might be holy with it. What a disgrace to their editors were those magazines, kicking about the yards, cellars—or rather arched spaces under the houses—and gardens! What a work, for one who calls himself a man, and for eternity!

CHAPTER VI.

FIRST CONVERSE WITH EX-SLAVES.

> He is one to whom
> Long patience hath such mild composure given,
> That patience now doth seem a thing of which
> He hath no need.   WORDSWORTH.

FIRE being now kindled in another chamber for us, we soon had our first privilege of speaking and listening to an ex-slave, as she came in, courtesying, to attend upon us. She seemed in good heart, tidy, and to have great reverence for the good doctor. Being asked of her religious state, she immediately glided into conversation respecting her mistress, her sorrow at leaving Beaufort, her hatred of the North, her silver, her daughters, but, above all, the wonder, over and over, expressed that she herself had never been a field-hand,—"neber!" This marvel was on account of the great riches and expectations of her mistress. And the wonder, scarcely less, was, that she had not been a common drudge, but "a mos' 'spectable servant in a mos' 'spectable family," all whose honors and wealth seemed to add to her own dignity,—in short, to be ner own.

"You would be glad to see them?" said we, animatedly.

"Oh, no, Missus! don't want to see them, neber, neber! No, mo'!"

"You feel free, then?"

"Oh! Missus, we's trusting and praying the Lord Jesus Christ for dat. He is able—we knows he can—we can do no mo' but trust him. Oh, Missus, chil'en all go to school now—all; and all go to Sabbath-school, ebery Sunday, ebery one Sunday. We's praise de Lord for what we do got, and trust him to be free.".

"What do you pray for about this war?"

"God bless! God bless! we must ask God first how to pray. BELIEBERS HAS NO COUNSEL IN ALL DAT JUDGMENT. You say: 'Lord, now show me de goodness, show me de meanness.' You pick and choose none for judgment. If you don't born ob God, don't know. Mr. Lincum hab de Christian heart. Presiden', dear presiden" good man ob God! Oh! we pray for God, add to him knowledge, wisdom, guard him, crown him! I lef' ol' mas'rs all to de Lord. I know de Lord by his word. Whosoeber beliebs him, on de right hand ob him."

"How do you pray for your old masters?"

"I ask de Lord: 'O Lord! look down 'pon de ignorant dis'bedient servants. Grant thy blessing, dat dey may see dat dey hab done wickedness.' I lef' dem all wid de Lord."

"Do you think they are awful sinners?"

"My dear missus," [raising his hands,] "all dat 'tween deir soul an' God! I was wicked gen'ration, stealin', lyin', dis'bedient, in de woods. You chain me to de tree—I bruise de tree. God hab mercy, I cry. Now I not sin; I gentleman! filled wid de Spirit ob God.— Walk in de spirit ob holiness now. Mas'r sell all, wife an' chil'en. Put de debil in me! Nor food for eat for two days, work hard all de time. Say: 'Please gib me one pint ob corn! one pint!' No! I get to de cubboard, eat some. Congress say: 'Wicked nigger!'— 'Stealin' nigger!'" The testimony of the superintendent and preacher was, that this was an excellent man and an excellent Christian.

This sentiment, reiterated from every one—from the devout with deepest uplifting of the heart and hands, and, even from the comparatively thoughtless, reverently, is most touching, and often brings tears. In short, were we obliged to describe the spirit of the ex-slaves by one text, it should be,—"We trust in the Lord Jehovah, for in the Lord Jehovah is everlasting strength."

Poor crushed and peeled race! While they honor, serve, and reverence the good man, their eyes are unto the Lord, their expectation is from Him, and they look with such a chastened, patient quietness, upon everything that is doing, for or against them, as touches all hearts most deeply. The most devout seem to see a hand you cannot see, to hear a voice you cannot hear, to feel a liberating Power approaching you cannot feel.

CHAPTER VII.

BEAUFORT.

"How much she hath glorified herself, and lived deliciously, so much torment and sorrow give her: for she saith in her heart, I sit a queen, and am no widow, and shall see no sorrow.

Therefore shall her plagues come in one day, death, and mourning, and famine.

And the merchants of the earth shall weep and mourn over her, for no man buyeth their merchandise any more.

The merchandise of gold, and silver, and precious stones, and of pearls, and fine linen, and purple, and silk, and scarlet, and all thyme wood, and all manner vessels of ivory, and all manner vessels of most precious wood, and of brass, and iron, and marble,

And cinnamon, and odors, and ointments, and frankincense, and wine and oil, and fine flour, and wheat, and beasts, and sheep, and horses, and chariots, and slaves, and souls of men.

And the fruits that thy soul lusted after, are departed from thee, and all things which were dainty, and goodly, are departed from thee, and thou shalt find them no more at all.

The merchants of these things which were made rich by her, shall stand afar off for the fear of her torment, weeping and wailing,

And saying, Alas, alas, that great city, that was clothed in fine linen, and purple and scarlet, and decked with gold, and precious stones, and pearls:

For in one hour so great riches is come to naught. And every ship-master, and all the company in ships, and sailors, and as many as trade by sea, stood afar off."—REV. xviii. 7, 8, 11–17.

ON the Atlantic coast in ever traitorous S. Carolina, is Beaufort, Búfort, or Bófort, as it is variously called by the Colored, a name contracted from "Beautiful Fort," erected by the French, in the sixteenth century, on the Beaufort river, four miles below, toward Hilton Head.

It is an ancient and drowsy town, or city, of over two centuries. Its business was mostly done on the river street. Its buildings, with porches and arbors, stand in military line and gravity, along the fine bank. Its old houses, sitting among the newer, in a gentle curve, upon these fair waters, like aged mothers, among pert, elegant and ambitous daughters, all seem in profound repose. Its alleys, walls, garden-walks, creep blindly along, feeling their way amid tangled shrubbery, neglected flower plants, and aged trees. Its streets, of either deep sand or turf, say, "It is impossible that real life, either in business or pleasure, ever animated them." The splendid parades and grand music of the military, the roll of drum, the universal gallop of the many mounted officers, seem only to rouse the faintest and doziest of echoes, and to stir the still air for an instant. The tide creeps languidly, hesitatingly disputing territory with the broad shores of white sand, but, like freedom, always in the end, triumphant, and some houses seem, having started, to stand pondering whether or not to fall. Most public buildings and walls show very imperfect building, and with suburbs, long neglect. In short, "slavery is written upon everything in such a look of shiftlessness," as a Philadelphia lady remarked. Nearly all marble monuments in the churchyard, for instance, are covered with singular black mold, which need only be removed once a year, to be kept away. Fences around graves, intended for ornament or defence, contain the dead limbs, trunks, rubbish, and leaves of years, and filled with weeds and rank, poisonous vines and briars, seem fit dwelling-places for reptiles; but some have been carefully kept. Marble monuments, when composed of several pieces, are falling apart, and showing their hypocritical brick hearts, while a few scared flowers seem lifting their lone heads as if to apologize. In the ancient churches, and graveyards surrounding them, nearly everything slants at every possible angle. Nothing is quite upright, as if in punishment to man for not being so. Beaufort is, in short, a complete specimen of slaveholding aristocracy. The showy mansion, the miserable slave "quarters," scarcely a place but has somewhere the tell-tale of poverty; or if not of that, certainly of most contemptible avarice or inefficiency. For instance, one mansion, with costly empannelled parlors, has back-floors slanting, back-stairs tottering, and "quarters" floorless, the deep white sand having become black and nauseous. Yet in this hideous place, every iota for the splendid table was cooked. The poor Colored woman, a saint of God, said, "I used to had to work till after de secon' crowing, den I would jes throw my bed on 'at kitchen table and sleep till mos' light, caus' I have to do task fo' I get breakfast." To one who has seen the pile of black rags, the poor slave calls his bed, and can imagine it, upon the only kitchen table, comment is unnecessary. But of course visitors were too well bred ever to look toward the kitchen, or take its odious breath.

Impressions, upon entering church here, were the most shocking—a den of thieves—a den of thieves—rings and rings through our mind in spite of all effort to the contrary. Everything conspires to heighten the impression, the high, square, angular, spindling pulpit, with its prickly teeth-like finishings is of black, the small trimmings covered with gold leaf; iron and gold, fit emblems of the ambition of most of those, who worshipped tyranny and mammon, here. In the galleries above the high, awkward fronts, rises, first, a cloud of dark faces, then, a cloud of turbans, high, and large, mostly of modest purple and white muslin, very clean, very stiff, and artistically put on. Poor race, how long have they sat there, to be edified by "cursed be Canaan:" "God made you for servants;" "He is a respecter of persons."

But now what an audience! Noble military, from the able and excellent General Stevens, to the common soldiers, in full dress and most dignified and reverential aspect beneath the folds of our sacred star-spangled banner, fill the place, and in all about five ladies are present, and from the holy man of God, goes up the prayer that all oppression, and slavery, may cease and liberty, righteousness, and love prevail. Oh it was magnificent, soul-thrilling! Still, the lies, there spoken seem to be yet reverberating, through the oppressed atmosphere. How has manhood here been crushed, how has childhood been embittered, merely because the skin was darker. Was ever such nonsense heard? to say nothing of the wickedness.

CHAPTER VIII.

VEGETATION OF THIS LATITUDE.

> That delicate forest flower,
> With scented breath, and look so like a smile,
> Seems, as it issues from the shapeless mold,
> An emanation of the indwelling life—
> A visible token of the upholding Love
> That are the soul of this wide universe.
> BRYANT.

VEGETATION, too, is singular. Even that seems to partake of the spirit of slavery. Trees, luxuriant, but misshapen, gnarly, ill-tempered, shade struggling blades of grass, and sickly weeds pushing up vainly amid sand, which forbids free development. The live-oaks look like uncommonly crooked limbed and overgrown apple-trees in general appearance, in town. But aged ones in forests, are like elms with many trunks, and one we saw, is estimated to be thirty feet in circumference. The orange and lemon trees are scraggy to the ground, and surrounded with shoots. But the rich enamelled leaves are beautiful, as are those of the fig-trees, which hide beautifully the most unsightly trunks and the crookedest of all limbs, as by one glossy apron. The streets are lined with the prickly pear cactus, its bloated tongues bristling with stings. But as sweet buds are beginning to crown them, so may not the beautiful buds, blossoms, and fruits, of liberty yet adorn, and honor, and flow from the tongues of former residents here, which so long shot forth little but stings and venom. The fragrance of the gorgeous flowers is delicious but stupefying. The forests in winter have an exceedingly tangled, untidy aspect, from the sameness of the color of the moss, a parasitic plant, with the trunks and limbs. But as April wears on, and the foliage becomes heavy, the contrast of the green crown of leaves above the limbs, with the long silver-grey fringes of moss below, hanging in tassels of from one to three yards in length, is beautiful, and waving from the tree-tops, which meet and arch over the roads, forms an overhanging bower of great beauty.

Still though there are here luxurious and stately growths, there is not as yet that hearty union of all plants in growing together, which in the vegetable world constitutes true beauty. Every splendid thing seems to overtop something which dwindles under its influence. How different from our maples, under whose fostering shadow the grass grows more thriftily, though our locusts, we must own, seem like some people, only to show their greatness by the number of things they minify. It is pitiful, to see the respect of the Colored for the fenceless flower-gardens. Truly, the foot does tread them down, even the foot of the poor and the steps of the needy. Singular, too, that they never pick flowers—excepting the spruce beau, a peony or rose, to ornament his hat for Sabbath!

Observing this a long time, we at last said to a child:

"You do not pick flowers for yourself, though you select such a pretty bouquet for me. Does your mother tell you not to?"

"Yes, Missus."

"Why?"

"Because I do not want them."

As other children made me the same answer, word for

word, doubtless that is precisely what their mothers told them. But a white child would have said: "She says I do not want them," if it were remembered at all. Do you see the difference of disposition?

CHAPTER IX.

GOVERNMENT'S TIME AND CLAIMS.

Honesty, even by itself, though making many adversaries
Whom prudence might have set aside, or charity have softened,
Evermore will prosper at the last, and gain a man true honor.
           TUPPER.

But the honest and conscientious reader—for there are such yet, and some even who live at government tables—says: "How could you, sent and rationed by government, honestly spend time to write this book?" This requires an answer, for which we must, in advance, beg the reader's pardon, if it be undignified. But honesty is worth more than dignity, and many could no sooner appropriate a quarter or dime from government's purse without rendering an equivalent, than from yours, gentle reader. Then to justify this appropriation of time to writing, which honesty, conscience, and love of the precious work, might seem to have demanded, should be used otherwise; we must say we were from the commencement of this mission, as the "chinking" which tried to be used in filling all ungainly, unoccupied spaces, and though often in comparative dishonor, thus consolidating the splendid parts into a solid edifice, and in that way really serving and effective, just in proportion as it is ready to be used or not used, crus outside or inside, up or down, concealed or revea .ording as the wants and inequalities of the splendi .rials around it demand.

But as chinking comes to hard pressure invariably, our strength was mostly spent early each day, thus leaving abundant leisure, if not quite the same mental vigor for writing.

Now, pray do not understand us as setting up a claim to " disinterested benevolence," for this scheme, having originated, as to earthly agency, in the brain of our own Moses, he having led this band of Ladies to this Red Sea, it was all important that it be crossed rightly and successfully, carrying the sacred ark unharmed. And it was, praise God. Our Miriams are already shouting victory on the hither side, while the pro-slavery host, their wheels already dragging heavily, are thundering on to the ingulfing, that they proudly and madly demand and defy. But the demands here forbade our going to New York to attend to publishing, so the manuscript, prepared in great haste, from urgent necessity, in the opinion of many, goes from here before an indulgent public, without rewriting. We have not aimed at smooth and elegant writing. The subject is too awful, too sacred, for polished periods. We only ask to draw faithful pictures—would they were more vivid! Oh, the contemptible poverty of words, smothering, hiding, what they would depict!

CHAPTER X.

CRUELTY REIGNS.

> My grief is all within;
> And these external manners of lament
> Are merely shadows to the unseen grief
> That swells with silence in the tortured soul;
> There lies the substance. — SHAKSPEARE.

THE voice of cruelty resounds here. This morn the blackbirds scream of it. The large crows that crown every dead tree-top, caw, caw, it. Horses, lean and weak, as well as cows and dogs, speak it in their poor eyes. Aged women, found on plantations, leaning on staves, are saying, shivering: "Oh, Missus, I so col'; I got no clo's but dese."

"What, no petticoat?"

"No, Missus, neber had but one, dat gone."

Children, and even infants, are sadly inured to rigid self-control, and when obliged to weep, run away to hide it; babies attended by those not much older, to the injury of the body, mind, and heart, of both, all proclaim it. No time, strength, patience, or heart, for sympathy have the poor "field-hand" women. They all have little feeling at the death of one, because all want to die who would, by grace, have the tenderness to feel.

On the corner of the next lot, lying upon a few rags on the hearth, too weak to cry, is a child of six years, in a dying state, from consumption or neglect. One of our ladies, on a second visit, said to the woman:

"You said that was your child. Is it?"

"No, ma'am; my sister's."

"There, I thought you told me wrong. You must take it up and bathe it, using some of this nice healing soap. We have brought all clean clothes and a bed" (a large clothes-basket filled with nice straw, and covered with soft cloths).

"Can't wash him; mus' go fo' rations."

"You must wash him; he is suffering so."

"I'll do it when I come home."

"You must do it now; we cannot leave until you do."

"I won't let my baby cry, and hold that big nigger."

"Only think how you speak, and he cannot live two days. How will you feel when you see him dead?"

"I feel glad, Missus, glad! Heavenly Father take five my children, I glad! I praise him! If he take dis too, and my own one child, all I got, I praise him" tears running down her poor face "'cause so much trouble."

So bitter, bitter! had been her poor life!

"But you must take care of him while he lives, else it is sin; you must wash him and put on these clean clothes; then we will put him in this clean bed. What ails his little head?"

"Maggits, ma'am, maggits."

Our sister, with uplifted hands, ran out and home to get remedies, we enforcing and superintending the washing.

"She shouldn't call'd my own poo' baby names," said the poor woman, big tears rolling down her thin cheeks.

"She did not; you misunderstood her. We are as tender of your own child as of this one; but yours is well, and it will not hurt it, so much, to cry a little."

"Yes, ma'am, it will; it will kill it"—having a weakness, as it proved.

The little sufferer's hips were raw, nearly skinless, yet there it had lain on the hearth and floor, upon a heap of coarse moss, from the top of which the small wet rags had been pushed off, and the floor under which, as we took a long stick and poked them out in the sunshine, looked as for a long time wet.

We said to the poor woman: "We pity you more than we blame you. We keep our sick little ones as clean as this dear little one is now; but we do not have to work in the field as you always have to do. Still, you want to learn to do things right, don't you?"

"Oh, yes, Missus, I do, 'deed I do!"

Dear sick boy, whose white father is probably advocating the beauties of slavery, Abraham's bosom received him in two days!

Looking into the basin on the hearth, we saw the tea given her the evening previous, a week's stock, all steeping and black, with an iron spoon in it. One would not think it possible that a woman could be so destitute of domestic knowledge. But we must do the poor woman the justice to say that her rags were all as clean as possible without soap, as many of them had none to wash with, her bed being a pile of rags, a bushel in size, laid upon a shelf, ready to be strewn upon the floor at night.

She will be attended to. Still some would have us sit in northern parlors, with hands folded, to entertain some caller, or even slaveholder, and let this, and a thousand other such instances, pass.

Said we last evening to a lady of wealth and luxury, of our own city, "What would induce you to leave this work, and go home?"

"Money would not do it," she replied.

So all feel, grudging themselves the needful rest, but each sure that the other is overdoing.

It has got to be a truism: "We may get sick in the work, but we cannot get tired of it."

But we merely named this instance in speaking of cruelty. As we returned to our dear Mission home, a most excellent Boston lady said: "It is not the whipping that is so awful. No; it is the dehumanizing influences of slavery that are so horrible, so horrible!"

But yet, is there not beyond, peace, liberty in the world? See, beyond the croaking, the cawing, the screaming of these birds of slavedom, in the blue distance down the river, is the beautiful white sea-bird, with unexcited mien and glistening wing, moving in gentle undulations, strongly, quietly and joyously. May not that bird, living not upon carrion or theft, but upon the pure, honest table that God hath spread in mid ocean, typify the sweet spirit of liberty, hovering near these shores, preparing to bless master and slave alike? Certainly, if the millennium does come, slavery must first cease. We think of the poor woman who occupied this home, this chamber, whoever she was, and who probably left it with so many tears, as many had to be carried to their carriages, crying, "My punishment is greater than I can bear!" We think how she would rest here with free laborers, serving her as heartily as they do us. Yet, let either of these, our good servants know that we had bought him, and seven devils would instantly take possession of him. Then we would be obliged to begin the vain attempt, with Satan to cast out Satan, if the spirit of liberty, of the revolution, of Washington, may be called Satan. Ah, this system has been upheld by cruelties unimaginable!

Every face, everything, bears the impress of it. In this dark land, torture has been a science, perfecting for long, long, weary years. A woman, found in a far worse case, if possible, than the foregoing, had a sister slave sick. Her master and a relative swore they would "cool her fever," and together they ducked her, keeping her under the water to the very point of strangulation, and

in the effort to do so, broke two bones; then they took her out and left her, and at evening she was found dead.

It is perfectly evident, from the incidental remarks of slaves upon plantations, that they always felt that Massah had power over their lives, and death has been the commonest of threats.

"Loss of property," one cries, "is a preventive." Then, if so, why do men lose fortunes in every other way to gratify passion? Yes! and when they fully believe and know they are bartering heaven for a few moments' indulgence. We had determined, as far as possible, to avoid description of sufferings, for adequately to do it is impossible. Accordingly, no instance is given but to illustrate some principle. Still, many instances are pressing upon our mind, as important to the true picture of slavery here. It is perfectly evident that these slaveholders thought their works would never see the light of liberty, or be reported from a free press, else they had done far otherwise. One year since, we could not have said all we must, or perhaps, should not have thought it duty. But they have shown out their true character, and now these facts are patent here. We sincerely regret, and blush for shame, that we must speak so of our own countrymen.

CHAPTER XI.

THE MISSION TO PORT ROYAL.

>   He did bring
> Life's warm affections to the sacrifice,
> Its loves, hopes, sorrows, and become as one
> Knowing no kindred but a perishing world,
> No love but of the sin-endangered soul,
> No hope but of the winning back to life
> Of the dead nations, and no passing thought,
> Save of the errand wherewith he was sent
> As to a martyrdom.   WHITTIER.

NEVER was a mission commenced under greater discouragements. A race to be elevated by the same people that had so long oppressed them—confidence to be inspired, in those of whom they had heard every lie that the heart of man could fabricate—in religion too, our only weapon that had riveted their chains, yea, bound their souls to be and have nothing here, that they might thus fulfill the curse, and gain heaven at last—loaded with the odious teachings, and more odious or harder borne blessings of the apostles of slavery—seeing thousands of their oppressed kindred, sold in the streets of Beaufort, under the ownership and sanction of prominent Christians—mothers screaming for their poor babes, until they reached, and were shut into the boat—to inspire hope for despair, confidence for such gloomy experience, and foreboding—courage for mean, timid compliance—industry for hatred of labor, intensified by every influence from infancy, knowing only the toil without the joy of work—to teach self-control to those weak of purpose from long tyranny—to produce self-reliance in those who had never known the luxury of providing for one's own—to call forth tenderness in every relation, where only brutality had been prompted—to impose the decencies of family customs in living, eating and worshipping, upon those so debased in habits and utterly irregular—in short, to lead up the mount of self-denial, and all goodness, those enfeebled by every influence, indulgence, barbarism and stimulus, resorted to by those who hoped thereby to improve their stock, or increase the number of "head" of slaves—an admitted fact,—all this was surely a work of such magnitude as can hardly here be conceived. But there is no measuring or describing the curse. And shall the perpetrators escape judgment in this world, or in that which is to come? He who says this, says, "there is no God." But, speaking of this mission, religion—true, pure, honest, undefiled religion—can do the work. She hesitates not, but longs to commence it, and for new trophies to the precious cross of Christ. None but the Christian could undertake the real work; yet *he* can, and love it too, above life itself. Nothing but faith and love, those two blessed angels, can lead victoriously through every impossibility, bridge every gulf, soar over every mountain, and lead up to God! to obey and honor him, in habits as well as heart. But for all this, it is in its full power, far more than adequate.

CHAPTER XII.

THE VACANT HOMES.

Both honor and Christian sympathy must lead one to speak tenderly of a home, in the absence of those who long loved it—of homes, made sacred by births, and loves, and sufferings, and holy vows, and marriages, and piety, and deaths. A deserted home! and that an aged one. What scenes have transpired within these eloquently dumb walls—what words spoken, what reliefs felt, what sorrows endured! In one instance, as a poor Colored woman was washing the floor, she looked up, and in their peculiar, soft, chastened, pensive manner and voice said, "Missus, der's ben tears 'nough shed in dis room by nigger girls to wash all dis flo'," and casting her beautiful eyes wistfully all around, went quietly at her work again.

But still we feel very, very tenderly for the absent, for who shall cast the first stone? So far as we know, no word is spoken that could wound them, were they invisibly present, excepting in reference to slavery, or rebellion, upon which a holy indignation, without capacity at least, for which, a man is totally without excellence, is quietly, and warmly expressed. But we tread their walks, or rather the government's, and these halls and rooms, and verandas, sadly, in their behalf, and when we criticise, it is the demon slavery, and his incantations, works, and rewards, and not them. There is no personal hatred in the heart of the North against the South. It is only the system of slavery that we abhor, as a foul cancer in a brother's body, slowly eating toward the vitals. Yes, we pass tenderly around, or rest, in these deserted mansions. We feel deep sympathy and sorrow that they, often so deceived, so sinned, so suffered. But suffering is linked to sin by every perfection of God, "the God of the poor, the needy, and him that hath no helper."

The flight from these homes was most hurried, Colored and White, all flying. Everything, that could go on wheels, used, roads clogged, and all confusion, ladies fainting, and restoratives used, as the carriages rushed furiously on. Fires were commencing in buildings, where report says many poor Negroes were locked in, and burned, alive! Please notice, we give this, as report. But the Negroes are said to be missing, and men whose names we have, had sworn they would do it, rather than the Yankees should get them. Still, the Colored do not refer to it, as amazing. Familiarity with suffering has deprived everything shocking, of power, to astonish! one of the saddest of features. These homes became dear. They witnessed much toil, and sympathy, for the Colored, but little conversation respecting slavery. One would check it in another, and gentlemen in charge, would check all, saying " this dwelling upon what you have seen, prostrates you more than the climate," so that, out of regard to health, slavery was almost a forbidden topic. When coming from plantations, where all the soul had been thrilled with sorrow, and sympathy, every allusion to it was checked with "let's sing." And we commenced sometimes: "Oh what are all my sorrows here?" Still, nothing seemed so inspiring and just appropriate as—

 John Brown's body lies mouldering in the grave;
  His soul's marching on—

with which those old oaks and pines were made to ring.

CHAPTER XIII.

SLAVERY A SEALED BOOK.

For God shall bring every work into judgment with every secret thing, whether it be good, or whether it be evil.

SLAVERY is a sealed book to all without its precincts; yea, to many within. There are thousands in slavedom who, if they knew of the agonies endured on their own plantations, would not suffer it—they would secede from it in some way—inured as they have been from infancy, to dire cruelties of the system. True, an aggravated case occasionally comes to their ears, or even their sight. But when the Master is tender of their feelings, the provocations are strongly dwelt upon, the "nigger" is made to appear as a devil incarnate. The overseer is scolded, sworn at, and charged in their presence, not to repeat his cruelties, or the driver, being a slave, is whipped. Thus treated, as a great wonder, children, and women in many cases, believe it is such, when it is only a little beyond what a majority of their slaves suffer, and that weekly, if not daily. But the slaves are inured to the most perfect self-control, and to hide their feelings completely.

Said a number of reliable Negroes, "When Massah or oberseer whip you, he untie you, den you mus' look right up in his face and smile, else you get jes as much mo', and when de people or strangers come roun' you must smile and say, 'Massah good,' 'Massah kind,' 'you'se so happy!' else you get whip so awful! You cannot tell Missus, else she think you oneasy and goin' to run away. Missus harder dan Massah, but she neber see we whipt, neber! You can't tell Massah 'bout de oberseer, he fin' it out, an' you'se nearly killed, when Massah away." So that after all investigation, we find that but one, or at most two dignitaries on each plantation, know all that goes on. These are, the overseer, a man adapted by nature, passion, education, vice, drink, and greed of gain for his work, and the driver, usually an athletic negro, and a skillful plantation manager, whose every blow upon the Negro saves two from his own back.

But one says, "I have seen the whipping." No sir, never! The whipping proper, is done in the dusk of evening, or grey of morning, and in the most retired place, and the poor sufferer knows that for every moan he makes, scores of blows will descend. But the torture, agonizing as it is, is not slavery's hardest feature, as we shall hereafter prove. We merely allude to it here, to show that slavery is actually a sealed book.

An intelligent lady, the wife of a United States Senator, raised amid slavery, said, "A person may be even raised and spend a life time among it, and unless he is of a very prying, pushing, energetic nature, he will know nothing that is going on. He must, too, be very early and very late upon the watch;" failings not common in self-indulgent families.

Since we came here, we are convinced that this is one secret of the universal outcry, made to strangers, against being out early, or late, in the morning, or evening, which has been so zealously asserted to be death here. And this opinion is confirmed by the fact, that our brave soldiers, exposed to both, are universally the healthiest men you see, not even excepting the Colored race, who alone are said to be able to bear such exposure, while we, who sit cooped up as directed here, over fires, in summer, mornings and evenings, are less so. But how convenient for the hard overseer, that the family, the guests, and even the Master, often, rise not, until all the plantation business is disposed of, except driving through the day, weighing, and reporting tasks after dark, and the whippings consequent. On most plantations you are shown the trees to which Negroes were tied, near the house, for the deception of all, in it. But ask, "Was the hardest whipping done here?" "No, Missus, way down dere," pointing to the most secluded place.

It is the universal testimony, that work in the field commenced when it was light enough to see, and continued till dark, or "at least till de sun was in de tree tops"—from which, till dark, is a very short time in these latitudes. So awfully were they driven, that laws were made to prevent it, and executed in most slave states, as this, for instance, in South Carolina:

"Whereas, many owners of slaves, and others who have the care, management, and overseeing of slaves, *do confine them so closely to hard labor, that they have not sufficient time for natural rest,* Be it therefore enacted, That if any owner of slaves, or other persons, who shall have the care, management, or overseeing of slaves, shall work or put any such slave or slaves to labor *more than fifteen hours* in twenty-four hours, from the 25th day of March to the 25th day of September; or *more than fourteen hours* in twenty-four hours, from the 25th day of September to the 25th day of March, every such person shall forfeit any sum not exceeding twenty pounds nor under five pounds current money, for every time he, she, or they shall offend herein, at the discretion of the justice before whom the complaint shall be made."*

* 2 Brevard's Digest, 243.

"How much longer than fourteen or fifteen hours per day, in winter and summer, the South Carolina planters had been in the habit of working their slaves, we are left to conjecture! But we know that 'the laws of Maryland, Virginia, and Georgia forbid that the CRIMINALS in their penitentiaries shall be compelled to labor more than *ten* hours a day.' "*

In Georgia and in Mississippi, there are laws forbidding the unnecessary labor of slaves on the Sabbath. This is all the information before us. In most of the slave states, there are no laws limiting slave labor. (See Stroud, p. 26.)

One single consideration is sufficient to show that the limitations just quoted are of no practical value. NO SLAVE AND NO FREE COLORED PERSON, IN THE SLAVE STATES, CAN BE A WITNESS AGAINST A WHITE PERSON. (Ib., 27.) Slaveholders would not be forward to prosecute each other for ill treatment of slaves.

Visitors, teachers, mechanics, might thus remain here months, and see positively nothing of the worst features of slavery, and yet honestly believe they saw all.

But one says, "I saw the quarters where they live." Did you. How many did you see, unlocked? The universal padlock was put upon most of them before light, or at least very early, and not touched till after dark, and those that you entered, were those of the laundress, the cook, or perhaps sometimes the favorite of Massah, called a sewing woman; but for deception's sake, they are situated among the others, and made to resemble them precisely outside, so that one would believe that, in seeing them, he saw a specimen of all.

There is no day when the quarters are not padlocked from sun to sun, excepting rarely Saturday afternoons and Sabbaths. Then, the poor dwelling has often the

* Jay's Inquiry, p. 130.

benefit of half a day's labor from the "field-hand" mother and sisters. On Sabbath, too, the one meal of the week is taken, the rest being a mere piece of hoe-cake, or junk of hominy, eaten lying, sitting, or running, as their "turn at the mill," the cooking, or worse, the time, will permit. This one meal is sometimes dignified with a little pork, given out on the best plantations, on Saturday evening. This meal, with the Sunday or clean suit, earned out of work hours, is enough to make the poor Negro jovial. Beside, the mere privilege of sitting down, or standing quietly, is a greater luxury than all that can be heaped upon a city voluptuary. Now if the guest walks out "for meditation" or sweet converse with the "good, kind Massah," he is as accidentally as possible led to see them out of their houses, where they ever are. He hears their compliments to "Massah," every one of which diminishes the danger or severity of their Mondays, or subsequent whippings. All this, together with their appearance of happiness, the greater from being a lull from so much distress, or agony in that lone dell or wood, whose name they dare not utter, the visitor sees, and he goes home, to Congress, or to the pulpit, with a lie in his right hand, his mind, or worse, in his heart.

The whole hospitality, etiquette, dignity, austerity, of plantation owners, and usages, ever forbade his going one word, or inch, beyond a certain line, in seeing, sympathizing, investigating. Yet to make the deception doubly sure, within that line, all seemed to be the most perfect abandon of freedom.

"The white people who came here used to talk to you, I presume," said we.

"Oh no, Missus! neber! 'cept Massah, dere; den we must praise him, or be cut up mo'. Neber had no chance to speak to nobody 'bout Massah, neber!"

The slave, too, conceals. He is never off his guard. He is perfectly skilled in hiding all emotions. The downcast eye, dull when he wills it, conceals his opinions, the hearty laugh his grief. His Master knows him not, except, possibly, as to what brute force will best subdue him. Nothing is more apparent now that the mask is thrown off, than that owners never understood their slaves. They were accomplished tragedians, the dullest of them, as will in many cases appear, in this work. But lest some think we err, and that Masters and visitors did understand them, we give from SOUTHERN WORKS, extracts from the OFFICIAL REPORT of the rebellion under Denmark Vesey, of Charleston. It says:

"He was for twenty years a most faithful slave. He maintained such an irreproachable character, and enjoyed so much the confidence of the whites, that when he was accused of leading the rebellion, not only was the charge discredited, but he was not even arrested for several days after, and not till the proofs of his guilt had become too strong to be doubted. Not a symptom of the volcano raging within him had ever appeared, and on close investigation of his whole life, nothing could be adduced by witnesses but that once he had said, respecting his children, 'he wished he could see them free.' Yet for more than four years, the enterprise for the independence of the blacks had occupied his whole mind."

That the Colored men cannot be understood when they will it otherwise, is further proven from the same Report. It goes on to say:

"It is a remarkable fact, that the general good character of the leaders, except Gullah Jack, was such as rendered them OBJECTS LEAST LIABLE TO SUSPICION. Their conduct had secured them not only the unlimited confidence of their owners, but they had been indulged."

"But," continues the Report, "not only were the leaders of good character, and very much indulged by their owners, but this was VERY GENERALLY THE CASE, WITH ALL who were convicted, MANY OF THEM POSSESSING the highest confidence of their owners, and not one reputed of bad character."

We merely quote this from Southern records, as being more convincing to critics—not as more striking, than many instances we have found. Of course, no sensible slave would be so out of love with life, as to say to his Master, "I desire freedom." And the more he was plotting for it, the more loving and contented would he appear. So, in everything, long habit has inured them to deception. Often, they act the opposite of what they feel, as it seems almost involuntarily.

Their accuracy in reading character from the countenance and appearance is amazing. This has been their life-long study. The deep thought it engenders is taken for dullness. Then, many of them are hated, abused, sold for resembling their Master, with all the spirit of his family swelling and boiling within them.

How, then, could visitors comprehend them, especially when on good terms with their Masters?

But the book of slavery has not only been sealed by ignorance, but by every device and misrepresentation which a ... f experience, tact, learning, and talent, could devise. ...e Master must make money, that is indispensable, and anti-slavery notions would ruin his business. Therefore they must not, should not prevail, and of this, and to prejudice all against the Colored man and in favor of slavery, he never loses sight, never!

Even now, at Port Royal, the seals of the book of slavery have to be forced. If, for instance, persons approach the huts of the field hands, they are met at the door by the whole family, who stand right before it, and with bows, courtesies, and docile actions and words, would beguile you from entering. This, however, they have tact enough to make appear as a mere matter of course. When, by a kind remark, you assure them that they are not responsible for their hard case, they receive it gratefully, but still no way can you possibly open to enter the hut, until you say decidedly, "I will go in, if you please."

Still, slavery is a sealed book, for though you have seen their wretchedness, you cannot tell it—words cannot do it. Most of our ladies at first, burst into tears, look around, and go out without speaking. Soon the whole abused, ragged group are around them; with streaming eyes, they tell them "that they feel for them, that we have come to help them, and to teach them to be worthy of freedom, in all their habits." We tell them "that the government, and their friends who have long prayed and plead for them, are watching to see what they will now do; whether what their Masters have long said is true, 'that they will be untidy, lazy, and improvident, will not work, and cannot take care of themselves.'" At which their eyes sparkle, and they say, "We can! we'll show 'um!" We tell them how Colored people live at the North, have good houses, beautifully dressed and well-educated children and family prayers, and sit down at table three times daily, to eat all together, so happy! all of which causes them to rejoice amazingly.

They invariably and warmly accede to all you say; and better still, when reform is made it is permanent, remarkably so. This is general testimony.

And still further, slavery is a sealed book, over the vast multitudes who die under its awful rigors, and tortures. We cite one, of hundreds of proofs.

"While attending the Baptist Triennial Convention at

Richmond, Va., in 1835," says Mr. C.,* "I had a conversation with an officer of the Baptist church in that city, at whose house I was a guest. I asked him if he did not apprehend that the slaves would eventually rise and exterminate their Masters? 'Why,' said the gentleman, 'I did use to apprehend such a catastrophe, but God has made a providential opening, *a merciful safety valve*, and now I do not feel alarmed, in the prospect of what is coming.' 'What do you mean,' said Mr. Choules, 'by Providence opening a merciful safety valve?' 'Why,' said the gentleman, 'I will tell you. The slave-traders come from the cotton and sugar plantations of the South, and are willing to *buy up* more slaves than we can part with. We must keep a stock for the purpose of *rearing* slaves, but we part with the most valuable, and at the same time the most *dangerous;* and the dem   is very constant, and is likely to be so, for when they go to those Southern States, their average existence is ONLY FIVE YEARS!'"

"The people, including church members, are not usually, though some are, better than their laws." †

Still who, who shall open the seals of this awful book? Would that hosts of able professional men from the North were here, to observe critically for themselves, the facts belonging to their various professions; that being thus first convinced themselves, they might report more adequately.

But slavery is a sealed book. You, having seen, cannot so report appearances but your auditors will get a lower opinion of these poor people than they deserve, or than you have. Nay, you cannot merely see them, and

---

* Baptist minister, formerly of New Bedford, and of Buffalo, N.Y.   † Goodell's American Slave Code, pp. 133, 134.

for ever so long a time, without the same result. You must converse with them, take them off their guard, watch them when tested, and then, unless they are convinced your interest is deep, real, heartfelt, you will learn little of them.

But to whom, to whom shall it be given to open the seals of this dire book? Would our Lord enable us to do it, we would cheerfully suffer almost anything. Life itself looks as nothing to surrender, could we only show slavery to the ladies of the North as it is. But, alas! all writers, even the ablest, the best, the most vehement against it, using the only and best lights they have, speak of those dear saints of God, so individually pure and dear to our heart, as a mere mass, or as a great body of debasement, and the natural inference of the mind unavoidably is, that they are so debased that it is, after all, little matter how they are used. So sealed up by long, and mean, and bitter obloquy from Masters is their true purity of heart and character.

CHAPTER XIV.

SLAVERY A VICE.

For he that but conceives a crime, in thought,
Contracts the danger of an actual fault;
Then what must he expect, that still proceeds
To finish sin, and work up thoughts in deeds.

But does one declare the alleged facts of the foregoing chapter, impossibilities? Listen! Slavery is a vice! It seizes and grows upon one, and holds him victim, just like another vice, as intemperance. He vents all the passions of the carnal heart upon his subjects. He glories in his mean power, procured under our benign government by mere dollars, at a slave pen. He requites himself by despotism here at home, for want of power, authority, and influence elsewhere. Said a talented officer, "it is not so much any profit of slavery, or what they get, or look for, from it, as a love of dominion, a glory in domineering over men, that these slaveholders consider, and are determined to keep. But what provokes me," continued he, "is to see them put the poor whites below their slaves, in every way, and teach the Negroes to insult them, just for love of domineering." If, too, slavery is not a vice, why do many Masters cause debasement, whipping and torture, just in proportion as they become intoxicated or debased in other ways? which is an admitted fact.

Besides, if whole communities could be thrilled at bull-fights, gladiatorial shows, etc., cannot the most debased find gratification in the agonies of a hated race? a race, too, whose wrongs and sorrows haunt their best moments, and horrify their worst, and who, the more they are sinned against, the more they are hated, by an immutable law of mind?

"But loss of property would prevent cruelty," one says. Then why does it not prevent all that is dear, yes life itself, being lost, yea, even the priceless soul, for the wine cup, gambling, or licentiousness? Is not the gratification of vicious revenge too, or slander, often dearer than life, or character itself? Do you, doubter, not believe cruelty exists in the human heart? Certainly. And does any evil exist there, which may not become a towering, tyrannical vice? Does not all vice grow by exercise? What cruelty too, toward animals, has there been in all ages? and can a man get as angry at a beast as at a man? Can he hate a beast as he can hate a man? Can the natural heart hate a wicked man as it can hate a Christian? Did not God, therefore, obviously never design one man to have unlimited power over another? And none dare bear witness, for if a slave is killed, other slaves dare not even talk of it among themselves, lest they suffer the same, that being the rule, especially as among those so degraded, there must be some traitors. But are you not convinced that one can find more gratification in cruelty than in gain?

A PICTURE OF A CONGRESSMAN—PROOF.

On a plantation, every Monday morning, the darkies are all assembled. They seem glad to see "Massah," flock round him closely as possible. He is going to have a treat. These poor people after working from light until dark, upon a peck of corn, the week previous, have washed their poor clothes on Sunday morning, done all odd jobs, got their wood for the week, bringing it home upon their heads, and are ready to commence the hopeless toil of another week. But Massah must have his gratification, and probably he apologizes to himself, or friends, that it will make the work go on better. So, behold the Congressman, elevated, his poor slaves all crowding close as possible to the stump or block, well knowing that severity in whipping increases with every moment's gratification.

"Sambo, do you want to be whipped?"

"Yes, Massah," and on go cuts enough to lay one not used to it, prostrate.

"That do, Sambo?"

"Yes, Massah."

"Go, Sambo."

"Good Massah, tank you, Massah."

"Jim, you want to be whipped?" he cries to one strong enough to push away the rest and be first.

"Yes, Massah."

He gets a little more, and with his "Tank you, Massah," leaves. And so this dignified gentleman, who, perhaps, has kissed a lady's hand in Washington, treated timid Congress freely, contemptuously! goes on, until he whips every Negro, including women, and all children old enough to go afield, making every punishment more and more severe, until the last is nearly prostrated. Then the driver comes in for his share; and one, a man of God, of whom his superintendent speaks very highly, call him a consistent Christian, told me he had received one hundred and fifty lashes, at one time, with their awful whip, composed of three or five thongs, for nothing but not driving harder than he possibly could. More of this man, soon.

What a spectacle of the morally sublime was that driver, that man, as he stood before us! What a chance for an artist to catch an expression, which would immortalize him! A beautiful, holy, expression of face is often seen when God cometh and dwelleth in man; but it is usually one of joy, of triumph, of bliss, mostly. But here, it was all that, mingled with agony, a vivid appreciation of the wrong, the injustice of man, in a mind cleared, and intensified by religion, a holy consciousness of having a manhood, and a life that the lash, and the still MORE DREADED SHAME AND CONTEMPT could not touch! and that the Master could not understand. All these, softened by perfect love, perfect patience, perfect soul chastening, sat in full simplicity upon that face. And some such face fastens the gaze in every meeting, and upon most plantations. But angels only could draw that expression. It is the smile of God, reflected, the smile he gives to those only who "have nothing, nothing! but Jesus."

WHEN SLAVERY COMES TO BE REGARDED AS A VICE, and is treated as such, then, will the testimonies of its advocates, and victims, be received for what they are actually worth. Then will the only cure of any vice, total abstinence, be applied.

That it is a vice will further appear, from the fact, that it vitiates the whole man. Qualities, which before were virtues, all shrivel into vices, under its wand. Frugality becomes avarice. System, order, punctuality, become tyranny, despotism, barbarity; what were dignity, is brutal imperiousness, as well to the broken-hearted wife, in many cases as toward those for whom she vainly intercedes. Chastity, becomes beastly sensuality; self-respect, towering madness at any restraint, or, perchance, in serving lordly self in any and every way. Now add all this to the fact that the Master has often, never been restrained, in one propensity, in youth, never governed, much less subdued, and you who know much of Southern society, know this is a fact, and know, too, from all testimony that young lads exercise perfect authority over all the Colored on many plantations. We have ourselves an instrument of torture, with which a lad of fourteen daily amused and gratified his premature tyranny, by torturing every child on the place, numbering between thirty and forty.

But that some who hold the relation of slaveholder are not such in heart, but the direst victims of the system will appear in other chapters, prominent among whom, are the wives of these tyrants.

That slavery is a vice, is further evident, from the fact that it absorbs, like all other cherished vices, the whole man. Property, reputation, true honor, life, soul, is each for a time swallowed up, lost sight of. The one daily o'ermastering passion, or vice rules. In the indulgence of this vice, so lost are some, that one is amazed at the utter waste of money, dignity, good name, family pride, life. The scenes that occur, where this vice is rampant, almost defy belief, and description, totally. That persons who sometimes appear manly, will so stoop, is almost incredible. The lives of poor slaves then are as nothing, or they will sacrifice one—which they can AT ANY TIME LEGALLY DO if he but lift his hand! to terrify the rest. It would absolutely be a comfort—since we have been told by such circumstantial and corroborative testimony of their barbarities—we say it would be a comfort, to believe that they actually thought them not human, so horrid were their cruelties, and sacrifice of life. But the government is now responsible. It has got to say, "I will not murder" or "I will." Nothing but the obliteration of the last jot of power, instanter, can save the awful responsibility and its ETERNAL CONSEQUENCES!— Nothing! If it does not put an end at once to slavery, we are a nation of murderers, willful murderers! And, if we say as a nation, "I will murder the innocent," whose helplessness should appeal to every manly heart, "one year, two or ten, or till it is convenient to stop," the soul-guilt is the same as if it were continued indefinitely. There is no escape. No Northern man, woman or child can wipe the mouth, and say, "I am clean," unless they each, after learning the facts, shall exert their very utmost energy to put away this horrid system.

Anti-slavery laborers should everywhere be thicker and more earnest, and thoroughly prepared, than ever political laborers were.

Then, it is a vice intensified by poverty, avarice, disappointment, remorse, constant failures. The vice is heightened too by the provocations of grudging, irresponsible unpaid, abhorred labor, endless, and most aggravating. and perpetually recurring. The Master brings robbery, oppression, agony to the slave; the slave, just in proportion to his actual manhood, brings discomfort to the Master. How would you do, in his case, reader?

Besides, it is a vice in the hearts and power of a class, many of whom are acknowledged by acquaintances, and advocates, and friends, to be demented by intermarriages of near relatives, a practice strangely common in many parts of slavedom, and becoming more and more so. It must too, inevitably, become worse and worse yearly; unless the dire system is destroyed; for while the temptations from many causes increase, the power to resist them diminishes with mental weakness, and will, until, if they remain a race of slaveholders, we shall have a race of actual fools, by the testimony of their own relatives, who are alarmed, as they have assured us. How much of the present course of the masses is to be attributed to this even now, it is impossible to say, for it is obvious, that let a Northern man be never so wicked, he cannot somehow equal them in blind, self-assured impudence, and in not seeing or feeling sound obvious reasons, and moral claims and relations. Where is the man in the whole South that compares with Jefferson or Patrick Henry? And how evident that, as a whole, they are strong only in overbearing, and bluster, and for all this we are all guilty.

We, and others, long wondered, and inquired why it could be that little innocent toddlers, of two and three years, should be whipped daily? what motive there could be for such brutality. But slavery is a vice. Reader, can you imagine from thirty, to fifty, little innocents, coming up in agony to Mistress, or her son of thirteen, to get their morning torture. Yet all this is absolute fact, and so common, that the query was passed around why, why? it could be? One said, of one, "she got provoked at one and so sure as she did, after punishing that, she punished every child on the plantation" for they are all under the care of one Negress, too old to work, of seventy or eighty, and in one case one hundred. One, thought they believed it made them grow, and many other reasons were suggested; but if slavery is a vice, it is explained. The love of oppression, and a debased, carnal nature is gratified. But, farther, we must say, that the most plausible reason given was, that it broke their spirit effectually, and forever, so that they would not even dream of liberty.

Now, let such a boy become a Congressman, and you have there one of the spirits that have caused this rebellion, that have ever moulded compeers, in a way that is incredible, and never, never! should have been tolerated. And these are the men that this day seem to rule this nation, actually, though just now behind the curtain. These are the men that must be conciliated! As well conciliate the evil one himself. These men are the persons that must not be exasperated; as well not exasperate the raving maniac. But its exhibitions, as a vice, are almost endless. Shall it be destroyed? at once? Speak, ye who make rulers.

CHAPTER XV.

SLAVES HELD FROM NECESSITY.

> Who bears no trace of passion's evil force?
> Who shuns thy sting, O horrible Remorse?
>   Who does not cast
> On the thronged pages of his memory's book
> At times, a sad and half-reluctant look,
>   Regretful of the past? WHITTIER.

THAT slavery or oppression is a vice, is further proven from the fact, that those who are as kind to those under them, as they know how to be, or as kind as they have liberty of law! to be in slavedom, are universally opposed to it. We challenge all investigation and proof to the contrary, on this point. But how shall we know that a given Master is kind? Appearances are nothing, though never so good, and never so long continued. Testimony of slaves so long as they are under his power, is nothing; for if you are on any terms with "Massah," such as even to permit you to stay upon the plantation, they will not trust you, sooner than they will him, with complaints. Their only hope is in propitiating their demon of a driver, or overseer, for they know "Massah, he won't interfere, he won't let Nigger speak 'bout driver or 'bout oberseer. You can't tell him when you lick'd, 'thout get mo'."

Then, to come at the truth, as to whether any one Master is kind, even to the very limited extent of his power, by law, and over the driver and the overseer, you must be invisibly present at the startings for work, before light, or at the weighings and settlings up of tasks after dark in the lone place, far away from the plantation dwelling—for we cannot say "plantation mansions" since we have seen them—or, you must take them, as we did, when Massah being gone forever, as they fully believe, they dare speak. We do not say that in every case the Master does not intend to be truthful. But, alas! what can he know unless present? and where is the Master that will be present in both twilights of every day? Or, where is the Master that dare interfere if he is, to the subversion of all plantation system, order, and success?

But of all, every one, of whom their people, now free to speak truthfully, assert that they were kind, wait a moment and listen! and they invariably assert of them, "O, dey was not for slavery! Dey did not believe in slavery!" One said, "O Missus, my Massah was the kindest, best man! Bless you; he not for slavery! Oh, you ought to seen him walk 'at yard dere, with his hands crossed behind his back, and sigh, and sigh; and he speak so kind to you, and to de chil'n, it make you cry. O! he not for slavery! he not for dis war. Oh, he de innocentest, best man. But, bless you, he couldn't do nothing, Missus was all for slavery. She not very hard; not hab you cut up, like mos' of dem, but she tight 'bout work—very tight. She all for slavery. Laws, Massah couldn't do nothing; he heart mos' broke. Oh, he good man! good man!"

Of another it was said: "Dat minister say 'he would not own slave; if he hab so much gold, he walk on it for pavement.' He not for slavery! But he wife, great for slavery; she own all de slaves, he can't do nothing!"

"I wonder he was not afraid to speak his mind so freely here."

"Why, bless you, Missus, dey knew 'at Missus great

for slavery. Dey knew she hab own way. Dey didn't mind what he say. But he good man, good preacher."

Three superior Colored women also testified to one kind Master. They said: "We could hab libed wid Massah and Missus foreber; dey kind. But 'twas de oder folks dere; de 'lations 'bout de house 'at make us have tight times wid work, get cut up. But Massah and Missus wa'nt hard, though he pretty tight for work. Sometimes give you task to take till dark, oder times get done long befo' night, 'bout dis time. O! he not hard; he not much for slavery, nor Missus eider. We could lib wid dem foreber, if 'twant fo' de oder folks dere. Dey all for slavery!"

The only other case of a kind Missus, we heard of in conversation with the Colored on twenty-five plantations, and in town, was from a light, genteel Colored woman, and her companions. They said "Missus did all she thought she could, for we. She couldn't do no mo'. She not hard, she not for slavery. She pray and plead 'gainst dis war at first. Den she pray and pray! God, to take her, fo' it cum. He did. He take her! She die just ten days befo' the taking of Hilton Head. She just scape all 'at confusion. Young Massah gone, we don't know where. She done all she could wid him, for we. Oh she was good Missus, good Christian."

These owners, were the victims, not of slavery as a vice, dearer, than all else, but as a system.

But does one ask, "Why did they not free their slaves?" We answer, how could they in a land where Thomas Jefferson with all his power, and abilities, and efforts, could not free his own children—as common report called them—but in his last will he himself " implores the legislature of Virginia, to confirm its bequests, with permission to remain in the State where their families, and connections are, then, dying under the uncertainty whether his requests would be granted, or his children sold into the rice swamps! One of his daughters, it seems, was afterward sold at auction, at the HAREM PRICE! And his grand-daughter was colonized, to Liberia 'coerced' perhaps by the 'cart whip.' A land of liberty for white people is it, when a Jefferson cannot bequeath liberty to his own children! In Georgia, had he lived there the attempt would have been an 'offence' for which his estate would have been subjected to a fine of a thousand dollars, and each of his executors if accepting the trust to a thousand more."*

So was it with Dr. Nelson, eminent for patriotism, learning and piety, whose work upon Infidelity is one of the most efficient popular appeals that has ever appeared. The following is from one of his letters :†

"I have resided in North Carolina more than forty years, and been intimately acquainted with the system, and I can scarcely even think of its operations without shedding tears. It causes me excessive grief to think of MY OWN POOR SLAVES, for whom I HAVE FOR YEARS BEEN TRYING TO FIND A FREE HOME. It strikes me with equal astonishment and horror to hear Northern people make light of slavery. Had they seen and known as much of it as I, they could not thus treat it, unless callous to the deepest woes and degradation of humanity, and dead both to the religion and philanthropy of the Gospel. But many of them are doing just what the hardest-hearted tyrants of the South most desire. Those tyrants would not, on any account, have them advocate, or even apologize for slavery in an *unqualified* manner. This would

---

* Goodell's American Slave Code, p. 375.
† Key to Uncle Tom's Cabin.

be bad policy with the North. I wonder that Gerritt Smith should understand slavery so much better than most of the Northern people. How true was his remark, on a certain occasion, namely, that the South are laughing in their sleeves, to think what dupes they make of most of the people at the North in regard to the real character of slavery! Well did Mr. Smith remark that the system, carried out on its fundamental principle, would as soon enslave any laboring white man as an African. But, *if it were not for the support of the North, the fabric of blood would fall at once.* And of all the efforts of public bodies at the North to sustain slavery, the Connecticut General Association has made the best one. I have never seen anything so well constructed in that line as their resolutions of June, 1836. The South certainly could not have asked anything more effectual. But, of all Northern periodicals, the 'New York Observer' must have the preference, as an efficient support of slavery. I am not sure but it does more than all the things combined to keep the dreadful system alive. It is just the succor demanded by the South. Its abuse of the abolitionists is music in Southern ears, which operates as a charm."

If Jefferson, and Dr. Nelson, then, could not free their slaves what could poor lone women do? Crushed for a life time beneath the awful car of slavery, acting up to the law of love, according to the light they had, weary of slavery, and sick of soul, this poor woman with one other of similar piety and bondage to cruel laws for whites! turned to the bosom of God and begged and begged for reception there by death, before the awful judgments, they saw impending should come. And God reached down and "took them and drew them, from the great waters, and from the hands of strange children."

CHAPTER XVI.

BOND AND FREE SERVANTS.

>   Woe to all who grind
> Their brethren of a common Father down!
>   To all who plunder from the immortal mind,
> Its bright and glorious crown!

HAD we to be put in prison, or upon a plantation or town estate, with the government of fourteen or sixteen or more slaves, as was the usual number in these large houses, we should deliberately choose the former even were the sin, of slavery, left out of the question.

To drive on in all the minutiæ of house labor—to compel care, in unwilling, grudging, revengeful hearts,—and revenge in some, has rankled desperately, and deep and long, and just in proportion to their ability, wrongs, and apparent docility—to force matters to desirable results—to attend to the buying, and making, of all garments, and to the health, of inefficient mothers, their children, everything, or have all go to wreck—to direct and invigorate and bring to proper issue the abortive efforts of aimless, hopeless, ambitionless labor, were a task, such as mortal can scarcely conceive of, and God never imposed upon man, and which no man, having the feelings and principles of a gentleman could impose upon a wife, provided he knew a better way.

Our little experience has already shown us, that were we to undertake this slave work, the lash must be the mainspring—and from its very nature, it is a mainspring that cannot aid with constancy, power, effect.

Never did we so pity ladies in any condition as such, obliged to meet the responsibilities of their station, with grudging servants, whose whole aim was to escape the curse, labor, and who were perfect adepts in the science of how not to do it. The Northern lady with her one, or two hired servants, competent, energetic, ambitious, is comparatively free from care, and lives often too easily. The Southerner with her fourteen, sixteen or more and the whole responsibility and care of all of them and their children, finds in each slave, weight enough to crush her. No wonder that they who can afford it, shut up house, and often a large part of the year. If we never believed their assertion, that "it was the mistress that was the slave," we do now, most cordially, from some weeks' experience with their servants. Oh why do men hold on to sin, the world over, just in proportion to its costliness its enervating, paralyzing, destroying power? But so under the sanctions of human nature, it ever is. One would think, one week of the sorrows of the drunken, dishonest, or cruel man were enough to wean him forever. So, one would think that one week of irresponsible, aimless unpaid labor were enough. It was enough for us. Our servants being detailed by the military power, and rationed, obligation to the government seemed to forbid explicit bargaining. Their future freedom too, being still clothed with doubt, all was chaos, as before. Every domestic thing therefore, seemed in our beginning here, to come short, as far as servants were concerned, either in the conception, execution, or "punctual delivery," and the more help, the worse, so that our efficient ladies began to look upon domestic responsibilities, with discouragement. Everything here, too, is so ill adjusted. Your kitchen or quarters being down six or eight steps, across a hot, sandy yard, up as many more steps into a small room, with either too hot a fire on the hearth, or none, and the sun pouring in at the door, servants who had either "forgot" or found it "onpossible," to do your bidding, quarters too dirty after repeated scrapings, and scrubbings, to sit down in, even did the room and the heat allow. Nothing remains, but to go into the "big house" and wait a time and go out and find some other "onpossibility" had intervened. One would think the young bride so situated, if conscience, or some other principle, did not forbid, would straightway follow Judas.

A lady, a slaveholder, calmly said, "Before I would have my daughters suffer what I have, in the care of my work, and servants, I would give up every slave I've got, lose every cent, and take my children and beg. But still slavery, is none of the business of you Northerners." Then murder is none of the business of him who sees it, and might interfere, and does not. But, it is a great mistake, that because Southerners have so many house-servants, they do not work so hard. They do, each and every one, has a harder time than one, North, who does all the work for a family, for their mistakes, dilemmas, shirkings, repinings, plannings, explainings, deliberations, commandings, resistings, domineerings, and all the further "ings," you can, or please to add, are a thousand fold more wearing and tiresome, than cheerful work. Beside so many "onpossibilities," etc., etc. But all this disappears when free labor comes, and shirking is out of mind.

4*

CHAPTER XVII.

FREE LABOR.

Come hither ye that press your beds of down,
And sleep not : see him sweating o'er his bread
Before he eats it. 'Tis the primal curse,
But ripened into mercy : mark the pledge
Of cheerful days, and nights without a groan.

BUT here comes in the remedy, free labor! free labor! These servants have been chosen with care, and detailed for us, by the noble and chivalrous Military, who look with great, just, scrutiny, upon our efforts. We give them presents ; still their relation to us, and to the government as well as their future, is a little cloudy. We having come to befriend the Colored, must succeed with them ourselves. We must not make a failure! as we are doing. Something effective must be done, and we ask wisdom. In the course of the day, we find opportunity to say, to them, separately, about thus, "There is a great difference in the treatment of servants in the North, and South, we never whip or drive, or in general, talk very much to them. We wait until we are sure they understand us, and know how, and when, we want things done, we talk always very gently to them, and explain our wishes clearly, and kindly. Then, if they do not remember, or do not do what we tell them, we often just go and hire others, before they know it, because if they do not try to please us, we infer, that they do not like our service, and as we do not want trouble about it, we get others and let them go." Immediately everything brightens. Capacities to hear, understand, remember, and accomplish, were suddenly and wonderfully developed, and everything went far better. But the stimulus of free labor, must be used like strong medicines, cautiously. In our ignorance we applied too much, and did injury. Our slippery Simon, ran the right way too fast. Peter, in spite of warnings from the ladies, scrubbed so very hard and nicely, and lifted so much at boxes, that he fell sick—John, too, the reliable, was somewhat ill—James was too much of a legalist, and being a little deaf escaped sickness—Susan, too, was sick. These ailments were real as was also their regret, at not being able to do for us. Our ladies began to exclaim, " We shall kill our servants by our energetic Northern manners." "We have got to be careful of them."

The impetus and enthusiasm of free labor, is so new, and the strange excitement such a tax upon their systems, that care must be used. Many will smile incredulously at this, but experience, under right influences and stimuli, will prove the truth of the assertion. Take a Colored laborer North or South and he accomplishes in a given half hour, less than a white. But in the day or week, circumstances being equal, he often does more, more quietly, and usually does it better. We appeal to facts well attested by those who have tried both races. However, our Simon, Peter and John are all doing well, and James is permitted to be absent.

If any think we have too many servants, let them remember, that in this land, where two women yet grind at the mill, and cotton is carded and spun as it was centuries since, everything to be done begins with the creation.

To our chambermaid we said—"I should think your Mistress used to talk to you, all the time about your work, did she not?"

"All de time, Missus."

"Well we do not; we tell *once* how we want things done, then, our servants remember and while they work, we often talk of other things, and they take more and more pains every day, to please us, and so learn to love to do things, just right. Would not that be pleasant?"

"Yes, Missus," said Phebe, her downcast eyes raised to ours with a new animation, and a most perceptible improvement, resulted. Still the fruits of slavery hang on every bough, and long—long—will.

CHAPTER XVIII.

HEART SERVICE.

All our actions take
Their hues from the complexion of the heart,
As landscapes their variety from light.   BACON.

This, beloved reader, if a slaveholder, you have never, never known. The sweetness of being served by those who freely prefer you, to all others in the world.

We would rather encounter again, all the difficulties connected with hired servants of our whole life, than those with which we met in a few weeks only, in connection with your former slaves. While not being hired, they had no especial new motive for serving us, so they were docile, but far LESS EFFICIENT than when hired.

We are candid and truthful. Do you believe it? The labor of driving a fellow-being through the world, is incredible. To have every act done for you without interest, is heart-sickening positively! That they have ever thus served you, is fully proven to others, whether you believe it or not.

But you think it dignified to own them. Yes! if it is dignified to be ruled by them, it is dignified to own them, or rather pretend to; for you cannot own them without their ruling you; causing you to run after them, scold them, be angered by them, made unhappy by them; forever keeping you waiting, teasing, disappointing, thwarting, annoying you; leading you into all unamiable and wretched and life-killing states of mind. and causing you at last to imbrute yourselves, in punishing them, thus at their pleasure or revenge forcing you to the meanest of all services, at all times, and to the inevitable pangs of a guilty conscience. They can too, and do! bind you to the bar of God, and to the terrible retributions of Eternity, by their awful imprecations of divine vengeance, for their wrongs—appeals which the God of the poor, the needy, and him that hath no helper, is pledged not to forget, and whom he first hears and avenges.

Now, your hearts concede the truth of all the above, in most cases, at least. Oh, are you not weary? Will you not permit a fellow-sinner to plead with you? to help you? These evils are in the system, and inseparable from it; not originally in you. You cannot reverse that system, that sense of right, of manhood, or love of Liberty while God is God, and man is man.

Will you not read the Scriptures upon this point of oppressing, turning aside the stranger from his right, robbing the poor? Then must you see that all the imprecations of righteous judgment, of vengeance, of all who have ever suffered, under the system, you use and uphold in all their privations, tortures and deaths, will fall upon you and yours.

We surely are not superstitious. But truly, rather than have these imprecations resting upon our head and the heads of our children, we say before God, we would cheerfully beg our bread with them. Yea, thankfully.

Hath not God promised that he will hear the cry of the poor, the sighing of the needy, and that he will arise to judgment, to save the meek, of the earth?

What has slavery done for you—what? Pray look candidly at it. But you say, I cannot work, and if I give up my slaves, I give up all.

Yes, you may give up all, if you give them up. But IF YOU DO NOT, you may, and MUST, GIVE UP LIFE. "For he that being often reproved, hardeneth his neck, shall suddenly be cut off, and that without remedy." How often have you seen this verified? How terribly now! So you have the word of God, commanding you to give up your sin or your life. Oh, may God help and bless you. But should you give up all and be poor, all the North is before you, labor is most honorable, and is it not as honorable, in integrity, in purity, to sit at sewing, as, filled with sense of guilt, and under the censure of the whole humanitarian, just, and Christian world, to drive around, and chase up and down, by day and night, a set of grudging, revengeful Negroes? To be their servant when sick, and whenever they so will it? Now, at the North, when servants do well, we get the benefit; if they do not, there are those to take the drudgery of attending to them, while we go quietly about honorable duties. We are never laid under the awful worry and responsibility of deciding that a man or woman shall be punished. Money could not induce, nor power compel us to cause the worst, so to suffer by our individual order. Never, never! Laws attend to all that, by appropriate officers and methods. We have no drudgery of serving servants, unless we choose it, freely. But, on the contrary, the most excellent help, usually.

In two cases, we have had the services of most competent girls two years, while neighbors were offering them higher wages. Yet for this long time, and until marriage in one case, and removal in another, intervened, were they heart and hand, with us. Of course, presents were not wanting, for we could not permit one to suffer by remaining with us; still as we gave high wages, we did not think it right or proper under the circumstances, to increase them. We do not set ourselves up as a standard, far from it; others have done far, far better. But almost first, among the blessings of our life, have been, dear, excellent servants, who were ours indeed and in truth, and, because ours in perfect freedom to leave, ours in heart. The number of ways in which they saved our money, comfort, and credit, and showed interest, zeal and love for the family, was amazing, and so it has been in most other cases. We say these plain, humiliating things, with the hope of influencing some candid ladies.

Our servants in South Carolina, so soon as they felt the spur, the animation, and the responsibility of free labor, began to improve, and now in eight weeks time, one does as much as two did, and does it better, and more easily, and has more spare time. They are far more respectful, more thoughtful, and with their present hilarity, fourfold more competent, of care-taking.

Oh we do pity you, who have been born and reared under this system, who have never, never! known the luxury of free service.

But does one ask what we do with incompetent servants? We answer, First, we show them sweetly, and after a few days, or at most a few changes, they become competent. It is amazing how the feeblest intellect soon succeeds, under the stimulus of free labor. But, if they cannot or do not, there is ample and kind provision for them, and nobody is imbruted in the process.

The blessings of free, competent, happy, honest labor may be yours; will you have them? We use the word imbruted above. We know it is very, very severe. But if it does not imbrute a lady to send one of her own sex to all the exposure, licentiousness, agony, of a public whipping, what can, what does? Yet the system absolutely compels this, in many cases, for the lash is the only force, and the mistress cannot use it, nor let perfect chaos reign in her house. O! let's away with the foul system. But it is duty to give one or more account of these awful whippings.

A slaveholder flogged a little slave girl, and put her feet in the stocks. She was found dead. A prominent lawyer, of a respectable family, was asked "whether the murderer of this little helpless child could not be indicted." He coolly replied that "the slave was Mr. P.'s *property*, and if he chose to suffer *the loss*, no one else had any thing to do with it." (Vide Weld's "Slavery As It Is," p. 54.)

The slave child was "property," and had only been *used!* "It is believed that no record exists of a *white* man having been executed in the United States, simply for the murder of a *slave*." (MSS, by Judge Jay.)

The subjoined account was written by the benevolent Dr. Howe, whose labors in behalf of the blind have rendered his name dear to humanity, and was sent in a letter to the Hon. Charles Sumner. If any one thinks it too painful to be perused, let him ask himself if God will hold those guiltless who suffer a system to continue, the details of which they cannot even read. That this describes a common scene in the calaboose, we shall by and by produce other witnesses to show. Dr. H. says:

"I have passed ten days in New Orleans, not unprofitably, I trust, in examining the public institutions—the schools, asylums, hospitals, prisons, etc. With the exception of the first, there is little hope of amelioration. I know not how much merit there may be in their system; but I do know that, in the administration of the penal code, there are abominations which should bring down the fate of Sodom upon the city. If Howard or Mrs. Fry ever discovered so ill-administered a den of thieves as the

New Orleans prison, they never described it. In the Negroes' apartment I saw much which made me blush that I was a white man, and which, for a moment, stirred up an evil spirit in my animal nature. Entering a large paved court-yard, around which ran galleries filled with slaves of all ages, sexes, and colors, I heard the snap of a whip, every stroke of which sounded like the sharp crack of a pistol. I turned my head, and beheld a sight which absolutely chilled me to the marrow of my bones, and gave me, for the first time in my life, the sensation of my hair stiffening at the roots. There lay a black girl flat upon her face, on a board, her two thumbs tied, and fastened to one end, her feet tied, and drawn tightly to the other end, while a strap passed over the small of her back, and, fastened around the board, compressed her closely to it. Below the strap she was entirely naked. By her side, and six feet off, stood a huge Negro, with a long whip, which he applied with dreadful power and wonderful precision. Every stroke brought away a strip of skin, which clung to the lash, or fell quivering on the pavement, while the blood followed after it. The poor creature writhed and shrieked, and, in a voice which showed alike her fear of death and her dreadful agony, screamed to her Master, who stood at her head, "O, spare my life! don't cut my soul out!" But still fell the horrid lash; still strip after strip peeled off from the skin; gash after gash was cut in her living flesh, until it became a livid and bloody mass of raw and quivering muscle. It was with the greatest difficulty I refrained from springing upon the torturer, and arresting his lash; but, alas! what could I do, but turn aside to hide my tears for the sufferer, and my blushes for humanity? This was in a public and regularly-organized prison; the punishment was one recognized and authorized by the law. But think you the poor wretch had committed a heinous offence, and had been convicted thereof, and sentenced to the lash? Not at all. She was brought by her Master to be whipped by the common executioner, without trial, judge or jury, just at his beck or nod, for some real or supposed offence, or to gratify his own whim or malice. And he may bring her day after day, without cause assigned, provided only he pays the fee. Or, if he choose, he may have a private whipping-board on his own premises, and brutalize himself there. A shocking part of this horrid punishment was its publicity, as I have said; it was in a court-yard surrounded by galleries, which were filled with Colored persons of all sexes —runaway slaves, committed for some crime, or slaves up for sale. You would naturally suppose they crowded forward, and gazed, horror-stricken, at the brutal spectacle below; but they did not; many of them hardly noticed it, and many were entirely indifferent to it. They went on in their childish pursuits, and some were laughing outright in the distant parts of the galleries; so low can man, created in God's image, be sunk in brutality."

CHAPTER XIX.

SOUTHERN CHIVALRY.

'Tis only change of pain,
A bitter change, severer for severe,
The day too short for my distress, and night,
Even in the zenith of her dark domain,
Is sunshine to the color of my fate.   YOUNG.

FROM Adam, the curse of God glanced to the ground, but it fell upon poor woman, and both her sorrow and conception, are multiplied. But will not grace at last triumph? Will not heaven be fuller?

Never, never! did we realize the curse, as in South Carolina, in the case of poor slave women. That there should be so much in poor woman's nature, that can be taken advantage of by barbaric natures, to torture, to kill, to debase her — debasement, surely, worse than death. If any one is troubled with doubts, as to future retribution, let him come here, and, without a word of argument, or even revelation, he will be a full believer in the fact, of future punishment, provided, he believes in the existence of a just God.

To commence then, saying, what were it not for a just indignation, our heart would shrink from, yea, refuse saying but which, under such promptings, it says, and dares and challenges the whole world, to hear, and conjures it to censure, to DISPROVE, or to REMEDY. It charges every man who has a mother, a sister, or who has, or hopes to have, one dearer still, to do the one, or the other, by every power he possesses, and not only every man, but every woman, every child. Yea, it not only challenges, it begs you to look candidly at the case. It begs with woman's tears! Will you, reader, refuse? Oh, no! You are manly, you will not.

In the name of God and humanity, then, we charge every man as far as lies within him, and no man knows what lies within him while in supine inaction, every man who deserves the name, to exert himself until he can say, before the womanhood of the world, yea, before God, I have done all I could; all! even to the offering of my life.

To begin then. The young girls must marry. But, usually, mild means are effectual, in a most affectionate race, where we have seen a love that actually made us believe the sacred thing is yet in the world, in spite of the fashionable life we have been obliged to see. For these poor, broken-down slaves, the moment they see you have a real sympathy for them, will almost invariably say, " Oh, I must show Missus my wife, or my husband," and with a love, that graces few pompous halls, they run to different cabins and bring the homeliest of old men or women, gazing at them as if they were angels. You try hard to look a little admiration, too, for their comfort, but you are amazingly afraid their keen penetration, has read the opposite, or at least, the lack of it. This frequent practice, is prompted, evidently, only by the poor loving heart.

So they bring their descendants, calling them their chil'n even past three " greats" in some instances. So that evidently from this, and numberless instances we could name, the Colored, are the most affectionate race living. Of course, a race that can so love, must be able to quarrel. But this is rare.

But, never, in all the miserable cabins we have entered,

and under all the different circumstances, in which we have seen them, even having husband and wife, both working together, for us, have we seen even a look between them that implied censure of each other. Never!

But to proceed. The poor bride is cheated even of, or in, the cheap ceremony, and feels it keenly, as is shown by many thankfully embracing the first privilege of being married even amid the scorn of fellows, and surrounded by their adult children. In other cases they say, "Missus, de Lord marry us, we live togedder better, dan 'em white folks, married by priest, sights better."

But instances are many, where they were made to believe that any man, who could read, could lawfully marry, and they say, "Missus, I'se married in de matrimony, wid de book."

But, in deepest anguish, when the heart is breaking over the sale of husband, or wife, they are often given to know that the horrid farther South, will be the penalty of failing to select another.

So does the cold, slimy hand of avarice lay its foulness upon the holiest, and the best.

Now the thoughtlessness, the jolity, of youth is passed with the poor bride, and all the woman stirs, wakes, rises, in her soul. Now the true tyranny over her poor nature commences, and if they can suffer it, can't we write it? cannot you read it?

To facts, then. Going into a cabin, on a plantation, belonging to a man, who pretends to be a respectable citizen of a Northern city, our eyes were met by the large, brown, soft, tremulous, eyes, of a small sized, delicately formed, fine looking woman, holding an infant of a few days upon her lap. She was beautiful, evidently of a most refined nature, and with countenance of one of the best expressions we ever beheld.

"You seem very weak indeed," said we.

"Oh, yes, Missus, I never gets strong now, no mo'! no mo'!"

"That is a beautiful boy at your feet; how many children have you?"

"Six, Missus, now. But I'se lost five."

"What, not you! so young!"

"Yes, Missus, I'se lost five, and six libin'."

"My poor woman! what was the disease?"

"Oh, no disease, Missus, strainin' and workin' so hard in de fiel', sometimes dead born, all mash! sometimes lib little while, neber ober tree or four weeks scarcely."

"But surely, I should think after one such result, or two at least, their own interest would prevent such cruelty."

"Oh, no! Missus, dey neber tink you die, or chil'n die till gone."

Oh that we could give the soft, plaintive, patient tone and manner in which all this was said, "softening our Saxon words, with Afric's mellow tongue." These words seem, in reading, as rude, but spoken, they are wonderfully soft, melting, and winning. She went on in that chastened way, as if past all complaining or vindictiveness.

"You neber 'lowed to drop you hoe till labor 'pon you, neber! no matter how bad you feel, you neber 'lowed to stop till you go in bed, neber!"

Incredible! for those awful hoes are judged to weigh variously from six to nine, or even twelve pounds, as a Bostonian judged, of some, and the large handle is from six to eight feet long. "How awful! But why not speak to the overseer or driver?"

"Oh, Missus! 'at aint 'lowed, can't do 'at. Beside, if

he not drive you, he only get cut up 'self, can't do you no good."

"Oh, it is awful! But you can't hoe all the year round, then you can't always suffer so, can you?"

"Den, Missus, when can't hoe, hab to go into de riber and bring up de mud in baskets and tubs, to rich de land."

"But you don't do that certainly when in such a situation?"

"Hab to do it, Missus, hab to do it to de very hou' you sick."

Now ought not that man to strut well upon Broadway, or Washington, or Chestnut streets, or at Newport or Saratoga? when he does it, at such expense? If he only have enough such women, how finely can he dress, and fawn to, and fascinate Northern ladies. He ought to be painted, with himself and all his estates, honors, titles, resting upon rows of such women, since they are the only basis, and foundation, of his dignity. Would you any more touch his hand, except in a work of necessity, or mercy, than a viper? Would you sooner entertain him, at your table, as an honored guest, than the lowest prostitute? Would you? Slavery has been dignified as an awful sin long enough. It ought to be treated as it is, as the most despicable, of all meannesses. Seldom have we communed with a more delicate, beautiful, refined, mother than this, for it does actually seem that the adornments denied to the poor life, were in many cases here, put upon the soul—how we did love her!

But we were prepared to hear of awful suffering at the last, from such labors, and inquired how it was.

"Oh, Missus, awful! I'se so awful sick, tree days and tree nights! den dey hab to go to Beaufort for white doctor [after she had gone all the rounds of ignorant practice] and he hab to use force, Missus, force, 'cause my poo' body so weak wid work in de fiel' I couldn't do nothing."

Strut! slaveholder, strut! show your obstreperousness to those who lick your hands for mean paltry dollars, or rather for false promises! You strut, at great expense! do it well, and so as to strike Northern sapheads, and steel hearts.

"Then you, so weak, surely could do nothing, or no work, at least, for a long time," said we to the poor, dear woman.

"Hab to do it, Missus, whether can or not. Hab to go in fiel' in tree or always fou' weeks and keep up wid 'e men 'e very first day and all time, or else get cut up so awful!"

Kiss the Northern lady's hand, slaveholder! You have many such women, and can afford the expense of drives, and balls, and revels, and, if funds get low, you can just send and have that bright, beautiful boy, or THAT BABE, or even THAT pure MOTHER sold, and to the lowest villain that walks the earth, provided he can steal, cheat or gamble into money enough. Our laws, or rather suffrances, deliver over that beautiful refined woman to your, and his, merciless power.

"Oh, my poor sister," said we, "soon I hope you will be free, and have a dear home of your own, with your beautiful children and that noble man, your husband, of whom the superintendent speaks so highly, as a laborer, a man, and a Christian."

"Oh, he is a good man! Missus," said she. And we left her, with her beautiful eyes swimming with tears of love, and hope. If this government dashes those, and such hopes, God will blast it, and good men will curse it, and the heavenly host will cry amen! Allelujah!

This is actually a sample of many cases, like in all respects, especially as to the extent, in time, and severity of suffering, and weakness, consequent, upon such incredible taxing of the poor body.

CHAPTER XX.

INCIDENTS IN SLAVE WOMAN'S LIFE.

> But chiefly Thou
> Whom soft-eyed pity once led down from heaven
> To bleed for man, to teach him how to live,
> And O, still harder lesson, how to die,
> Disdain not thou, to smooth the restless bed
> Of sickness and of pain.

LEST some should doubt the foregoing or think we mistake and that poor woman's wail of nature's agony would be heard, we insert some facts, which like all others in this work are proven.

A poor slave woman of about twenty-five years, went to her Master and tremblingly told him she was unable to work in the field. He exclaimed, "it was all laziness, and he would cure her." In vain, now, she plead to go to work. She had committed the awful crime of telling of her illness, and must suffer the penalty. A large hole was dug, she was made to stand in it, to be buried alive, as she supposed. The heavy sand was filled in around her up to the shoulder-blades, and she left in the broiling sun, in intense agony.

"Did they pack the earth around you?" said the excellent Superintendent.

"No, Massah, it was no need. It was so heavy I to't I die ebery one minute."

But not to dwell upon further minutiæ too horrible for record here, she was left there six hours, suffered awfully for days, and then gave birth to a dead infant, her constitution, and spirits, broken forever. Her mistress, the severer of the two, was the daughter of a governor of South Carolina. Another instance, proving that these poor women have usually no hope, but awful danger in appealing to Massah, must suffice. A very young girl in the same situation, ventured to say to the overseer, "that it was impossible for her to work." She seemed to have little power to move, as if paralyzed. He instantly caught her, swearing, and thrust first her arms, then her head too, into a barrel, then he commenced beating her. "She soon was silent, begged no more, and he beat her until her poor body laid against the barrel like a piece of meat." She was then taken by her poor fellow-sufferers into a hut. It was evident she could not live any time, and her poor mother, a favorite, and very valuable, slave at the town estate, was slily sent for. She implored her Mistress to let her go, especially as it was Sabbath. Her Mistress refused, was inexorable when entreated. The poor mother fell upon her knees, and with tears and blessings, and prayers, begged "only to see the last of her poor daughter." She does not seem to have even implied a censure upon her Mistress for keeping such an overseer, as it was on her plantation it occurred. Her Mistress, noted for charity and piety, refused her, positively, sharply, and very possibly partook the holy sacrament that afternoon.

The poor slave mother went about her toil, not seeing her poor daughter, and, as we understood, though we cannot assert that, without attending her funeral. She worked on, and wept on, until in a few weeks she died of grief. Our informants said that "because the same overseer had killed two of her children, before, and she didn't die, so, her Missus thought she wouldn't this time, but she saw the others before they died." It seems always to be a great surprise to these oppressors, when their slaves die, and always unexpected, for they live through so much that they seem to expect they will live through any, and everything. Doubtless this Mistress felt badly, especially as she lost three, or the same, in the operation. Probably her "charities" suffered a little also.

But, nothing could be done with this overseer, he was such a favorite with his Master, brought in such good returns from his plantations, and the losses by deaths were only sworn over. He must not be spared and only sworn at awhile, threatened, and for these murders, he goes on irresponsible to any earthly power. For, if a slave is killed, how easy for him to swear that that slave resisted him, then, by the laws of South Carolina, he is exculpated. But even what poor laws they have are not enforced of late.

Many other instances might be cited as, of poor women in the same situation being tied, or drawn up by the hands, whipt most cruelly, and subjected to many other agonies for the same offence—not being able to work— told us by credible White witnesses as well as equally truthful Colored ones.

Of course, the suffering and weakness consequent were awful, as every one at all acquainted with the human system must know. These sufferings lasted for a week at times. But that children were also often born in the field, was true, and more or less common. A dear pious "Aunty" pointed out to us a fine little Colored girl, saying, "L—— born in de fiel', brought home wid moder on de cart. Didn't die—de Lord good to 'em." But all who know the commonest truths respecting slavery know that this is sometimes the case.

'That such waste of life should be suffered is amazing,

but not more so, than most facts connected with slavery. Of course, if complaints were heard or indulged, indolent ones would take advantage, and who could judge who was and who was not able? The evil is inherently in the sin of compelling unpaid labor, and can never be separated from slavery, so that, if that is right, all its necessities are.

CHAPTER XXI.

RESULTS TO POOR WOMAN.

Through suffering and sorrow thou hast past
To show us what a woman true may be.

In consequence of what is hinted at in the last two chapters, where are the poor women of the field hands— where? Under the sweet clods of the valley! The agonies undergone resulted in their death. Scarcely one in ten reach the age of fifty. This, many close observers have reported as a remarkable fact, others are doubtful of the number.

You see some old women, usually one, two, or three upon a plantation. But generally their work has not been in the field, or they came from Africa, and have better constitutions, have no children, or there is some peculiarity in their case. But you ask them, or use your judgment, and see how many young women, in their time have died; and in those living, internal weaknesses are almost universal. Another cause of these weaknesses is, that when sick they are not permitted to lie down, lest they "get lazy," the one unpardonable crime with the laziest people on earth. This is an incredible number, but in a mere economic view, how characteristic of slavery!

But though the end of these poor women is awful murder upon the part of oppressors, how sweet is the thought, that they went so early home, to be

"Forever with the Lord."

And how deeply beautifully is the precious image of Jesus

blended with the marks of death upon many that are left. Their dear illuminated countenances are engraved upon our heart, among its choicest images. Oh, how much of Christ was there in them! how quiet were they! past all eagerness, past all regrets. Still in God, and looking down to see what you are doing with their fetters, or rather the fetters upon their poor body, almost as an angel might be supposed to do, leaving the impression that great eternity is almost here, and that it is of far more moment to us how we use them than it is to them.

How beautifully this moss hangs from these live-oaks, over the graves of these poor people! Well does a New York lad observe, "It is far more beautiful than anything in Greenwood." It is of ash color, hanging in beautiful fringe from every tree, and to within a yard of the ground; with a soft rustling moan, both waved and breathed, a kind of sweet audible silence. Beneath, are the graves of these oppressed ones, folded in the cool, pure embrace of mother earth, where they hear no more the voice of the oppressor. They have gone up to join the fellowship of all the noble pure spirits of martyrs! of Colored women who have given up life rather than chastity, of whom we and you have read and heard, and thousands of others, of whom no record exists, below that of the recording angel's, but which shall challenge the admiration of the holy, when EVERY MAN'S WORK shall be MANIFESTED of WHAT SORT it is.

CHAPTER XXII.

WOMAN AND CIVILIZATION.

And down the happy future runs a flood
 Of prophesying light;
It shows an earth no longer stained with blood;
Blossom and fruit, where now we see the bud
 Of brotherhood and right.   LOWEL.

THERE is not a spot upon the globe, where woman toils equally with man in the field, and they live in a civilized manner. It is impossible, utterly so. Even in brisk New England, with all her excellent domestic management, it requires the aid in care, if not in labor, of mostly the whole female part of the population, to live in a civilized and refined manner, and most housekeepers everywhere, have extra help. This being so, with all the conveniences, and excellent domestic training, tact and skill of the highest civilization, what must it be to those of little experience, and skill, and no teaching?

No. If our government cannot afford to let women confine their labors mostly to the house and garden, at least, it condemns four millions, still to live in a half-civilized manner; it condemns them whether it frees them or not, since it has THE POWER to free them; it condemns them to claw out their hominy from the pots with their poor fingers or with clam-shells, as is often done now, and other equally uncivilized practices.

But some superintendents say "they finish their tasks by noon or even before, as they begin by light." Very well. If they do this, and the women work equally with the men, we are not the ones to insist that they shall thereafter do the work that should have occupied the entire day.

No, they must live like beasts, all eating, dressing, living as they can, until the women are permitted to study household good, to get three *regular* meals, and to make, wash, and iron, so that all can change their garments frequently.

It is said, "many are willing to look miserably all the week, if they can only make a show on Sunday." But, what credit do they not deserve, for making a neat appearance on Sunday, when laboring equally with men in the field all the week? We often say to the superintendents, "We would make a difference, were it but of half an hour, between men's and women's toil, so as never, never! to have to feel or acknowledge, in after years, that we had made no distinction between them in field work." But "present expediency," as usual, is against it, for present expediency never does, and never did, anything that will bear the light and the gaze of half a century thereafter.

But it is the opinion of scores of good judges, upon the spot, with whom we have conversed that not in the whole world, is there to be found a people that show so much ambition and real effort for decent civilized life, as these same poor Negresses.

When, in accordance with teachings, and the necessary tools being provided—not a broom, for instance, being found on whole plantations—the cabin is whitewashed, out, and inside, cleaned thoroughly, and chaos reduced to system, there seems to be no bounds to their appreciation and enjoyment of it, and they keep it so to a remarkable degree for persons so raised. All accord to them a taste far, far, beyond their ability, in every department of civilized life, and excess in taste for dress, and good style of living.

Then, if Government makes them free, and gives them the chance, all they need and ask, though not all they deserve, and have earned, we shall soon have the highest civilization among them. If Government does not, she may have but very, very short opportunity together with the power. God hath arisen and is contending for the Colored man. Happy will it be, if our nation HAVE THE POWER TO SEE IT, and to side WITH HIM FOR THEM.

CHAPTER XXIII.

CRUSHED INTELLECTS.

But, bitterest of the ills beneath
Whose load man totters down to death,
Is that which plucks the regal crown
Of freedom from his forehead down,
And snatches from his powerless hand
The sceptred sign of self-command.
WHITTIER.

ONE sees many poor Colored people who seem to have been crushed in mind by some great blow. It is perfectly clear they are not what they once were. Some of them seem to contemplate, in dull, heavy, terror, some past event, the recollection of which fastens their gaze, and stupefies them. One such, we saw yesterday;—a mother;—an aged Colored woman, with very fine mental physique, but now seeming to dwell in almost stupid abstraction.

Her husband, a very dignified, grey-bearded man, was speaking of slavery in answer to our queries. Her lips kept moving, her dull eyes almost closed, but, as if peering at something in the distance. As if suddenly noticing the moving of her lips, I said—"What did you say?"

"Two hundred lash! two hundred lash!" was her only reply, entirely respectful, but with mental gaze fixed on the dim past, or upon some object contained in it. Her husband, with a look of tenderness, pain, and of consideration for her, immediately began as follows:

"Ole Massah charg'd ou' son wid stealin' corn. He

was innocent—but was so frightened dat he ran 'way to de Main. Word com' to Massah, 't 'e was dere. Massah send me, 'cause he say he come wid his fader, an' den he won't punish. I go. Dey tell him dere, 'not to come.' Beg him; tell him, 'Massah whip; don't go.' I say, 'I tink's Massah won't.' He come wid me; he wou'dn't come wid no oder, but I brings him. I say, 'Massah, for my sake, don't whip him, 'cause I, his own fader, bring him.' Massah tie him"——

"Tie his hands an' feet, so," interrupted the poor mother, crossing her toil-worn and deformed hands, and shaking her head. "Onspeakable!" "onspeakable!" was all she could say.

"He gib him two hundred lash," said the father, with that inured-to-endurance voice and manner, which is so melting. "Oh, how awful I felt, 'cause I, his fader, brought him! but had to smile when Massah come roun' an' say—'You did right, Massah.' Must do it, or git just de same, Missus. Must say it for self-preservation; but God know de heart; he know cou'dn't help it, cou'dn't, no way."

"I'se walkin' up an' down dis yard, tendin' baby, 'cause I'se nurse," said the poor mother; "cou'dn't tell whedder on my head, or on my heels" [with a shudder], "to see my poor boy whip so awful."

Can you bring this home to your own case, parents? Can you see that boy of yours thus tied, and raised from earth, and mangled, and you obliged to laugh and say, "he deserved it; all right?"

One of many instances of heroism, was in the case of a very tall and strongly built Colored man, with an exceedingly fine, manly expression of countenance, but upon which, as upon most, suffering, tenderness, and endurance, were most strongly impressed. Said he:

"I was driver many years; cou'dn't help it—had to do it. When task not done, dey all get whip'd. I, too, for um; I'se had mo'n one thousand lashes in my time. Had to whip chil'n, too, so awful; dey break plate, or fall 'sleep, waiting for do something, or for Massah, gi' 'um twenty, thirty, lashes. Massah say —'you go barn, whip dis Nigger;' I go; know de poo' chil'n hain't done not'ing; don't deserbe it.

"So sorry for poor little chil'n, 'cause can't get away from Massah, no how! no way! neber! So I tells 'um: 'scream while I whip somet'ing else, wid all my might.' Massah hear; t'inks it's dem. People knows 'twasn't. If dey tell, and Massah hears it, I gets fifty or mo' lash, awful! But mus' try to save chil'n, eben if I did suffer so."

What a noble example of suffering to save others! And this is found in many Colored drivers. But not only do many show the devastating effect of awful shocks and hopeless agonies, but many also of blows upon the head. It is the universal testimony, that infants, so soon as they can handle a stick or the poker are at perfect liberty to strike their poor mammy over the head with it. "And," said one, "I neber dare make a sound as if it hurt me; if I did, Missus would seize it, and lay me ober with all her might." Incredible! say you. So is almost everything, connected with this, as other, awful sins.

But such severe and protracted toil must have a deadening effect upon the brain, both from that part being an expansion of the spinal column, and from many other reasons. In short, nothing, short of the resurrection, will obliterate the dire marks of their servitude, and abuse.

CHAPTER XXIV.

THE INNER LIFE OF THE PIOUS.

On piety humanity is built ;
And on humanity much happiness ;
And yet still more, on piety itself,
A soul in commerce with her God in heaven
Feels not the tumults and the shocks of life,
The whirls of passion, and the strokes of heart.
.YOUNG.

How rich, how unfathomable, how glorified is the inner life of these poor people! How they seem to look out from that inner, spiritual, hidden existence, or nature, upon you! All is for the time transformed, or rather seen in the light of eternity.

They are your judges, your tests of sacrifice for God, for principle. They are yet field-hands—those women. What of that! The seal of death is upon their faces; yea, the seal of God, the sweet seal of his ownership, his claiming, his coming. The power of man over them, will soon, and forever cease.

Toil on, ye ransomed, ye sanctified ones! Lift those awful burdens a little longer; to-morrow ye shall be with God, to go no more out forever! What though every lift seems to be the last, and "makes your heart all sink down," and "all fall within you." It is but a moment! Jesus is at the door! Yea, more, is he not dwelling in you, and with you? He has come to receive you unto himself, that where he is, there you may be also. And he walks with you through the last, long, toilsome, life-crushing days, or years. His holy image is upon your brow, more visible than the hated color of your skin.

But while I thus speak, your patience breaks my heart! O! were there more earthliness in you, we would not weep so! Did you rave, or even complain, we could bear it better. But your meek giving up of everything in life, yea, of life itself, so quietly, so patiently, so gratefully, breaks our heart.

But do ye not die for a noble government?

Is it not an honorable government?

Will not your last of life's summer's work put dollars into the treasury?

Will it not buy coaches, dresses, and entertainments?

Is it to be expected, that so noble a government, can, all at once, abolish field-labor in aged women? Remember, it is not sex merely that this noble government considers—not woman, as woman—else you should be shielded.

No, it is not the woman, but the color of her face, the accidents of her birth, training, education, and the tinselry thrown around her, that this noble government considers.

Can you not die for such a chivalrous government?

Can you not toil hard in the field, five and a half, or six days in the week, until you thereby learn housekeeping?

Is it not fitting that the whole nation should turn woman-drivers just for a treat, or for economy, before it takes a farewell glance of the blessed institution?

Beside, the *Christianity* of our great cities demands it. They send down their noblest sons to execute it. Those sons may never curse the day in which they fulfilled their noble requisitions, AND THEY MAY.

"Patience! noble, pious ex-slave women! the government is in debt!" It needs aged women to toil upon burning sands, and under fiery skies, to help it out!

"It will free you when it will cost nothing." Is not that magnanimous?

Take your plate of hominy, and sit down as usual, as your unavoidably neglected children do, upon the floor, or in the ashes, a little longer. We are not the ones to ask you to set the table, when you have kept up with the strong man all day, in the field. Not we!

Other women under government's care, must have many personal servants, so you must pay for it, by doing all your week's work in half-a-day, and then you, and yours, are expected to be as clean at preaching as any one. Beside, "men, among your poor race, would be jealous, if you were not to do as much work as they do." This is gravely asserted by men! men trained in the North! and it will not do for this noble government too suddenly, to lead men to treat their wives with tenderness, "giving honor to them as to the weaker vessel," as God distinctly commands.

How preposterous, that women especially at, and past middle life, are not to do the same work as men! Some say they work faster.

Yes, indeed! So they do; and so does a watch for a time, after the mainspring is broken.

O bruised and crushed ones! We have felt as if we desired to go out and take the hoe, and sink in the furrow, and die with you. But no! we will live and lay our daily tribute of poor woman's tears, upon your memory! and thus help the good to keep it green, so that you shall be inhabitants of two worlds at once.

But, at last, where falls this censure? Hath not the present government gone to the utmost limit of its power?

Have not the noble Saxton, Dupont, Sherman, Benham, Stevens, Hunter, the last preëminently? Do not many censure our noble Secretaries of the Treasury and of War, that they have exceeded their power? And has not Mr. Pierce, the government agent here, gone to the utmost of his instructions? Has not Mr. French? Do not our noble Superintendents do the same? Where? then, where? falls this censure? Upon the people? They are responsible—whose voices should thunder through the ballot-boxes, and echo, and reëcho, through the land, "We will have no woman-driving under our government!" They are the guilty, who should have elected the most anti-slavery men to the high offices of trust, at the expense, if need be, of every other or opposite consideration.

CHAPTER XXV.

THE GENIUS OF SLAVEDOM.

Ah me ! from real happiness we stray
By vice bewildered ; vice which always leads,
However fair at first, to wilds of woe.
THOMSON.

TREACHERY seems written upon everything in this land of deceit, slavery, and cruelty. It is in the soft air, in miasma ; in the cool, grateful evening breezes, in chills; in the clear water, in warm nausea; in the smooth looking roads, in deep sand ; in every hedge, in unseen prickles; and even in the dull oyster, in poison ; to the Northerner, at this time, at least. Slavery is here never out of your mind, WE HAVE THE TESTIMONY OF MANY TO CORROBORATE OUR OWN. It seems here to bind you in a spell, as an invisible power. Everything looks to have been stolen. You see a fine house, carriage, plantation. Your mind cannot dwell upon its beauty, but the thought that chokes, smothers, all others, is of the unrequited toil, the heart-breaking, it has cost. Even the innocent flowers blush, or deepen in color, that they have been planted in anguish, by the spoiled. But worse still, you come to feel that all "in that immense, microscopic realm of human life, down below human law," is tainted with injustice, extortion, theft. You even come to have a vague, wierd, confused, and most uncomfortable feeling, that you yourself have been thieving, that your companions have, that the man, woman or child, you meet has been thieving; that what is in their bundle, or basket, has been stolen. Your distinctions of mine, and thine, become confused. You ask yourself, does this article actually belong to me? Let's see where? when? how much? did I pay for it? Yes, it is mine. That fact is settled. But it has no more effect upon the muddled state of your mind, or clearing it, than dropping a pebble into a muddy stream. You cannot see a fine equipage without wondering how it was obtained, and you involuntarily ask, "Is it, or that book or horse or furniture, any more his, than mine?" In short, confusion invades everything,—you now have charity for Floyd, and his compeers, for you see, that under the long influence of slavery, they actually mistook thine, for mine. For you argue, if all this damage is done a mind, which hates slavery, what must it be to one who hugs, yea, deifies it? You strangely feel, that nothing is in the hands of its true owner, even if there is such a person, that nobody rightly owns anything, that nothing is valuable or worth much care. You are tempted to say, "the world is out of joint. Let the unjointed thing go on, while I catch what I need." You feel "nobody is honest and nothing has any permanence—nobody can be trusted if tempted enough." In short, the spirit of slavery strangely invades, blights, glooms, darkens everything. But all description fails of the actual reality, of this state. But, for an instance, to illustrate it, feebly. Your shoes are tight for so much walking, you go to see if there are looser in the Mission boxes. Yes. You have a new and strange feeling, that if you set a price upon them, you shall steal, you go, and get the "committee" to price them, grumbling all the time at yourself, that you have come to dare not to trust yourself. The committee come, and show the same spirit, that haunts you, by putting them too low. You think that is too low, and covetously say, "I should have priced them higher," pay for them, and go up stairs, saying to yourself, "I shall wear them out in the service of the mission, I get no pay, I might as well have taken them without all this fuss." You are indignant at this thievish spirit, and cry down! down! but it will not down, or at least remain so, in this atmosphere, charged with theft, and you cry to the Strong, for strength. Under what an odious, ruinous influence is this to bring up children, leaving out of view, other most destructive tendencies. All this, and much more, which cannot be coined into words, is the universal and legitimate effect of contact with slavery. Wonder ceases, that travellers under all these influences, lost all power to oppose it. God hath so constituted the human soul, that it cannot be opposites at the same time; as dishonest, and unjust in one department of the soul, or even mind, and honest, and just, in another, however it may flatter itself to the contrary. The fact, that dishonesty was recognized and most strenuously guarded against, here, is most evident, proven by the barrels, and barrels, of old writings, scattered about deserted dwellings. Not a dollar's worth, it seems, could be bought or sold, but the most strong, and correct, legal writings were exchanged. Everything in business, was tied, doubled, and twisted, and locked. The writers seem to have been friends, by the letters, but as shy and suspicious of each other, as Arabs. Everything you see, here, shows that it was the opinion of these Southerners, that honesty does not exist in man.

CHAPTER XXVI.

AVARICE OR POVERTY.

He turns with anxious heart and crippled hands,
His bonds of debt, and mortgages of lands,
Or views his coffers with suspicious eyes,
Unlocks his gold, and counts it till he dies.
                                    DR. JOHNSON.

The parsimoniousness, so often asserted in these pages, would seem impossible at first, in gentlemen. But this disappears, as one sees the actual appearances here. Poverty, Poverty, Poverty, is written upon everything, and stalks boldly abroad. All government stores cannot conceal it. It is proven that in the Barbadoes, slave labor costs seven per cent. more than free. This is proven also in the whole history of Jamaica, where one-third of those rich plantations were deserted from utter poverty, and where a majority of the debts that had eaten up all owners, were of one hundred and more years' standing. Slaveholders are not able to be liberal, however it may seem at a glance, or whatever ants may show. They were determined slavery should be profitable, and made the most desperate efforts to make it so, but in vain, generally. The testimony of all appearances, account-books, persons—show that. Many ex-slaves assert that they did not get over six quarts for a peck of corn per week, and that without salt, or anything with it at all, in most cases.

"The measure did not hol' a peck, Missus," said one, "it was gone by middle of week."

"What did you do then?"

"We have to get corn by selling chickens and such."

"What did you get for a chicken?"

"Sixpence for some, for some less, for some mo'."

"Then how much did you have to pay for corn?"

"Dolla' a bushel, Missus."

But lest some are not convinced, we give an exact copy of items from an account-book in possession of an officer, a mere sample of the whole:

"Set one turkey-hen on 20 eggs.

" three 'common hens,' 26 eggs.

Peg sick one day, Moll one—two, gave them all 21 grains of calomel.

1 needle has been furnished to each grown person.

8 buttons to each woman.

12 " to each man.

1 needle to every two children."

But if not poor, they were incorrigible misers, for everything about the "quarters" shows the most economic planning and long usage.

The servants too, who attended these tyrants upon Sabbath were sometimes the same who toiled hard all the week upon plantations, during every moment of light. As an instance of this, a gentleman well informed, and very moderately anti-slavery, at least, said: "The lady who occupied this house, had a plantation ten miles in the country. Her servant, after attending to her, and other labors, in the morning, had to walk into Beaufort ten miles, arrive before her mistress' carriage, to dress her, then to follow her to church, carrying her book, then precede her home, wait upon her at table, undress her, and walk back to the plantation, and be ready to attend upon her there, making twenty miles walk beside all other labors." This was, we presume, one of her good days, in which Missus, was peculiarly kind. Little did that woman think, she should end her illustrious career in a runaway, and that forced too, (for the inhabitants of Beaufort had bound themselves by dark oaths, taken in the Sanctuary and on the holy Sabbath—all to go when the federal army came, if any fled, and that he who broke this oath, should be shot in his tracks.)

But slavery, like all other sin, is ever beguiling by fair promises. The young clerk can prove, that by sacrificing conscience he can become wealthy, or the thief, that such and such prizes will make him forever rich. But though that thief, clerk, slaveholder, never, or seldom dies rich, still the mirage glitters as before. Still, many think the assertion, that slavery is profitable, can be proven by figures which cannot lie. But the true fact is, slaveholders are poor, men would not live so, if they were not. No Northern farmers live so; but their barren acres are crowned by a home, while not a home have we yet seen on all these rich lands. There are such, we are told, but we have seen but one house on twenty-five plantations, where we could think of remaining one night, unless duty, or necessity, absolutely required it, and then we should prefer a tent, were it possible, so old, ill-scented, and filthy are these houses.

"Do you say you lost all your children?" said we to a pious and very respectable-looking woman.

"Yes, all gone."

"Of what disease?"

"No disease, Missus. Work so hard in house, lib so poor on peck ob corn, as Massah called it, but won't a peck."

"Why I should think you, a cook, would get more."

"No mo'! Massah, or Missus, dey measures or weighs ebery bit you git, den you must have jest so many buscuit and everyting." This was said by the many pious, reliable servants of a minister, and, in one case, confirmed by a local preacher, and is further confirmed, like all the facts stated in this work, by general corroborative testimony. "Den he whip us so, if break anyting or fail in work. Take away ou' 'lowance ob corn. But must smile to visitors, say Massah so good, so kind; say don't want anyting for eat, when you starving most, else get cut up so." "But driver whip field hands; Massah—the minister— 1'y whip we house women and men." "Massah 'ligious! No more 'ligion dan dat grass." "Oh, he! too bad, work too tight, too much; but we pray he will be saved, don't want no hurt come to him, on'y pray! pray he neber come 'gin! and Jesus hear prayer, promised to, won't let him come 'gin."

These instances of measuring and weighing are from scores of evidences, of most desperate efforts, at economy, coming to light in every possible way.

Now what Northern farmer—even where it is said "they have to sharpen sheeps' noses to enable them to get the grass, among the rocks"—would stoop to measure flour, and count the biscuit, as this Southern pompous minister-planter, and others did. But we forbear.

We are convinced that their financial embarrassments, are one grand reason why masters so generally hate their slaves, and they hate him equally in return. But should you walk with him among them, you would see the low courtesy, the hearty smile, or that they would even kiss his hand, if they dare. But all this is to escape torture. But the Master is determined to adhere to slavery, and to make it pay, and every step, and year, is deeper, in the mire of debt in most cases.

This is evident from account-books, from all the ideas, and habits, of the Negroes, and in all habits and appearances upon plantations. We, with others, thought at first this poverty-stricken appearance might be from avarice. But avarice could not be so universal. It must be poverty. Beside, this country is not richer than the Indies, which, under the influence of the same system, were fast becoming depopulated of whites, from absenteeism, in consequence of debt. Still, there are said to be within ten miles of Beaufort some three, four, or five splendid residences, with appropriate surroundings, and the wonder never ceases to be told. Just imagine a person, asserting that "there actually is a fine house on an island near New York, Boston, or any Northern city, or village," and continue to assert it, as if it were almost incredible, and you have some idea of the difference between liberty and slavery.

If one is not convinced that the actual motive for this war, is, to cover up debts, and failures, in many cases, he need only go South to be fully convinced of it. In fact, they were bankrupt, owing millions in New York city alone. The immense interest on the money invested in slaves, and the many deaths of slaves, and especially infants, the vices, extravagance, pride and indolence, attending slavery must keep them poor, inevitably.

CHAPTER XXVII.

EMBITTERED SPRINGS.

The heart laid waste by grief or scorn,
  Which only knoweth
  Its own deep woe,
Is the only desert. There no spring is born
Amid the sands ; in that no shady palm-tree groweth.
FREILIGRATH.

THE wrongs heaped upon this helpless race, had seemed enough, had not their religion been made an instrument of torture. Had this one spring been left unfouled, they had not quite fainted in the dark, stifling desert of slavery. "I am exceedingly disappointed," said an eminent D.D. here, " in what I have considered the alleviation of slavery."

" What strikes you as most remarkable ?"

"The fact that to them religion was so dispoiled of its true character, and made such an instrument of oppression and bitterness," said he.

Then the possession of manhood—what a dignity, joy ; but with the slaves, more especially those gifted by nature—and many such there are—the robbery of this is the greatest bitterness. For a man or woman to know that they are imbruted, as far as Massah can do so—how agonizing ! To have an endless, inward whispering of taste, manhood, conscience, respecting what they ought to be, contrasted with what they are, must, especially to the ever self-conscious Negro—be most awful.

The patronizing air, that many put on, or the fact that not a word or action of his, but must be weighed against his color and condition. Added to this, is the fact that most persons consider him inferior, and remarks of his, to which a philosopher would listen with interest, are considered weak and contemptible. But the bitterest cup, some think, is the knowledge that his Master has unlimited control over him—his body—his wife and his children; and is subject to gusts of furious passion, and is yet amenable to no earthly power. All this keeps up an intolerable but unavailing struggle in his soul against such despotic tyranny. But others think the bitterness of their full cup, is the total contempt with which Massah regards them. And as impressions are received by the mind in some states, with awful vividness, and ever after stand out in colors of more than real life, so is the disgust with which Massah, and in most cases his family also, regarded them, so impressed upon them, that at the least allusion to it, the whole face is distorted with shame and agony,—but not a particle of anger. This in most cases has been most touching, melting, to all hearts.

"Massah touch a Nigger! Ah! you do' know nothing 'bout Massah. He no mo' touch a black Nigger than a black snake!" said an aged saint of God. "He say so, he hat us so awful! You go work fo' light, work good, get task all done, come home, dark, so you hardly see way out of fiel'." "You come near Massah, you want to speak to him 'bout some things, he kick at you and scream, 'You mean, good-for-nothing, black Nigger! Will you speak to me? Go 'way, you old black cuss!' Oh, Missus, he never touch Nigger but with whip, not to save you life. 'Lazy Wretches,' he says, 'I send you to Cuba.'"

Most of them, too, not only know that they were hated,

but loathed, and never seen but with disgust, or heard or thought of but with anger and malice.

"Massah can't love no Nigger! Come from Beaufort! Neber glad to see you, he boot you!"

This, added to the toils and sorrows, has seemed in some cases, the bitterest draught in the cup of slavery. But more who have conversed much with them, think, the separation of families the sorest grief; and WE KNOW, from universal testimony these cost many lives.

But every power or faculty, of body or mind, becomes an avenue or spring of sorrow. Every family tie, every affection, passion, power, of the soul, is a fount of agony and bitterness, and SHALL NOT THE MOST HIGH REGARD IT?

CHAPTER XXVIII.

THE APOSTLES OF SLAVERY.

Thus said the Lord unto me, The prophets prophesy lies in my name: I sent them not, neither spake unto them: they prophesy unto you a FALSE VISION, and divination, and a thing of NAUGHT, and a DECEIT OF THEIR HEART.

ONE said, speaking of preachers, "Some good, but couldn't preach as dey want to, must preach as Massah 'lowed; no furder; no open Gospel! no furder. If dey did, hab to alter preaching next time. Dey come 'gin, preach right oder way. Preach must be humble—obey Massah, do ebryting for Massah, and noting for self, else de Lord would not save your poor soul." But we give the testimony of Dr. Nelson, a slaveholder, the author of an able work on infidelity:

"But nothing is equal to their harping upon the 'religious privileges and instruction' of the slaves of the South. And nothing could be so false and injurious (to the cause of freedom and religion) as the impression they give on that subject. I say what I know when I speak in relation to this matter. I have been intimately acquainted with the religious opportunities of slaves—in the constant HABIT OF HEARING THE SERMONS which are preached to them. And I solemnly affirm, that, during the forty years of my residence and observation in this line, I NEVER HEARD a single ONE OF THESE SERMONS but what was taken up with the OBLIGATIONS AND DUTIES OF SLAVES TO THEIR MASTERS. Indeed, I never heard A SER-

MON to slaves but what made OBEDIENCE TO MASTERS by the slaves the FUNDAMENTAL AND SUPREME law of religion. ANY CANDID AND INTELLIGENT MAN CAN DECIDE WHETHER SUCH PREACHING IS NOT, as to religious purposes, WORSE THAN NONE AT ALL.

"Again: it is wonderful how the credulity of the North is subjected to imposition in regard to the *kind treatment* of slaves. For myself, I can clear up the apparent contradictions found in writers who have resided at or visited the South. The 'majority of slaveholders,' say some, 'treat their slaves with kindness.' Now, this may be true in certain States and districts, setting aside all questions of treatment, except such as refer to the *body*. And yet, while the 'majority of slaveholders' in a certain section may be kind, the majority of *slaves* in that section will be treated with cruelty. This is the truth in many such cases, that while there may be thirty men who may have but one slave apiece, and that a house-servant, a *single* man in their neighborhood may have a hundred slaves—all field-hands, half-fed, worked excessively, and whipped most cruelly. This is what I have often seen."

A most reliable, intelligent, fine-looking Colored "member" said, "Our preacher curse. He curse God for doin' what he doin' in the war. We bless him all time! But preacher will learn God yet! You know 'e hymn says,

'When my faith is sharply tried,
I find myself a learner yet.'"

One who had evidently drank deep into the cup of sorrow, said: "We couldn't tell, NO PREACHER, NEBER, how we suffer all dese long years. He know'd nothin' 'bout we." What a pastor!!

The owner of that mansion upon which we now look,

so sure as he drank freely, which was often, went out upon his plantation, and had a chair brought into the yard, and regaled himself with seeing his slaves whipped. Yet doubtless the next minister that sat at his splendid table simpered and smiled, and cried, "Cursed be Canaan," licking his hand, while he pierced his soul.

But many not only taught by word, but deed. One such, used to preach pathetically, here, while he had a poor slave chained in his cellar for grieving because he had sold his wife. All keeping their people on a peck of corn, measuring and weighing out materials for dinner before going to church, and counting and measuring afterwards, so that the poor cook left the kitchen faint, as many told us, and "went to her hut to cook a little corn for self."

"Why I could not tell within one biscuit," said we.

"Dey could tell, Missus. Dey used to it; you couldn't take bit, but dey know it, and whip you." And yet the pompousness and irritablity of those ministers could awe whole Assemblies, Conventions, Conferences, and cheat them out of common sense, to say nothing of religion. But we give a few facts:

"'I know a minister, a man of talents, and popular as a preacher, who took his Negro girl into a barn to whip her, *and she was brought out a corpse.*' This is the testimony of Mr. Geo. A. Avery, of Rochester, New York, who states further that the friends of the minister seemed to think it of 'little importance to his *ministerial standing.*' Of course he was not indicted! This was in Virginia.

"A minister in South Carolina, a native of the North, had a stated Sabbath appointment to preach, about eight miles from his residence. He was in the habit of riding thither in his gig or sulkey, after a very swift trotting horse, which he always drove briskly. Behind him ran his Negro slave on foot, who was required to be at the

place of appointment as soon as his Master, to take care of his horse. Sometimes he fell behind, and kept his Master waiting for him a few minutes, for which he always received a reprimand, and was sometimes punished. On one occasion of this kind, after a sermon, the Master told the slave that he would take care to have him keep up with him going home. So he tied him by the wrists, with a halter, to his gig behind, and drove rapidly home. The result was that, about two or three miles from home, the poor fellow's feet and legs failed him, and he was dragged on the ground all the rest of the way, by the wrists! Whether the Master knew it or not till he reached home, is not certain; but on alighting and looking round, he exclaimed, 'Well, I thought you would keep up with me this time!' so saying, he coolly walked into the house. The servants came out and took up the poor sufferer for dead. After a time he revived a little, lingered for a day or two, *and died!* The facts were known all over the neighborhood, but nothing was done about it! The minister continued preaching as before; and another slave of his, unable to labor or walk, was seen laid under a shed, near the house, where he would have starved, but for the food thrown over the fence, to him by some mechanics working near by, and which he devoured ravenously. He was sent off to the plantation, and soon after died. When that minister comes up to our General Assemblies, Annual Conferences, or May Anniversaries, he can, doubtless, tell us all about the 'innocent legal relation' of slaveowner, and how kindly the slaves a. J treated by their Masters! We should not publish *this* narrative, which has never before appeared in print, had it not been told to us by an eye-witness, with whom we are well acquainted, and in whose statements we can implicitly confide—Mr. John W. Hill, Green Point, near New York city. He saw the gig when it came up, with the slave dragging behind, and saw the minister alight and go in."*

An instance in illustration of the standard of ministerial character is seen in a Preacher in Beaufort, who having sent his slaves out of hearing, into the basement, raved about the war and the North. His son said:

"Father, it is of no use. We can and must see that the Lord is with them."

The father jumped from his seat, and violently stamping his feet, cried:

"Get out of my house this instant, or I will shoot you"—suiting the action to the word—and the son was obliged to seek safety in flight.

In short, one cannot become familiar with their history and course without agreeing with Parson Brownlow, in his awful but appropriate language, that they are, as a

* Goodell's American Slave Code, pp. 216.

class, "infernal apostatos" and "Judases;" though as Judas repented, perhaps he should not be slandered by being classed with them.

True, there were noble exceptions, so far as personal character was concerned. But they went on, in fellowship with these, and so by countenancing, became partakers of their evil deeds.

COLORED AMBASSADORS.

The real spiritual benefit of these poor Colored people, instrumentally, seems to have been mostly derived from a sort of local preachers, Colored, and mostly slaves, but of deep spiritual experience, sound sense, and capacity to state Scripture facts, narratives, and doctrines, far better than most, who feed upon commentaries. True, the most of them could not read, still, some of them line hymns from memory with great accuracy, and fervor, and repeat Scripture most appropriately, and correctly. Their teaching shows clearly that it is God in the soul, that makes the religious teacher. One is amazed at their correctness and power. They say: "God tell me 'you go teach de people what I tell you; I shall prosper you; I teach you in de heart.'" They open their mouth in simple faith that God will fill it, and are not disappointed. How dear to God, must be their perfect humility, perfect trust, perfect love.

> Richest by far is the heart's adoration,
> Dearest to God are the prayers of the poor.

But they are remarkably humble, and seem almost pained if you call them preacher, saying quickly and quietly, "No, Massah, I not preacher, I talk to 'e people, 'at is all; I not preach, only try for help 'e people." But there is in them a richness of imagination, a seeing of the invisible, a clear realization of eternal realities, which is indescribable, and powerful in effect, upon their audiences, and learning from the Bible alone, their standard of action, and experience is very high. But to speak of their conscientiousness, requires another chapter.

CHAPTER XXIX.

PRAYERS OF THE EX-SLAVES.

The prayers of the poor slaves, are proven to have had great value, in the minds of their Masters, in scores of ways. They argued, and begged, coaxed and threatened, broke up meetings, punished, to make them pray " fo' de confederates." It is proven to have been so from the fact that so many refer to it, as a known fact in so many incidental ways; for instance—"Massah say, we pray for de war, say we shouldn't, mus' pray for de 'fed'rates. We pray mo', pray harder. Den dey wouldn't let we hab meetin's, broke up de meetin's, but didn't broke our hearts, we pray mo' and mo', in de heart, night and day, and wait, and wait, for de Lord. Oh how we did pray for Pa Lincum! all ou' people call him Pa Lincum. Oh we pray for de Lord to come, to hasten his work. Now he come, we save by de Lord. De Lord done it. We all so happy now, all work good; 'spect to work, used to it, and not'ing else. We so happy, we hear de firing at Hilton Head, and when we see de ships comin', we tink we 'mos' in heben." Such was the faith of these dear people, in the success of the North, that they rejoiced at the knowing that there was actual battle as if it were victory.

Said an intelligent woman—"Some ou' people sick, all 'long, befo' 'at time, not suffered to lie down, must sit up all time, else Massah say you get lazy, sit up till you all so hot inside, all dried up, all life gone. Some, after cryin', O Lord how long? so long, get 'scouraged, tink de good time neber come, so say 'ey mus' gib up, can't bear no mo', no mo', no way. Then cryin' and prayin' to God fo' 'em, I hear a voice in my soul—voice say 'which side I am on will prevail. You will see which side I am on,' an' I knew I would, an' I did. God did promise a Savior, de Savior did come. We knew ou' enemies should be ou' footstool. We love you all, but we praise God."

A deeply pious ex-slave, said, "When I see de ships come to Hilton Head, I go into my little cabin, and fall down 'fore de Lord, and pray all night; I neber stop all night. I pray dat God bless you, and gib you success! Massah angry, but mus' pray for de comin' ob de Lord, an' his people."

Another said, "I knew God would bless you, an' give victory, I feel it when I pray. Massah angry 'cause I pray for de North, can't help it, mus' pray for de whole worl'. Massah say, 'No! Pray for de 'fed'rates.' But I knew God would bless de North. I say to de boys, 'Work on, work on de fort, work good, boys, 'twont be long, dis fort wont do no good for rebels; work on boys, God will soon set his people free.'"

These are samples of scores of testimonies.

CHAPTER XXX.

AMALGAMATION.

Finally, brethren, whatsoever things are pure, whatsoever things are honest, whatsoever things are true, whatsoever things are lovely, whatsoever THINGS ARE OF GOOD REPORT, if there be any virtue, and if there be any praise, think on these things.

AMALGAMATION is the progeny, and sure follower, of slavery. In every clime and age it has accompanied it. It is ever sought, and practised by oppressors. Strangers, are lured to their ruin, for its profits. Yet pro-slavery men cry Amalgamation! when they can produce no other prejudice.

Now, where, in the free States, is there any amalgamation? Where in the slave States is there not? There, it stalks boldly forth; here, if in some very rare cases it appears, it hides, because of just sentiments.

The Colored do not seek it, first, the world over. They wisely prefer their own people. There is not in the Caucasean the warmth of soul, to adapt him to the African. There is not the Colored adaptation to him.

Great efforts were made in Oberlin College, Ohio, for years, and in their most excellent society, to produce more association between Whites and Colored, for the elevation of the latter. But, it was found impossible, even under the liberal-minded and deeply-Christian influences there, and the great talent of many of the Africans who graduated there.

We have been to rehearsals preparatory to public concerts there, and seen the Colored most honored, both as singers and in preparatory business. They evidently felt quite at home, if not a little elevated, by their more expensive color. But the moment business was done, they as naturally drew apart from other pupils, into companies by themselves, as water runs down hill. In relation to this, an excellent professor there said, "We have given up producing much association between the races here. We have made every effort, thinking thereby to benefit the Colored. But it is of no use. They are always in circles by themselves, and we conclude, now, it is all right."

So it ever is. When did one find a Colored person in his way, or making himself sociable, in any place where he had not actual business? So it is in South Carolina. The company of the Colored is far more sought by the Whites, than the opposite. When you see Colored men talking with soldiers, it is nearly always evident that it is the latter that make the effort to prolong it; and so everywhere. It is only by constraint that they favor Amalgamation at first, and in almost every case where it has actually occurred, it has been the Whites that have made advances.

It is far *better that the races are* distinct. The pure African is often superior to the Mulatto in the South. It is robbery that the race should be cheated of their best specimens, as in slavery it ever is. But, if you would see Amalgamation, read the following, the legitimate and sad fruit of slavery:

"Are we dealing in romance? Come, then, and we will introduce you to a Vice-President of the United States—a very singular man, to be sure, though not singular in being a slaveholder, nor singular in having beautiful Colored daughters, to be sought after—in some sort—

by white gentlemen; but singular in giving his Colored daughters a good education, attending them in public *as* a father, and insisting that whoever admired and sought them should do so only in the way of honorable marriage! The singularity of Colonel Richard M. Johnson attracted the nation's attention. He was *so very* singular as to treat the mother of his Colored daughters as though she were his wife; to give her the charge of his household; a seat by his side at his table, addressing her as 'Mrs. Johnson'—to do all this, instead of selling her in the market, as some other great statesmen have sold the mothers of their Colored children. When 'Mrs. Johnson' became religious and wished to unite with the Church, the good minister felt it his duty to tell her that there was an obstacle in the way—the scandal of her living as she did with Colonel Johnson. She immediately communicated the fact to the Colonel. 'You know, my dear,' said he, 'I have always been ready to marry you, whenever it could be done. I am ready now, and will call on your minister about it.' He did so, and requested the minister to marry them, after explaining the facts of the case. The good minister was now in a worse dilemma than before! What! marry Colonel Johnson to a *Colored* woman! What could he say? He could only say that the law would not permit such a marriage. 'Very well,' retorted Colonel Johnson—who was not a Christian—'if your Christian law of marriage will not permit me to marry the woman of my choice, nor permit her to marry the man of her choice, it must even permit us to live together *without* marriage.' So saying he walked away, and that was the last that was said about the marriage. Whether the lady was received into the Church, we cannot tell."*

* Key to Uncle Tom's Cabin.

Nothing is more evident to those who actually know the Colored, than that while they respect, value, and revere, the good, they want little companionship with the Whites. The fervor, we repeat, of their natures, makes the frigidity, the self-love of the masses most distateful to them. Then, too, they are most highly social, and even where they do not respect, as they should, their love for each other is wonderful.

While they honor, and reverence, their teachers, while they are patient of any amount, of conversation, where they can do or get good, still, when all is done, they fall into their own circle or color for companionship. This fact amazed some of our most excellent teachers. They exclaimed, "They seem not to tire of our teaching, and to prize us more and more, but they seem, after all, to want little of our company."

This is precisely the testimony of Oberlin, to which we again refer. She has for twenty-eight years received the Colored freely to all her privileges and honors. She has even seemed to foster them most if possible. She thought the way to elevate them was to bring them into close association with her ablest, most excellent scholars and Christians. But, after years of trial, she has given up that the Colored must be allowed to follow their nature, which is to seek companionship with each other. NOT THE SHADOW OF AMALGAMATION has fallen there, while in slavery IT HAS RULED THE DAY.

We have the personal testimony of Oberlin professors, upon this point, that the Colored and Whites go forward most harmoniously, and profitably, together as learners and laborers; but that for companionship they turn to their own, particularly the Colored. There has not been a case of attachment, or at least engagement, between the races, in all the noble Colored scholars that college has raised, and not a barrier has been apparent upon that point, as we can ascertain.

AN INCIDENT.

We were most amused, when in the care of the Xenia Female College. A devoted lady, from Cincinnati, was spending some days with us. As a meeting was going on in the Colored church near us, she frequently attended, and labored, in every way, for souls, most acceptably. She was cordially received, and in fine spirits about the meeting, but soon began to droop, as we had expected. We most deeply sympathized all along, but it was one of those cases that interference never helps, and cannot help. Soon she began to say, "The meeting goes on finely, powerfully, but somehow they do not seem to need much help." Again, "They are polite, but actually I think they had as soon I were not there." This was the result we looked for, from all our experience, as we now comforted her, by assuring her. And so it ever is, and will be. Religion sanctifies, but does not destroy nature. In all the institutions and churches where they have been received, and fostered, not an instance of marriage has occurred. The more pure and elevated the soul becomes, the more does it see the fitness of all things.

Who would so wrong either the White, or Colored, as to lead to unions that must be unhappy from nature's inflexible laws? It is the privilege of each human being, to be himself, in purity. It is slavery alone that amalgamates, that outrages nature, that confounds everything in one mass of corruption, that renders the South "the African bleaching ground."

CHAPTER XXXI.

OUT OF LYING.

Falsehood puts on the face of simple truth,
And masks i' the habit of plain honesty,
When she in heart intends most villainy.

The proficiency of these slaveholders, in lying, which we would not intrude upon the reader, but to show the necessary and legitimate work, and results, of slavery, the effect having been the same in every place, as Russia, Turkey, France, Great Britain, etc., etc., where it has existed, and to show how much credit can be given to their assertions, which are as yet taken after all by the masses, as the expose of slavery, or the light it is seen in. We say, their proficiency in lying, would seem Satanic, were that dignitary fool enough. For instance—though these lies are so odious, we are loth to have the repetition, defile this work, still as our object is to draw faithful pictures, for the best effects, we must not exclude this ugly weed, nor leave it in the background—to proceed, then, pious, tested, truthful servants said, "Massah told us 'at de Yankees would put us in harnesses made in de shape ob a man, and we would hab to go on all fours, hitched to great wagons filled with stone 'at hosses couldn't draw. I bein' FREE TO SPEAK, NOW, 'CAUSE THIS WAR, say to him:

" ' 'At would be onpossible. We could not move um if a hoss couldn't draw um.'

" 'But,' said Massah, 'dozen men will stand and whip

you, and, if you don't go ahead, they will pierce you with their bayonets, and kill you.'

"'At would be wasting money, sure, for de man cost mo' dan de hoss. Can't be possible!'

"'You'll see; dey'll do it,' said Massah.

"'Dey all say de Northerners live in bar'ls and casks and sheds, in de street, der chil'n born in um, dey die in um, dey hab nothing for eat but roots and sich.'

"But I say, 'dey send us most all we gets; 'at is strange again!'

"'Dey do 'at fo' ou' money, but dey hab nothing to wear.'

"''At strange too, when we get calicos and all cloths, from dem! Can't be! onpossible!'

"'Well they make it all out of ou' cotton. We'll keep 'at now, den dey can't hab anyting, hab to go naked.'"

For three weeks many poor slaves wandered in the woods, after our troops took possession. In other places they established a regular patrol of men, hiding their women and children.

This was done under the belief, or at least, fear, of being shot, cut to pieces, roasted, and eaten by the Northerners, which their Masters had told them, was the way in which Yankees used Negroes, and though they did not fully believe it, still being so often reiterated and sworn to, they feared us somewhat.

One said: "Massah—a Congressman—swore 'at de Yankees would not come, and if dey did, de world would turn back, and we all be killed."

"But," said she, "de war did come! Massah gone! Praise de Lord! and it is jus' de same world. De sun rise dere, and set dere, jus' where it always did! It's de same world, and de same Jesus!"

Evidently the oratorical talents of the Congressman had been finely used, for they had been exceedingly frightened.

This amiable Congressman, in whipping his poor women, because "couldn't do task;" "could not;" "onpossible;" would cry, "call upon the devil! needn't call upon the Lord! Call upon the devil! I'll whip you till you do!".

"But," said the poor woman, "couldn't call upon de debil, when poor body suffer so! So hab to call upon de Lord, and hab to be whip mo' for 'at. Massah say soldiers kill we, eat we, carry we to Cuba, grind up our babies to make sugar in Cuba. I say:

"'Why, Massah, 'at would be flesh, and bone, and blood, and not sugar.'

"'Well they'll do it—you'll see.'

"But, Missus, we not 'fraid o_ de soldiers when dey come way up 'long 'at fence with deir great guns, and all deir tings all shining so. We go right out to meet um, 'CAUSE WE FEAR DE LORD. Dey put deir hands right out to shake. Oh! den we so glad, so glad! But, we didn't tink dey kill we, cause Massah hate um so awful! We gib um best got for eat. When dey come 'gin, dey kill ou' chickens and pigs, and all, most, but we can't care, 'cause dey fights for we, and ou' chil'n, dat we be free. Neber been in such peace, neber! Neber tink we could: work! nothing to work! in such peace—no driving, no cutting up, no whip when done. We work mo', 'cause so peaceful—willing to work, for make something. Oh, so glad, so glad! for dis good time. Didn't know I live to see such time. Put all hopes on Jesus. Oh! my poor chile whip, so swell all up, kill it. Oh! my Lord! Now times so good, don't know what to do, too much! too much! Work! task done! come home here, so peaceable, too comfortable! 'bliged to praise de Lord ebery minute!"

Would that the reader could have seen her radiant face, her grateful, loving, pure, expression of countenance, her plate of hominy, her hut, her rags, and heard her praises! Oh! it was a sight for an angel!

"Massah not so hard," she continues. "Driver hard. But Massah no let you tell what driver do. He cut you up so, tie up ebry woman hands crossed so, stretch way up dere so, 'cause task not done, so hard! so much, couldn't do it, couldn't! onpossible. Whip mos' thirty on dis place ebery night. But Jesus been 'mongst we, for help we all dese long years. Oh, if it hadn't been for him, couldn't lived, couldn't!"

A servant was speaking of Mr. Lincoln's being so awfully homely, when her employer, an officer, took out a bill, saying, "he is not so very homely, see, there he is." The poor woman most modestly but fervently seized the bill, and kissed his portrait, exclaiming: "Good man! good friend to ou' poo' people." But it was with difficulty some could be made to believe he was not a Colored man, who went around, begging for jobs of rails to split, till he was made president. But never but once, did we see uncontrollable laughter, among the Colored, and that was when we said to them, "Your Massahs said they loved you." Then, we seeing how amused they were, and withdrawing inside the door, that they might freely enjoy the laugh, they went on, with ho! ho! ho's! till all rang again. Then one would say, "Oh, yes, Massah —— love Nigger!" then the he! he! he's! and ha! ha! ha's! would be uproarious. Another would say, "Oh, yes! he lub you! he neber cut you up dere, and dere, and dere," putting the hands on different parts of the poor body. "Oh, yes! he neber cut you up dere, he lub you." Then another would say, "Oh, Massah ——— lub Niggers!" and the general laugh would again be uncontrollable, and we presume, from their appearance, that that simple remark lasted for a subject, of merriment, for weeks.

Yet these are the men, WHOSE TESTIMONY has IMPLICITLY been received respecting the characters, labors, and the usage and happiness, and far worse, the degradation, of these poor creatures, isolated here from the whole world.

President Lincoln was reported a mulatto, as was also his wife. An effigy of the new black president was drawn through the streets, and finally burned. The Colored say, "we knew it be a lie all de time, for de Lord 'sure ou' hearts 'at he be ou' friend, and 'at de Lord will deliber us out ob de hands of all his enemies." Repetition of these falsehoods is painful, and disgusting, but one cannot avoid giving it, in order to give a correct picture of these Southerners. But, to recount all their lies, would require a volume. Indeed, like all other liars, they injured their own cause, by them. The veil, too flimsy, only revealed the fear, avarice, and hypocrisy it was meant to conceal, and weaned those whom now they sought to concilitate.

CHAPTER XXXII.

MANLINESS.

> Say, what is honor? 'Tis the finest sense
> Of justice which the human mind can frame,
> Intent each lurking frailty to disclaim,
> And guard the way of life from all offence
> Suffered or done.—WORDSWORTH.

WHEREIN consists manhood, gentle reader, can you answer? Surely it is not, in purse, social standing, a seat in Congress, or any one of the thousands other less seats, more or less dignified. Surely it is not in the shade of complexion, the education, the gracefulness of manner. Wherein, then, does actual manhood, in its largest, noblest sense, lie? For however it may rise in splendor, it must have a base, an actual foundation. Is it in religion? Is it? Is every one who is truly religious, manly? Would it were so. He is far more manly than he would be without it. But does every Christian man treat his mother, or one in that more sacred relation, wife, even, in a way that can be called manly in all respects? Would it were so! No. The great majority of the world are ashamed of the actual manliness they have. How often would that son, most fervently have embraced, kissed, that aged and dear mother. How would he have said, "Forgive me, mother." How blessed had both been by those acts? How noble were they! How Christian! How would such nobleness smooth down to the grave that mother's thorny path? Why could it not be done?

Why cannot you, reader, do equally, when prompted by all that is best, holiest, within you? Why? Is it not because you have not all manly principles? Ah, yes, there it is at last. It is manliness! Manliness in the PRINCIPLES! Yes, a person is manly, whatever is his complexion, just in proportion to his principles, and his energy in carrying them out.

But here, chaos, meets us, again. What one principle is the leading one, the noblest? You say, "In man it is reverence for right, for justice, for woman, for God." Well, we will not argue that point. Take your definition. Then, in the following cases, who is the man, not to say gentleman, Christian, as we might, justly, but who is the man? You shall give in the decision. Not we. In Brooklyn, a large audience is listening to thrilling words. "I saw," says the noble advocate of freedom, "I saw a Colored man who was literally covered with large welts from his head to his heels." What was his offence? Reader, put close thought, ingenuity, upon the rack, and imagine, and answer, What could have caused a manly, civilized person to inflict such blows? What? Hear it: HE WOULD NOT WHIP HIS OWN MOTHER! That was his crime. He WOULD DIE, but he would not whip her who bore him. WAS THAT MANLY? Which, in that case, was the man, the civilized man? the cultivated, the Christian man?

Another case we give. It is of a little girl. Few know of her existence. But in her one lone little heart, is shut up a rich world of womanhood. But, he who stole her, at her birth—stole, we say, for no one dare lift his hand to God, and say, "Thou madest a slave." No! she came from his hands free. This man, because he could do it, stole her, seized her, and ever since, he has regarded her as a thing! a thing that had hands, and feet, and could therefore be used instead of his own, or some one whom he could honestly hire. She, too, can suffer. "Good!" he cries, "that gives me power over her. Good! she shall serve me; she has no rights." But while waiting in an ante-room, overcome by fatigue from tasks to which her little frame is unequal, she commits the crime of nodding.

Oh, how she starts! Visions of awful whippings, rush upon her, she raises her little hands and thanks God, for waking her before Massah saw her. She rubs her poor little hands and her face, and eyes; and stands upon her feet, for fear the awful crime of yielding to nature's exhaustion should subject to horrid mangling her little body. Yes, now she is quite awake. Now she can surely sit a moment and rest, and be ready to spring to her feet if she hears Massah coming. With little heart glowing with gratitude for her safety, and this privilege, she sits down to rest, just for a moment, for in this house, one person wanting her so early, another, so late, little sleep, and hard toil have exhausted her delicate little body.

But in an instant she is gone! asleep! She sees the Savior, folding little ones to his breast. Ah, she is advancing, advancing, toward him. She, too, will soon, soon! be in his arms. Yes, some sweet influence in that holy place, draws her toward the dear bosom of the Man of Sorrows! soon that throbbing head will be upon his dear bosom. When lo! a stunning agony passes through her frame. She is upon the floor, and looking mildly up, her poor eyes rest upon her infuriated Master. He follows the blow that levelled her, with kicks, upon those tender limbs. In vain the little hands, and streaming eyes are raised, for forgiveness. There is not a feeling in his unmanly soul that can be touched, by that mute appeal, for she dare not utter one word, she has learned better.

He calls the driver; and a powerful Negro, six feet tall, and strong and with a most determined look, appears.

"Here, Massah!"

"Take this imp away to the barn, and give her twenty-five lashes! Now lay it on well. I'll see if she can't keep awake!"

"Yes, Massah."

The driver has no particular knowledge of the child, no particular interest in her—she is only a little "Nigger." He takes her away promptly. Oh, righteous God, why is innocence permitted such agony as that little heart now suffers on her way to torture? He walks fiercely on before her. Her imbruted Master watches them from the veranda, and enjoys, even in anticipation, the feast, that her torture spreads, so familiar, that he can see it mentally where he is. They get into the barn. The driver turns and looks upon her. What is she to him more than any other child? But he is a man. Now if he does not obey, his own agony, must pay for it. Massah is listening to regale himself with the sound of the blows, and the assurance of the agony that is so familiar to him. Reader, you are capable, by nature, of becoming just such a person, under the influence of slavery. The noble driver says: "Poor ting, she can neber, neber get away from Massah. Men, dogs, guns, nature's barriers, are all 'gainst her. I will shield her 'is once. The chil'n will tell, likely. Massah will hear it; I shall be cut in pieces by his lash, under his eye. Yes, it will likely be so. Yes! but I will shield her 'is one time; I can suffer it easier 'an she."

All this passes in the instant through his soul, even under that fierce face, while he is reaching the place of torture.

"Now," he says to the frightened girl, "now you

scream while I whip dis, or something that will sound, like it was you," and the deception is carried out.

She falls upon her knees, and thanks him, and screams at the right time, and laughs, gratefully, in the interval, and is taken to her poor bed, in his strong arms. Massah seeing this, thinks it all right, and so it is, when he does not find it out. When he does, he superintends the torture of the driver himself; and one such told me, "When Massah did fin' it out, 'e punishment was awful, onspeakable," and that he thus shielded children over, and over, with full expectation of it, and his words were amply corroborated. His was one of the finest expressions of countenance we ever saw.

Now, reader, can you see, by imagination, these two men. Which had character? manliness? But one more fact.

A walking creature, that calls himself a man, has a girl for sale—for he is honorable, and must pay gambling, and other such bills. He advertises:

"NEGROES FOR SALE.—A negro woman, 24 years of age, and her two children, one eight and the other three years old. Said negroes will be sold SEPARATELY or together, *as desired*. The woman is a good seamstress. She will be sold low for cash, or EXCHANGED FOR GROCERIES. For terms, apply to
"MATTHEW BLISS & Co., 1 Front Levee."
—*New Orleans Bee.*

The day arrives, the young woman is brought forth, placed upon the block. She tries not to look beautiful, but dares not look sad. A company approaches, containing many smoking, vulgarly strutting, spitting, swearing, creatures, fancying themselves men, and thinking to add more to their manhood by the influence of purchasing this slave. They walk up, and examine her poor face, count teeth, feel limbs and chest, all which are accompanied by remarks appropriate to their morals. Now some would think she was the despisable one in this crowd, but where is the crime, the disgrace, the contemptible, unmanly, conduct, the base insult to womanhood? Who is the barbarian, who is the low beast in everything, but mere outward form, and immortal soul, which soul is robbed, too, and will quail, when the judgment is set, and the books are opened?

But who now is disgraced, the poor slave or those more than contemptible men?

We say, she is not disgraced, though so awfully wronged. No one man can disgrace another, forcibly. True dishonor only can be, by our own action. By what we stoop to be, or to do, only is our character actually lowered.

But, of the two, this woman and her purchaser, whom does this action dishonor most? Suppose you had to be one of the two, absolutely, and there was no escape! reader, which would you prefer to be? Which would you, in the presence of all the pure, of Jesus be? Which would you be willing to look back, from all, all! eternity upon having been?

On which side, in all these cases, is the civilization? the respectability? the manliness?

Now, where is respectability, in slavery? The poor slave obeys his Master involuntarily, and only so far as he prefers that to death. He obeys him merely with his body, which is not the man, except as it becomes so, in the bestial man. While he does that, he! is often, in most holy communion, reading his Redeemer face to face. His study is God! God revealed to man, and more and more clearly revealed, just in proportion to his actual needs and hungerings, and his actual and constant hanging upon him alone. He comes nearer to Jesus than the angels; for there is a song that none but the redeemed can sing. There is a place for them next the throne.

But, while he is thus in communion with all the holy, yea with God, and merely in body serving his Master, what is that so-called Master obeying? How can we turn to the revolting picture. We will not, fully. But he is a voluntary slave to every mean passion—passions which the least child can call up, to rule him, to his utter misery here, his utter disgust at himself, in lucid moments, and eternal death.

That there are noble exceptions does not weigh anything against these general and awful facts.

But in all these cases, where is the civilization? the manhood? the Christianity?

In short, travel through slavedom, you see the Negro subject to the White; but to whom, to what! to what! is that Master, that Mistress, in most cases, subject?

But we must give one more illustration of manliness, a sketch of a speech made by Prince Lambkin, an ex-slave, on Sabbath, August 10, 1862, in Fernandina, Florida, on the occasion of a visit of Gen. Saxton.

"The Lord send on me so much trouble. I was in the world, in the horrible pit, and when my hands were tied, I was whipped, and I could hold up no longer, just sinking, the Lord he reach out his hand and save me. Let us all pray. The Lord send deliverance, if we pray. I don't 'spect my liberty will do me much good. Slavery has worn me out. There ain't much left for me and you, my brethren; but liberty will do the rising generation good. Our children must work for it—must fight for it. O, my brethren, I haven't got only half my body here. My wife and child are with the rebels. It make me feel so bad. I work hard, I earn my bread; but O, my brethren and sisters, I can't eat it! It don't taste good, for I don't know my family has a mouthful. Rebels all so wicked, I fear my family starve. I can't eat, (with great emotion,) but, brethren, I thank God I live to see this day. And I do so much bless the Lord, and am thankful to him that he send his true ministers, who preach to us the full Gospel so as we never heard it afore in all our lives. It do my soul good. I love this Gospel, and the Lord bless these faithful servants for evermore. O, thank God, I live to see this day and the old flag! Once that old flag, just like as Saul, persecuted us; it was our enemy. We loved the Lord; we were good people, but our masters were wicked. They swear, and drink, and gamble, and sell us, and the flag be their friend and our enemy. Now it get converted, and it become good, like the apostle, and he go and bless the same people, and do them good he persecuted. So, my brethren, the old flag is converted now. It looks sweet now. It protects us now. I love to look at it now, it looks so smiling! And, as the general was saying, if we would fight; why now I could fight. They say 'we have got no country. We don't want any home.' Why, my brethren, we got a home over in the promised land; and, by the grace of God, I mean to hold out faithful. And, my brethren, we must all pray for the general and all the officers who have come down to help us. They ain't fighting for themselves. They are fighting for us, and we must pray the Lord to have them in his keeping. And the soldiers; they get sick, and many of them die for us. O, they be so kind. We must all pray the Lord to bless the soldiers, and give them all the crown of life. And, my brethren, I feel like fighting for the old flag; don't you? I mean to fight; and if the flag, which now be our friend, go down, we will all go down with her."

CHAPTER XXXIII.

ENERGY OF THE COLORED.

Whatsoever thy hand findeth to do, do it with thy might.

> ' What are we sent on earth for ? say, to toil;
> Nor seek to leave thy tending of the vines,
> For all the heat o' the day, till it declines,
> And death's mild curfew shall from work assoil.
> God did anoint thee with his odorous oil,
> To wrestle, not to reign."   MRS. BROWNING.

To prove that they excel in energy, it is only needful to point to the whole and individual testimony of the military in all reports, letters, and documents in which their noble, brave, energetic, patient course has been referred to, to show that the energy of the Colored under sufficient stimulus is amazing. They will put forth most patient and long-continued effort for an object they much desire, and consider attainable. And this energy seems more natural, or at least developed earlier than in most races. One, or two, instances we give. A Colored woman said to us:

"After de rebels run off, dey come stealing back, to get deir slaves. Dey come sweeping round dis house, scouring de place, to hunt um, to care um to the Main. Some dey caught, 'cause come so quick. Dese little chil'n—of about five and seven years, we think—ran down hide in de mud, 'cause tide is out. Men come 'roun right here—within ten feet of um—but didn't see um, all but faces cobered up. Dey git in, but dey couldn't git out, hab to dig um up."

Where are the white children, of the same age, that would have done this? Their aged parents, the rebels did not want.

Another instance. Two of our ladies, in visiting a plantation, said to a woman, in the presence of two little ones, just fairly able to walk:

"Why do you not wash their clothes?"

"Missus, it is onpossible, haint got no soap, nor a thing to put on 'em while I does it."

"Well, you must have some sent you; but you can surely wash their faces."

Soon, the ladies returned, and were electrified with laughter, to see the little todlers, both stooping over a basin, and rubbing their faces most energetically with their own little hands, fully determined to be clean, and this, at an age, when white children would be screaming in nurse's arms. Superhuman efforts, too, to escape from slavery, show great energy, their only other encouragement being faith that God would help them.

In one instance, to save his wife, a man crawled two miles upon his knees amongst deadly enemies and pickets thickly placed, and was successful. Some crossed Broad River, three miles wide, upon boards, exclaiming, when arriving: "God brought we ober dis Jordan, into de good land ob liberty;" or, "God provide de way;" "God give we de boat;" "I ask him, he say he will, and he did, he keep we."

A most excellent chambermaid said, "she came from de Main mor'n thirty miles through rebels," most deadly in pursuing, and killing the Colored. She came on foot, and with only another girl, for company.

"How did you dare start?" said we.

"Why, Missus, I'SE A MEMBER—church member—and I ask de Lord to bring me safe, and he say he would, and he did. Nobody spoke to we, nor hurt we, nor scared we. De Lord brought we."

Many of them do much work by moonlight, to get necessaries, and respectable dress. But upon the hardest plantations, they are not allowed a garden, of any extent. We suppose this is for fear of leading them to think of comforts, and that, leading to seeking their liberty, for what other reason could there be? when so much land goes to waste around their huts.

In a church, upon a large plantation where the Master would not afford them a floor for it, and where, while listening to a sermon, a poisonous lizard sprang upon our lap, then glided away among the naked feet of the dear little Colored boys, a pulpit not being furnished, the poor slaves had twisted withes, and wound them with the grey moss, and by great effort, had made a pulpit that was beautiful. Windows, too, could not be furnished, but rude, door-like shutters opened in the places of windows. This is but a sample of the poverty-stricken appearances, everywhere, and this, when the law gives the master fifteen shillings per day damages, if the slave is disabled from work, by another, not under his employ. For so does the love of flogging prevail, that slaves are often stript in the roads and whipt, and, as the white man's oath alone can be taken, this is done with impunity, except in rare cases.

But, the energy of the Colored is further shown in their herculean efforts to make a 'spectable appearance, with little means, and in most ingenious and excellent mending of injured articles; all pronounce their work remarkable.

An instance: A Colored man had a coat presented,

about two sizes too small. What was to be done? Most people in that class, would have let it be strained out. Not so, this woman. But as the coat was of a bright snuff-color, she obtained some dark-blue cloth, and put into each seam, of the body of the coat, a piece, some three inches wide at the centre, and tapering regularly to both ends of the seam. It was beautiful, so neatly done, with such a look of completeness, and a good fit. One said— "If a New York tailor was here, he might get a hint that would be of great value to him." We merely give this as an illustration, of their ingenuity and energy.

The fact is, everything comfortable has had to come by their wits, even with extra work, in some way, and if those wits are well developed, in more than one way, it is the fault of oppression.

Our Peter said, his "Massah awful scared, said 'Peter, Hilton Head is taken, de Yankees are coming, we go in de carriage, we run fo' life. You take de slaves into de swamp, and camp out dare and take care ob um. You understand, Peter?'

"'Yes, Massah.'

"'You take um way, and take care on um?'

"'Yes, Massah,' said the meek Peter.

"When Massah gone, I TAKE CARE ON UM, I brings dem all cross de land, den cros de riber, den to Beaufort, to dis land ob freedom. I get um most all over—one hundred and fifty in all—in de night, de last load come on de boat when sun two hou's high in de morning. Pickets shooting at we, few yards off. But I not 'fraid, 'cause de Lord he help us."

Hundreds of instances of such energy might be recorded. Many, it might not answer to name, until the war is over.

LEARNING TO READ

How sadly isolated are these poor people! Of the world, the world of man, the world of love, of sweet homes, of Christians, of philanthropists, of scholars, of sufferers to spread the kingdom of Christ; the world of those in deepest devotion to God—of all these, how little do they know.

What volumes upon all these points are yet to be opened to them; and how anxious they are to peruse them! There is nothing, about which they manifest such desire, and intense eagerness, invariably almost, as reading and writing. They say far more about this than even freedom. This seemed singular at first, but it seems to contain freedom, in their minds. And they do learn.

One lady said she taught the alphabet to a whole school in one hour, and when they came the next day, all, excepting two adults, knew every letter. A large number at Port Royal, some think three hundred, some more, now read the word of God. All are anxious, even those whose eyes are dim with age. And what is most encouraging, is that every one, as soon as he learns a letter, becomes a teacher to one who is ignorant. Every Colored man carries his spelling-book in his pocket, and groups are seen in all imaginable places, and attitudes, even in groups on street corners, conning their books, and assisting each other.

When we visit them, mothers bring the spelling-books at once, to show us how far their children have gone; and the interest continually increases. Old people, children, and grand-children, all are seen reading out of one book, and all seem equally ambitious and animated. If you have a spare moment, in visiting a plantation after their tasks are done, you have only to commence teaching one person, old or young, and in a single minute you are surrounded by an eager group, kneeling, standing, leaning in any position unwearied, so as to get eyes upon the book, and whom no occurrence diverts, for one instant, from your instruction. And when you must leave, they say,

"O! Missus, please read us one hymn befo' you go;" or, if they are writing, even if it be with a stick in the sand—"Make us one mo' letter, please Missus."

Such eagerness and constancy must soon be rewarded by good scholarship. A minister from Washington City says: "The intense desire of the Negroes to learn to read, is beyond anything I have ever witnessed elsewhere, and their progress is fully equal to that which you will find among any other class of learners. I was giving a lesson the other day at the Navy Yard, where the class had but an hour at noon both for their dinner and their lesson. One of the men, not satisfied with having spelled out and read the lesson given him the preceding day, had actually mastered four lessons in advance. Overflowing with delight, and perfectly chuckling over his success, he said at the close, 'Wal, now, Massah, I reckon I'll git larnin', won't I?' Another, not satisfied with spelling out the words, looking on the book, wished me to hear him without the book, and I found he had the whole lesson perfectly.

"Our Alexandria school is greatly successful. During my last hour there, they answered questions with such fluency I was driven from card to card—we teach by large cards hung upon the wall—from capitals to small letters, from punctuation marks to figures till I was at my wit's end to find something they could not answer on our elementary cards."

CHAPTER XXXIV.

NEGRO QUARTERS.

And meekly still the martyrs go,
To keep with pain their solemn bridal.
MASSEY.

THERE is no work extant respecting the Negro, but misrepresents him. Not one! Not even the works of those most warmly enlisted in his favor, do him justice, or speak truly respecting him, at least, as he is, in America. Not one. The reason is obvious. The only light in which he could be seen, was that cast by slavery, for no other power had access, real access, to them. Many travellers, and others, may have imagined, they had access, saw things, as they were, but it will yet be universally acknowledged that THIS WAS NOT SO, and that, however candid, and open appearances were, they saw in these dark places, merely, but just what the Masters chose, they should see, and nothing more. They heard just what tales the poor Colored, knew it was for their whole skin, and length of days, that they should tell, whatever appearances were. The "greenness" of the traveller, or transient resident, who imagines that a Negro would dare be sulky, or sad, in appearance, or otherwise than jovial, wants a name, or, that the Negro, would dare act himself, in any one way, freely.

All this, is said now to prepare the way for the refutation, of that awfully mean and contemptible falsehood, that has been rung, and rung, through the world, by those whose life's study, and science, it was, to prejudice the world against the Negro, "that they herd together like beasts." This is a falsehood, to express the meanness of which, no adjective is sufficient.

IT IS NOT SO! Let the world hear. Let the warmest friends of the poor Colored, so long imposed upon, know, IT IS NOT SC. They do not so herd together. But in their poor huts, without a window, without a chimney, without a floor, without a decent chair, or table, from the misers, to whom every day's work of theirs, is worth fifteen shillings*—which can be collected by law, if one is disabled—without any of these things, they have yet partitions that divide their huts, probably twenty or twenty-five feet square, INTO THREE APARTMENTS, so that they do not "herd together" s much, as persons in many other cases.

These partitions are most ru , but they are there, invariably. They consist of puncheon usually, or trees split instead of sawed, and inclose just the length of the bed, a sort of berth. The door is hung by wooden hinges, in this land of poverty, or old soles of shoes, BUT IT IS THERE. The poor hut is the work of the slave, and usually, out of labor hours. Perhaps when a Master is "oncommon good," he gives the poor man a day or two, with the help of a mechanic. But we never heard of this, but the opposite. So, that, these decencies cost the poor Negro great toil, usually, but the toil is given, the decencies are had. So one of the refuges of lies, one of the falsehoods, under which slaveholders have hid themselves, is exposed. We call every one, who has been to South Carolina, the deepest dark, of the dark land of slavedom, to witness the truth of our assertion, that, invariably, however rude or cheap the hut, there are

* Goodell.

three apartments in it, however small. We do not say that there is none not so, but in entering hundreds, we saw none.

The slaveholder, has long seen, that nothing, so reconciled the Northerner to slavery, as the impression that the Negroes were almost beasts, and therefore, it was little matter, comparatively, what they suffered. Now the entire opposite, of all this, is the fact. Never, have we seen such effort to make poor rags shield the form, never such effort to live decently, even though it was with scarcely a bodily comfort.

But these quarters are horrid. We have been in those, which having no floor, because boards could not be afforded, or gotten, had been swept out until the ground was like a dish, and the poor inmates, said, that in rainy times, the water stood, so that they were wet to the knees, in spite of all effort to prevent it. One woman had suffered terribly from this exposure. Yet very near, there was high ground, unused, and a competent mechanic certainly could have moved the whole structure in a few hours.

But wisdom has been denied these poor slaveholders. This fact strikes one, momentarily, everywhere, upon their plantations. But every, every failure, has gone to make the sufferings of the poor slaves more and more acute.

A pro-slavery man was visiting Beaufort. The minister whose guest he was did not argue much, but simply took him out upon an ordinary plantation. When he came to the huts, he raised his hands in horror, exclaiming, "You do not say the slaves lived here!"

"I do."

"What liars! were their Masters! What liars! Why I would not put a hog in such a place. I cannot believe my own eyes!" said the man, with many other epithets. But common epithets, and facts, were far better forgotten, so only the cause be removed. FOR THAT WE LABOR. Suffice it to say, the minister had to preach to this man charity for the ignorance, training, and prejudices, of the slaveholder ever after.

Said a minister, "If one is possessed of a pro-slavery devil, let him come here, and it will be cast out, without a word." Yet in these awful huts lived many of whom it is true, that "they shall be mine, saith God, in the day when I make up my jewels." They lived, toiled, suffered, died here, but not alone, not alone, praise God! The Man of Sorrows walked with them through these fires, through these floods, through these agonies, through these tortures, through death. O! the body, the poor body, how crushed; the soul, how triumphant! Many, many go up from these dark huts to join the great army of martyrs. Many have died under the lash rather than tell falsehoods! saying, "Must sabe soul! couldn't sabe body." Many, rather than part with chastity! many, or some, rather than whip their parents or wives. The simple, heart-rending story, of those only, of them who survived, is told; the great majority have no earthly record. And it was not because their Masters were brutes, or at least, originally so, it was a fruit inseparable from the tree, slavery. Those Masters did not intend, usually, to k'll, but to torture to the very extreme of endurance; to crush the manhood out of them, and terrify all the rest into surrender of their manhood. But the means failed. The submission was only external. The Colored man rose, in God, far, above his tormentor, and felt that the real man was out of his reach. Still torture,—Ah! torture! of the poor, poor body, was just as hard for him to bear as for you and me, reader.

Nothing is seen growing around the Negro quarters on most plantations. Nor even is there a stump or block of wood, or anything where one could sit a moment. An old leech, or crib, would be a beauty, anything, that took away the look of desolation. Nothing but sand, poor weeds, and a few rags. Nothing but the great hoes standing against the hut, yet land enough wasted around many of them to support a family, with intelligent labor. But the poor slave cannot have a good garden without learning to think. But thinking is dangerous; and one thought may bring on another, until he will think of freedom. So, as raising chickens, admits of no improvement, inspires no new thought, that is the only thing he is allowed to do, on some plantations.

The only furniture inside the hut is a washtub, in which water is carried on the head often from long distances; hominy-pots, ever stewing in the ashes, boards propped up so as to form a kind of table, evidently not used or washed for weeks, some few dishes on a shelf against the wall, or on the table or floor, some children eating garden beans from small wooden buckets, a bench, and sort of berth, where a heap of rags shows it is used as a bed, and sometimes one or two old chairs, and some boxes.

How we did often regret, that lack of time forbade us to show them, and have these poor rags washed, sewed together, filled with moss, everywhere hanging from the trees, or with prairie grass, since straw, in this land of poverty, could not be afforded. But field-work, no soap, no water, no kettles, tubs, fires, or wood, would seem to make it impossible. Indeed to keep away all ideas, especially new ones, of personal comfort, evidently has been the aim.

Then the filth, no boundary between the ashes of some chimneyless huts and the deep dirt upon the floor or bare earth, passes all description. Wood chips, kindlers, always in the hut, mixed with rags and dirt that had not been moved for weeks certainly, for the poor women were formerly in the field during every moment of light usually. They seem to have not the least idea that any one will enter, and it is evident and proven, that, in the time of their Masters, no white person ever did. In short, the most perfect absence of all appearance of comfort. Yet some, during all this time, lived tidily as possible; swept their poor huts with pine bushes by moon-light, and the space of ground around them.

But in these huts the villainous darkness has long reigned, only darting behind boxes, and piles of rags, when the poor door was opened, then resuming its sway. But it will now be cast out. Windows and furniture are now being provided by the Freedman's Relief Association, so that a pattern hut may be erected and furnished on each plantation, for some aged couple, who will keep it nicely—and THERE WILL BE NO FAILURE THERE—in order to stimulate all others. Already the great improvements in furniture, and neatness, and habits, that have been made, through the efforts of the noble Superintendents and ladies of the Mission, are amazing; and soon, under freedom, steam-mills will convert the large wasting pine logs into boards, which now it is almost an utter impossibility to obtain. Comfortable dwellings will rise; and how will these good Colored people bless, by their kindness, their TRUE piety, excellent dispositions, their knowledge of *farming*, and their capacities and hearts for labor, whoever shall have the care of these lands until they have their dues out of them. There could not be a more delightful position, provided they were hired and paid honestly, though it were very little. They seem as much to belong here as the palmettoes. The land would mourn without them, and be desolate under any other labor. No one, who has had the care of plantations, could think of parting with the majority of them, but would consider it an insufferable deprivation. But this subject requires an entire chapter.

We visited a plantation yesterday, now for two weeks under the care of Mr. Fox of New York, and found two cabins whitewashed, clean and comfortable, and the inmates neat, and happy as birds. Such a sight never greeted us in Negro quarters before. But now (six weeks later), on many plantations, it is common. They say "the free hoe flies easy, and quick; before we work for lick, now, for wife and chil'n." They say, "we do not care what work we do, or how much. We will do anything, and we thank God for it, for work, and for we see dis good day, and for dis good chance. De Lord, is trying us, to see what we will do, wid freedom."

Indeed such are the improvements, already under the labors of those under the auspices of the Freedman's Relief Association, that many masters would scarcely know their former "quarters," or people. Still, never can their dwellings be homes, until the women are allowed to devote their time mostly to them. This is a vital point. Their readiness and zeal, in present improvements, prove that this will be done to good effect, and with taste rarely equalled among persons of that class. How will this land smile under freedom! Free, manly men, going forth in the mornings, to labor, leaving good, neat, well-filled, and well-kept dwellings, and returning to all home-comforts, and the family altar instead of the lash. Then will the products be, as in the West Indies, vastly increased under free labor. Then will all see, that not the curse of God rests upon the land—as under slavery, was most painfully evident to all—but His blessing, that maketh rich and addeth no sorrow.

CHAPTER XXXV.

PREJUDICE AGAINST COLOR.

The poor slave knows men, Christians, only by tales of cruelty and despotic power, every effort being made by lying Masters to induce him to shrink from contact with the world. Of religion, too, beyond his experience, he knows little except that it is made by odious teachers to engrave the bondage, deeper than the lash striving to write it, upon his soul, in its most susceptible moments. Yet something within, which is divine, says that this teaching is all unjust, untrue. Still, they have had no real pastors, but those of their own color, equally crushed and suffering. "All other ministers must preach as 'Massah low'd,' and we had no open Gospel," say they.

But they will have true apostles. There are those who will be willing, glad, to labor with them, when, to do so, aright, is not to rush into death. There are Ashmuns, and Drummonds, and Wilkinses, and Wesleys. And these must and will, labor for them in the Gospel.

This is necessary. For, just in proportion to his degradation, does the Negro despise his own race. This is one of the direst wounds of slavery. So often, and so long, has he heard his race called "Nigger," with just such a prefix as avarice, hatred, revenge, or meaner passions, suggested. But the prevailing epithet has been so long one expressive of contempt, and disgust, so constantly falling upon the bare hearts, of a most impressible race, that upon the least occasion, those feelings appear, and to be called a "black Nigger" embodies all that is odious—so that just in the ratio of their degradation, are they dependent for instruction, upon the Whites, especially in the slave States. We scorn to plead with the Whites on the question of color, but for the comfort, and benefit of the Colored, we insert the following:

"On my late tour, in August, 1825," says Dr. Philip, "I first came in contact with the Bechuanas. I have seldom seen a finer race of people; the men are generally well made, and had an elegant carriage; and *many of the females were slender, and extremely graceful.* I could see at once, from their step and air, that they had never been in slavery. They had an air of dignity and independence in their manners, which formed a striking contrast to the crouching and servile appearance of the slave."*

On visiting a family of this tribe, Dr. Philip observes: "I had in my train a young man who was a native of Lattakoo; and when they found out there was a person in our company who understood their language, they were quite in raptures. I think I never saw two finer figures than the father and the eldest son. They were both above six feet; and their limbs were admirably proportioned. The father had a *most elegant carriage*, and was tall and thin; the son, a lad about 18 years of age, was equally well proportioned, and had *one of the finest open countenances that can possibly be imagined.* The second son was inferior in stature, but he had a fine countenance also; and, while they indulged in all their native freedom, animated by the conversation of my Bechuana, or began to tell the story of their misfortunes, expressing the consternation with which they were seized when they saw their children and parents killed by an invisible wea-

* Philip's "African Researches."

pon, and their cattle taken from them, they became eloquent in their address; *their countenances, their eyes, their every gesture, spoke to the eyes and to the heart.*"*

"Teysho, chief counsellor of Mateebé, King of the Wankeets of South Africa, is a handsome man," says the same writer; "and the ladies who were with him were fine looking women, and had an air of superiority about them." †

We have the testimony of another recent traveller, and resident for some time in South Africa. Thomas Pringle, in speaking of the Bechuana, or great Kafir family, says: "Some of them were *very handsome. One man of the Tamaha tribe, was, I think, the finest specimen of the human figure I ever beheld in any country*—fully six feet in height, and *graceful as an Apollo*. A female of the same party, the wife of a chief, was also a *beautiful creature, with features of the most handsome and delicate European mould.*" ‡

It has often been asserted, that independently of the woolly hair and the dark complexion of the Negroes, there are sufficient differences between them and the rest of mankind, to mark them as a very peculiar tribe. This may be the case to some extent. Yet from the foregoing remarks of accredited travellers, it is evident that the principal differences are not so constant as may generally be imagined. Many Negroes, we have been informed, strike Europeans as being remarkably beautiful. This would not be the case if they deviated much from the European standard of beauty. Slaves in the Colonies, brought from the east coast of intertropical Africa, and from Congo, are often destitute of those peculiarities,

---

* Philip's "African Researches". † Idem.
‡ Pringle's "Sketches of South Africa."

which, in our eyes, constitute ugliness and deformity. "In looking over a congregation of Blacks," observe Sturge and Harvey, " it is not difficult to lose the impression of their color. There is among them the same diversity of countenance and complexion, as among Europeans; and it is only doing violence to one's own feelings, to suppose for a moment that they are not made of the same blood as ourselves."*

Most here, love the pious Colored, tenderly; true, we did not kiss them, as was asserted, not one of them, for we would not, by so doing, CREATE AN EXPECTATION IN THEM, and thus PUT IT IN THE POWER OF OTHER WHITE LADIES to slight them. In short, in all our dealings with them, we tried not to prepare the way, for those whose black is not of the face, to wound them. We imagine their impression of us, was that the NORTHERN LADIES' MANNERS WERE NOT AS AFFECTIONATE, toward them, AS THOSE OF THEIR BROKEN-HEARTED MISTRESSES.

Now, if one is so ignorant and narrow-minded that he decides upon another by the color of his skin, and loves him accordingly, let him once fairly own it, to himself. The admission will do him good. He could not have associated with some of the fathers of the Christian Church, its ablest divines, with Euclid, etc., etc., because, forsooth, they were Colored.

A really intelligent, large-minded man judges of character, much by the expression of countenance, and here, will you compare the Colored, man, with the White. Walk Broadway, or Washington, or Chestnut street, and once have your mind upon the expression of countenance of the persons you meet, and see how you are affected at the contrast of Colored with White. Ah, we are coming upon better times, when better tests of excellence will be

* Sturge and Harvey's "West Indies."

used, and required. England is reaching it, for though the most barbarous laws respecting the Colored, in this land, were passed under her government, perhaps in her parliament, in 1705, she NOW GLORIES IN HONORING THE AFRICAN. Yes, she often DOES IT, JUST TO SHOW HER SUPERIORITY TO US, IN CULTIVATION, and large-mindedness and just sentiments. As an instance of this, the truly Royal Victoria, among the very select number of guests at the nuptials of her daughter, not comprising a score, beside the royal family, had one full African lady.

It is well known that the English love to bring the Colored in company with Americans into their houses, as guests. At least some credible travellers so assert.

But it is well known that just in proportion to the lowness and vulgarity of a writer, is he prepared to spew forth his low prejudices against color, and *vice versâ*. Investigate this, we pray you, reader. OBSERVE THE MORAL STANDING OF THOSE WHO LOVE, AND THOSE WHO HATE, the Colored man. That, is all we ask. We have editors, who equal the lowest slavedealer, who ever cracked a whip, both in prejudice, and low cunning, and, we presume, in other respects, their real characters are precisely similar, and they would, doubtless, hold with them, the very sweetest converse, and mutual communion of black souls. THESE WRITERS HAVE MERELY MISTAKEN, in the seat in which they sit; their MEANNESS IS THE SAME, precisely. Should you, or I, stay in that climate too long, and permit the Sun to look upon us too freely, these noble, honorable, men [?] would think the slave-gang, slave-ship, or rice-swamp, exactly appropriate to us.

But, seriously, will you, candid, noble minded reader, take one walk, not for dollars, or new bonnets, but TO WATCH THE EXPRESSION OF COUNTENANCES, and decide for yourself where the superiority, as a whole, lies?

We do not wrong, nor prejudge, these writers. We leave it to the intelligent reader, whether it is not the same qualities, which would have made them good drivers, etc., of women, good sellers of babies, that prepare them to drive on the community toward bestiality, by administering most adroitly to the lowest of prejudices, passions, instincts, thus acquiring a most loathsome popularity, having even deacons, and class leaders, in tow. But one thing is sure, NO MAN, WHO LOVES THE HUMAN FAMILY, CAN ENDURE THEIR WRITINGS. This popularity may put money in their purse, and momentary power into their hands, but will leave stench enough around their sepulchres to nauseate the centuries coming, yea, to sicken every really noble, intelligent man, that shall arise, until this polluted earth is purified by fire, and the new heavens and new earth, wherein dwelleth righteousness, shall come.

But, how sick, is the soul, at seeing that no writer, no! not the bravest, best, realizes what slavery actually is, what the Negro is. Scores of best writers should have seen all, at Port Royal under the first smile of liberty there, and returning with glowing hearts and words, moved mightily the masses. Surely, then government had acted to the saving national honor, and purity, and the precious lives of tens of thousands of noble soldiers. Surely, this curse, slavery, had been lifted, instead of settling down more sternly, plunging us into deeper oppression. Surely, when Fort Donelson was taken, poor patriotic Negroes had not been delivered over to torture from Masters. Surely the rebels had not been invigorated, by our weak, cringing measures. Surely the nation had not settled down in warfare to the barbarity of the rebels. When the Lord MAKETH REQUISITION FOR BLOOD, he forgetteth not the cry of the humble.

CHAPTER XXXVI.

THE SOUTHERNER.

Oh, how unsufferable is the weight
Of sin ; how miserable is their state,
The silence of whose secret sin conceals
The smart ; till justice to revenge appeals.
QUARLES.

It will not be denied that the Southerner is brave, generous, hospitable, warm-hearted. He seems formed to be the noble, honorable gentleman, frank, and faithful to a friend. There is but one thing that spoils him, one thing that gives too tight a coat, and eminence upon a tree with an uncomfortable cravat, to his hospitality; that is, provided, his visitor is manly and out-spoken. There is but one thing that arrays him in antagonism to the philanthropic world, one thing that sets his hand against every man's hand, and thus, transforms his brother into an enemy. There is but one thing that makes him a traitor, a presumptive, heir of perdition. That is slavery. How sad, even if he become happy, and rich, and honorable, were it to pay such a price for it. But when the contrary is the effect, how intolerable. How sad at death, to leave an appellation to his name, that shocks the world, as does the word slaveholder.

The Southerner too, is certainly better, than the system, under which he lives. He does not, as a general thing, become such a swine in sensuality—we beg pardon of the swine—as his opportunities allow. He restrains himself more than Job did, because he has so much more within him to restrain. He makes more resolutions to be kind, amiable, and good, than St. Paul himself did. His is a life-long fight against himself, his home, his country, his slaves, the world, and he lies down at last, the most weary and soul-sick of mortals, to die. And what does he gain? He gains the mean glory of tyrannizing over others by the mere paying of dollars, a thing in which he can be equalled by the most base and contemptible of men. He gains less money than if investing none in Negroes, he hired them honestly, and sold no babies. We know whereof we affirm. We know that Virginia exports $12,000,000 in babies, or slaves per year. Still, is not Virginia the poorest of States, considering her age and advantages? Then, think of the intolerable meanness, of living upon such profits, of having babies sold to buy your bread and butter, and tobacco and whiskey, without which stimuli, the thing could not be done. He gains the privilege of locking and barring, and bolting, and arming, and terror, and sleepless nights. He gains domestic anguish, and heart contempt, in life and after death. He gains strife with the whole world, in which, it is sure to have the last word. He gains certain condemnation in the millennium. He gains the companionship of the very meanest men of the North, men whom without slavery, he would scorn. He gains sighs, around his habitation and grave, which sadly say, "he's in perdition." He gains all the imprecations of all, who in agony, and death, have called for vengeance upon oppressors. He gains disquiet, terror, death of soul. Yea, before that dire event he gains the knowledge and consciousness that he is actually brutalized. How does that graduate of Yale College feel in his lucid moments about dropping the hot pitch from burning pine-knots into the quivering flesh of poor helpless dependents, to say the least, merely because they are sick and cannot work. We have his name, but we will not stain it, hoping others may yet honor it.

How does that man, his companion, feel, who being afraid to ride about without a body guard of two Negroes, yet has them strip the lone stranger, the travelling Colored man, and flog him unmercifully, merely for happening—mayhap in weighing his internal sorrows—to forget to bow low enough, in passing him. This is a fact. He has such stripped, tied to a tree, and whipt severely, merely for not being obsequious enough though he bowed most respectfully. And the laws allow him to kill him* with impunity, provided he makes the least resistance. But the Southerner gains poverty eventually in himself or children, unless he have sense enough just at the right moment to sell and get into a free State, which is sometimes, but rarely, the case.

Finally he gains an early death. We were credibly informed, over and over, that few slaveholders live till past middle life. All its ripe and holy decline, and long, beautiful and quiet evening, they lose.

This known fact, DEATH THE GAIN OF SIN, is attributed by good judges to worry, excitement, but mostly to dissipation.

BUT, SUPPOSE HE GIVES IT UP? He gains what words cannot express, of peace, quiet, conscious honesty, accredited honesty; the hearty approbation of the good, fraternity, with all men, except a few slavedealers, and petty despots, and their avaricious, or contemptible, abettors. He gains a name, of which his descendants will not be ashamed, in the millennium, or in heaven. He gains honor, comfort, good conscience, union with the good of earth, and, the heart being pure, heaven. Now let none

* Goodell's "American Slave Code."

say the idea of descendants being ashamed of ancestors being slaveholders, is a forced idea. They are so now, in the North, in England, Prussia, Russia, yes, even in France, and in all the Orient. We have seen persons of wealth, standing, and pro-slavery, also, in this city, evade, in every way, owning the fact that their ancestors were slaveholders, within one week, and must not this inevitably increase, as righteousness shall fill the earth? Moreover, wealth, gotten by slavery, it seems impossible to hold—so let it be given, while so doing will bring honor, not dishonor. For "wealth gotten by deceit, is soon wasted." Children are censured for not holding that, which God hath cursed, "both in the basket and in the field."

CHAPTER XXXVII.

INNER AND OUTER LIFE.

*Our real life in Christ concealed
Deep in the Father's bosom lies.*

THE distinction between the outer and inner life, is very, very, obvious here.

The heavy hoe is in the hand of the poor, failing, body—the hand of the soul is upon the crown of life. The throe of anguish quivers through the frame—the glow of irrepressible love to God and the Lamb thrills through the soul!

They say, "Oh, Missus, I'se worked in de fiel' till I'se so hot inside!" or, "till all burn up inside;" or "till heart fall all down inside!"

But it is evident that these pangs do not touch their "real life, in Christ concealed." They glide quickly into talk of Jesus, as naturally indeed as the face of the suffering babe turns to its mother's bosom. If their Master is alluded to, a shade of remembrance of how he despised them, passes over their countenance, for that is still, and ever, the most vivid earthly picture before their minds. Then, with heavenly expression, they almost invariably say, "Oh! Missus, he was a hard Massah; a hard Massah! work from befo' light, leave here when stars shining; work till can't hardly see to get home, then whipt so awful, if you not done task. Hands stretch 'bove you' head so—raising the poor hands—

whipt so awful, ebry one 'at not done task, whipt thirty or forty on dis place ebery evening, and couldn't do no mo', no mo'! Lie down while corn cook, fall 'sleep on dis flo'—hominy all burn up. Grind 'fo' light and make mo', or, try borrow. Sometimes couldn't lend—dasn't. Go widout till night, den if you couldn't do task, whipt 'gain."

Oh that we could give the plaintive, tremulous, voice, and the manner with which this was said. But, as we commenced to say, the burden of talk among the pious ones "'bout Massah," is, "don't wish him any ebil. Hope he won't want for not'ing." At this exhibition of Christian endurance and forgiveness, our indignation glowing through all former recital of wrongs endured, finds vent in tears of approbation, and praise to the grace given. But not observing our emotion, as much as one not acquainted with the human heart under the constant pressure of great griefs would suppose—for they have learned not to place too much reliance upon the moods of the Whites—quietly, but without the least disrespect, they go on, "Wish Massah may repent. Oh, I pray, I pray he will be saved! He may hab forgibness; I pray God for it!"

"You would like to see him?"

"Oh, Missus, neber, no mo', neber in dis worl'! We pray he neber come back no mo' for 'buse we; neber hab dominion ober we, no mo', no mo'! But not wish him any ebil. Only come back no mo'. Want to die in peace, in peace! ou' Missus! an' no peace for Nigger where Massah is, he hate us so; he call you 'black cuss!' 'black Nigger!' say 'he sell you, he whip you pieces, he kill you!'"

"But he would not dare kill you."

"Laws, Missus, you don't know Massah."

8*

"But men on other plantations would interfere."

"Oh! Missus, dey doesn't know! If Massah shoot Nigger, dey don't know, don't care for black Nigger, don't interfere. Laws, Missus, dem people in Beaufort all relations; dey don't care for Nigger. Dey aint goin' to make one 'oder mad for we!"

It is as evident as the light of day, that Colored men in this region thought "Massah" had authority over life. It leaks out in scores of ways, in their conversation. There doubtless were exceptions both in persons and plantations. But it is well known that legally, any, any Master is in effect ever safe in taking life.* But suppose a Master was kind, he must have an overseer, and a driver. Suppose a Negro is shot, is the whole work of the plantation to stop until the Master can go away into the world—for we seem out of it here—to get another overseer; or cannot the overseer make his own representation? Could it be presumed that such a man would not lie? To know how isolated most plantations are, one must be here, and then he will readily see, that the most awful deeds could be easily covered. Hedges are so high, and thick, that you ride miles without a glimpse of plantations, except through gateways. Moreover, all are guilty, more or less, if there is any reliance to be put in human testimony.

BUT THE SUFFERING, THE AGONY! IS TRANSIENT, the joy, eternal. The presence of the one, is just as real as the other, to their minds. Hence their answers almost invariably convey an unintentional reproof. They see the INVISIBLE, so clearly, that light must shine through all their answers. Could our Congressmen see, and hear many of them talk, how differently would they regard them. How would they see that God hath, indeed,

* Goodell's "American Slave Code."

arisen for their help, and that in dealing with them, they are dealing with Him; for "inasmuch as ye have done it unto one of the least of these, ye have done it unto me," HE SOLEMNLY DECLARES, and the opposite.

When spoken to respecting their freedom, they say: "Ou' trust is in Jesus," in a way to make one weep, common as that saying is. How wonderfully is he with them—inspiring the deepest gratitude for the least kind word, or even look, and a gratitude increasing daily.

They are little moved by anything that occurs around them, excepting when "ou' sojers killed, dat come to fight for we." Then they say, "my poor heart 'most broke for dem dea' sojers, and deir moders. Don't you think, Missus, dey will be saved, dyin' in dis holy war, fightin' for poo' we, even if dey not members?"

"God is merciful," we say. "Oh, pray for the poor wounded, not Christians, that they may this moment seek and find the Savior."

"Oh, I does, Missus, ebry minute, ebry minute," and some of them have spent the whole night in prayer for the North. Going unexpectedly to the quarters of our help one evening, we heard them, in the garret, in united prayer, though they had been in at worship with us. One said: "Oh, Lord, hab mercy on ole Massahs. Oh, Lord, dey are at defiance wid God and man. Oh, shake dem ober de brink ob hell, but neber let um drop!"

CHAPTER XXXVIII.

THE TRUE DEBASEMENT.

The Colored people do not incline to magnify their sufferings, even were that possible; nor yet their patience, in a self-righteous, or self-flattering manner. But rather in genuine humility and love, they magnify every kindness ever received, even the least, especially from "Massah," from whom it ever seems a perfect miracle; and it is spoken of in their first remarks to you, as a wonder of goodness.

Said such a woman, light-skinned, gentle and amiable evidently, whom we overtook, with a basket of wood upon her head, in reply to a remark from us—

"My Massah oncommon good. He neber 'quire me to do anyting but wash and iron; when dat done ebery week, time my own."

"How many children have you?"

"I got twelve chil'en, Missus."

"You must have felt awfully to have them all slaves."

"Yes, but den Massah bery kind. He neber whip me, neber."

This fact, spoken of as such a marvel—her apathy respecting her children, and her evidently superior love for her Master, were more startling and heart-rending than the terrible tales of punishment with which most abound. "Can a mother forget her sucking child," said we inwardly, "that she should not have compassion upon the son of her womb?" Yes, slavery, and love, in poor woman's heart, for an unwomanizing Master, can cause her to do even that.

"Her children are her Master's," is a common, unblushing remark. Yes, even made, at times, with apparent respect, on account of her honors, and surroundings. Alas, poor victims of the basest passions, of the lowest of men sure to end in being victims to his hate, then to his foul calumnies traducing her in every way, for a debasement low as himself! and which he forcibly produced. Is there, can there be, another such meanness out of perdition? Besides, a man cannot drive one woman afield, and respect another deeply and truly. If one can override the laws of his State, and country, he cannot fully ignore the immutable laws of God, written upon his own soul. Therefore to be IN HEART an actual and successful slaveholder, he must sink in soul, to the level of those, whom he so debases. Nor can he prevent this result, until he can dethrone God, and change eternal right to wrong. It is, doubtless, this sense of debasement, in spite of all arguments, pleas, theories to the contrary, that renders so many Masters and Mistresses so miserable, so excitable in regard to slavery, and so revengeful. So HARD doth our holy, benevolent God make it, for a mortal to DRIVE HIM AWAY, and to TAKE HOLD ON DEATH. All the slaveholder's power is intensified by the influence of religion upon the poor slaves, who are taught by slavery apostles, that their soul's salvation depends upon obedience to their Masters, acting so irresponsibly in these dark places. So, obliged to obey implicitly, and by deceit and sin, to adapt themselves to unrestrained natures of so many contradictions, they become adepts in duplicity. But the warmest love is often felt for the base Master by the poor injured woman, ever ending, of course, in sure heartbreaking, and the foulest slander from him. Of course he is far more agreeable to her than the black man, who shares his honors, and whom this poor woman calls husband; but whom he kicks and cuffs around with unwonted satisfaction, even for him, because of that very fact. The children of this woman are often pets, until, by showing such decided resemblance to her Master, as to provoke to the utmost, persecution, from his family, they lead to his exposure, and their sale.

From such circumstances, it seems the universal conclusion of this keen, discerning race, that little connubial happiness existed among their oppressors. In short, it is as evident that those oppressors felt that they were resting under a curse, as that they lived. They would not see it, or confess it, but could not escape its presence, or its baneful blight.

Said one of these poor women, "If I didn't know Jesus Christ, I go crazy all dese years! If he is not in our help, it is not'ing. Jesus is my trust. He keep heart right. If I do right, Jesus take me. When he send for me, if I can on'y meet him, I satisfied. Distress and hard labor drive me to Christ. So heart-broken tired; heart all fall down inside! I go hide me in de grave-yard"—with a shudder—"to rest; HIDE 'MONG DE DEAD. No woman could carry de hoe as I could, when dis Massah buy me. He broke me down wid work in fiel' ebery day till baby born. Trust I hab no mo'. Tink hab no mo'. Aint 'bliged now; young women's 'bliged." But the debasement, SO FAR AS OWNERS ARE CONCERNED, is too horrid to dwell upon.

"If dey praise God, if dey had one speck ob Jesus, dey would do we better. Sell baby! make woman work in de fiel' till last minute; dat girl born in de fiel', bring home on cart, not die, God keep um! God good! God help! O 'ts past awful. My two chil'n dead. Glad!

glad! when dead, 'cause you can't speak when oberseer lick um so; can't talk, him hab own way. Massah not hear you. Some drivers an' oberseers make girls mean to save lick, an' DEY MUS'N'T EBEN LOOK SORRY, but glad. Some can bear it, some can't, so GET MO' TASK, AN' MO' LICK. None fall dead on cotton fiel' or dis plantation, 'nough on oder do, on dis island. Prime people on dis place, all works well."

Now, reader, what do you think of the virtue of the Northern lady, or any lady that will say one word in favor of slavery, or be displeased when it is named, and is opposed to agitation about it? Is she so ignorant as not to know all these evils? Impossible. What then do you think of her actual, inner soul virtue, who can coolly hand over the poor Colored girl to such a fate? Who can honor the perpetrator, or one of his class, as such, and advocate slavery, which she knows has its whole root in these sins, and its increase from these awful wrongs? And yet she would be considered amiable, virtuous, pious. But great allowance must be made for ignorance; still, how long will THAT, BE EXCUSABLE?

CHAPTER XXXIX.

HEART CHASTITY.

Cast my heart's gold into a furnace flame,
And if it come not thence, refined and pure,
I'll be a bankrupt to thy hope, and heaven
Shall shut its gates upon me.
MRS. SIGOURNEY.

THE Colored women, are an enigma in one respect. They have many of them been victims to brutal treatment, in their most vital being, chastity. But it is impossible to believe it, while conversing with them. Impossible! So all testify here. For ourself, we may be pardoned for saying, that we have been closely associated with ladies in different States, and in all the great cities, North, as well as in Canada. We, too, only extol the great work, to which our Lord deigned to call us, when we say, they were among the very best ladies of all those places, and, we solemnly aver, and those ladies will rejoice to hear it, that never, have we conversed with a more genuinely modest set of women, than those dark daughters of the South. Never. As we said, they are a puzzle to us. Such immaculate purity as there seems to be in their inner soul. Now some will curl the lip in scorn, or laugh derisively, and say, "Ah! what credulity! It was all put on, the counterfeit, modest mien, of the magdalen." Far from it. That mien, we can pierce with words, as easily as possible, when it is duty. This is, innately, or by grace, a part of the very being of these poor women. We had many, in our mission, ladies of superior abilities, long used to labor in the cities, and certainly capable of approaching any one properly. But their experience accorded with our own. We could question a magdalen where NECESSARY, which is, very, VERY RARELY, but these Colored women never! Never! The fact is, these women have not parted with true delicacy, true virtue. That is evident, whatever they may have suffered. There is no great gulf between them, and the pure, as there ever is, with the voluntarily fallen. We do not explain all this, cannot, even to ourself. We only state facts, which all the pure, conversant with them, will corroborate.

As you meet and converse, with one, and another, and another, of these pious, refined Negresses—for they have a refinement of soul you rarely see equalled—you involuntarily say inwardly, "This one has never become familiar with vice;" and so on, and on, until the number is so great, as to make it impossible that all have escaped. Then you are more amazed. You would ask them, you think you will, as you want to know and promote only the truth, and from the best of motives, you would get the most correct idea of them, and of what slavery actually is. But you can no more ask them, how they have fared, than your own mother. You review it, think you are failing to get knowledge, that the cause, the truth, righteousness, demand that you get, that you may advance appreciation, purity, and holiness. You resolve to do better next time. But the impassable barrier is before you, high, and pure, and beautiful.

But one thing, is absolutely certain. Vice, cannot put on the impress of virtue, as these dear dark sisters wear it. Impossible. Virtue, and vice, have each, a language written upon the countenance, the latter on many who little suspect it. But virtue, is vividly written upon these. How winning they are! What an expression of purity, endurance, love, tenderness, patience, and, a quiet defiance of earth's wickednesses, and griefs, that it makes you weep, to see.

Oh, ye jewels of our Lord! How doth he love you! The writer had long been privileged to feel that she was about as dear, to our Adorable Savior, as most of those, with whom she worshipped, but, when she listened to you, in those poor huts, in their shades, in the sacred groves of the dead, she felt that you were nearer the heart of our precious Jesus, than was she. You have been tied to the uttermost, and not found wanting. In some instances, those who would have wronged you have quailed before that purity, that quiet, strong, trust in God. In many cases, how many we know not, it has been given you, as a shield. In others, your fellows, have died martyrs to purity.

Yet contemptible Whites, who have nothing but color to value themselves upon, and others in ignorance of actual facts, write you all down, as debased, and degraded—favorite words with those beauties—and feel themselves elevated in the process, and the higher, still, the lower they can put you, when you have a Christianity, a purity, they never dreamed of, and greater than aught else earth has ever yet shown us. Oh, ye jewels of my Lord! most of those that despise you, despise him, also, our dear Divine Master. Is it not enough for a servant, that he be as his Lord?

For his dear home with you, is in your soul; and he gives no one power over the soul if it use its utmost energy, to avoid the contact, and resist the power of sin, and cleave to him for purity.

THE WHOLE MATTER OF SLAVERY IS OFTEN A GREAT

TRIAL OF FAITH. That God permits one, to exercise such power over another's body. But the SOUL IS HIS OWN, and cannot be stained, in fact, but by its own consent. If the soul actually wills it, he will cleanse it, whiter than snow, and keep it so, all his own, a garden, inclosed; a spring, shut up; a fountain, sealed; all pure, all to himself.

So it evidently is with many; still many, alas! have fallen to the level of their tempters; but never, in one case, did they refer to or hint at it. It is only in the third person, or what "they," or others, suffer of which they can speak, and then, it is the pious, and who confide fully in your deep heart-sympathy for them, and in your just appreciation of their subjection.

Doubtless, we say, many sink to real debasement. But many, many! will sooner die, than sin, and some way, almost miraculous, is sometimes made, for their escape.

One poor Aunty said: "Oberseer raise me wid a pole high as 'at corn-house, wid clothes ober head, fo' take away my shame, so I be mean. He did, Missus, but"—clasping her thin hands above her poor head—"but Jesus keep me, O, bless Jesus! He keep me! Bless Jesus! Ebery lady ough' to praise Jesus, for me."

No effort, or means, that all ingenuity and learning and talent of man, and of ages, have invented, to destroy respect for the Negro, in the North, has been wanting, upon the part of slaveholders and their abettors, far meaner than they. For, in proportion as men despise them, are they content that they remain slaves, and all effort, for their emancipation, is paralyzed. Astonishing!! that their word has so long been taken.

So, they have made apparent docility, of poor slaves, to appear as eagerness, because they SUPPOSED THAT

WOULD NAUSEATE, MORE than any other lie. APPEARANCES HERE, ARE EXPLAINED, in this chapter.

We say our heart is breaking over their woes, and our government's inefficiency. It seems to be to most, in this nation, as nothing, that the present race should fade away and die under these awful evils, provided, in some future age, freedom may come to their descendants.

To prove how deeply our soul is stung with their wrongs, and agonies, we may be pardoned for saying that we cannot see company since returning. It makes us weep, to see our ladies so tenderly cared for, so prized, so pampered, while their dark sisters so suffer. So the most beautiful sights are blighted, and actually turned into anguish. But this, we name, only to induce the same feelings in you.

Going out, with mind intent on mercy-errands, we met the bright, beautiful, cherished throng upon Broadway. In contrast, the dark but beautiful ones we had left, were instantly before us, with their wrongs, toils, agonies. Tears gushed, and gushed, until weeping ruled the hour; and, that we were observed, seemed of little moment, amid these stern griefs. Giving up errands, we sobbed, and sobbed our way down to 320,* where we could do a work for them. But as Saturday evening approached, we were obliged to go to a milliner's, and, having in a measure become calmed, we went in—when in came the happy milliner-girls, and taking from their work-boxes bonnet after bonnet, they bestowed upon each a fond, admiring gaze, as they placed them in the store boxes. Then, rising, first upon one tip-toe, then, upon the other, while rolling up the ribbons, they peered out of the full windows, upon the passers-by, as full of life, of joy, of expectation, as any lady in the city. And these are the girls,

* Building occupied by the Freedman's Relief Association.

whose lot is compared to our poor dark sisters, suffering all of toil and indignity that man can heap upon them. They observed our heart-agony, and looked as if to say, "Poor woman, she has lost some one, in this war," and tripped away.

In the evening, we were obliged by sickness of a friend, to go into a most sumptuous chamber. There, is the beautiful sick daughter, so luxuriously couched, and attended, everything in the city, laid under tribute, for her comfort. Again, then we contrasted the hard lot, of our poor dark sisters, who, in the most weak, and agonized, states, are not permitted to lie down, not even upon the floor, or ground, "lest they get lazy," and were entirely overcome once more. This, is the history of one afternoon.

This day a sweet letter came from our precious, only daughter, and her doating husband. They "are to hold a reception for their parishioners, and mother must be there." No; mother cannot go, does not want to go, does not want to see that daughter, who has been a chief blessing of her life, as thousands know. No! mother does not want even to see that daughter, after four months' separation. Her heart is so sore, that she had rather hide and weep, over her suffering dark sisters, and brethren, and her country's sins, and try to labor for them. Weak! do you say? We would be weaker than infancy, if thereby, we might only touch your heart, for when the hearts of the masses, are PROPERLY moved, the powers that be, MUST FEEL, and ACT, and work is done.

Sister, who reads this, you would feel so too, or more, could you see slavery and its dear victims, as it is, as we have.

But so long, so able, so persistent, have been the efforts of Southern Congressmen, and all others in the interest of 'avery, that they have thrown a false coloring over the whole system; and Northern writers and speakers write and speak under the influence of that coloring, and while they lead you to hate slavery, they innocently lead you to despise the Colored; to you, therefore, seeming as a great moving, mass of darkness, and impurity; to us, mothers, sisters, brothers. Then there are those in our midst, who actually think, they have seen matters upon plantations, as they were; when, so far from it, even the mistresses of those plantations, knew little, or nothing, of the dark deeds there committed. The Master, too, who mayhap, would be comparatively kind, knows what the overseer does, only by his own report, and he knows not what the driver does, only by his report. So that, when the exact truth is at last reached, it is Sambo or Quimbo, unrestrained—for, if the poor slave tells on them, they nearly kill him—who govern the poor victims.

Massah, too, in the far South, was out upon a carousal, nearly all night, and must sleep much of the day, in nine cases out of ten, as we were assured, by those who knew, and Mistress, too, without her wine, is too dispirited, and with it, is too inspirited, to care for them properly. Beside, who but the driver can bear that tropical sun? and can he carry forward the work without the lash? when the lash is the only propelling power? Certainly not. So Sambo, or Quimbo, must have unlimited power. There is no escape from it, but to let everything go to wreck upon plantations, OR HAVE FREE LABOR.

Yet Christians, Christians! North, can shield those who coerce poor woman to every brutality, or to daily torture inconceivable. Oh, if they could die! If masters would kill them! But no, it is torture, torture! torture! scientifically used, TORTURE! the ONE SCIENCE OF SLAVEDOM. Yet many are martyrs. They can die, but they cannot sin and sink to the level of their masters, overseers, or drivers.

We say it, before high heaven, and an outraged world of ladies, that the martyrs to chastity now upon earth, are our dark women of the South. Oh! could you hear as we heard a dear saint of God say, "O! Missus, dey makes our women mean, to save mo' task, and to save de awful whipping," and adding, with their plaintive, melting, tone, "an' 'ey mustn't show 'ey feel bad, but make um tink 'ey glad. O! 'ts past awful! past awful! Some can 'dure it, some can't, so dey gets all time mo' and mo' task, and mo' and mo' lick. When oberseer come 'gin, you task all done, he say, 'not done good, you go way be lick,' bab to go."

As she said this, too delicate to glance at our face, though glowing with indignation, she gazed down the beautiful river into the pure blue distance, as one who pondered, and pondered, long, and deeply, and looked for a great future, a great retribution! Yet, with characteristic refinement, she soon bade us good evening, without looking up, started in the direction we were gazing, and our eyes never again met. We shall meet at the judgment, and you will be there, reader, and answer for your part in opposing this awful, inexpressible iniquity. Our saying, Lord! Lord! I felt so, and so, had such, and such, visions, and joys, will be nothing, there, if he shall say, "I was sick, and in prison, and ye came not unto me. I was a stranger, and naked, and ye clothed me not, ye took me not in. You did not do unto the least of these, as ye would that others should do unto you, so ye did it not to me." Now what would you have others do, were you in slavery? YOU KNOW! PERFECTLY! AND CAN NEVER say to the Judge "I did not know."

We say again, that in the ardent labors of a score of years, we have never seen their refinement of soul surpassed, and are they not Christ's? Then, do you not do to him, as you do to them? Oh, could we touch the heart, of the Christian North, yea, even of the ladies, deeply! how joyfully would we lay down our life! Could we so startle, and awaken, ALL OF THE WOMAN in every lady's heart, that in the closet, over the cradle, or rising in some sacred hour of silent night, she would raise her right hand to heaven, and vow in the name, and strength, of Him that liveth and was dead, and is alive forevermore, that she would leave nothing! nothing!! in her power, undone to dethrone this demon! Could we do this, we would suffer anything.

Oh, what can be done, to rouse the indignation of the virtuous, against this perpetual insult to their sex? For there is virtue. There are thousands, who, rather than see a servant suffer what is the daily doom of poor, poor slave women, would interpose their own lives to protect them. Why, then, should the mere fact, that they are a few hundred miles farther away, quench this just anger? And even supposing slaveholders can, by a long or short influence, lower one, so as to entice others, does not that make the sin, the debasement, a thousandfold more odious? You say, "there is this sin in the North." We answer, "show us a case," clearly involuntary, and if the law does not reach it, the whole power of the citizens, yea, of Northern ladies, will. Let it be known, that servants of a family, are forcibly detained, and coerced to this sin, and the whole community would be frantic. But what, oh, what? can make the North feel equally for slaves?

Different reports, are, doubtless, one cause of indifference. Thousands get impressions from slaveholders, who will no more injure their business than rumsellers. Many see the Colored man through their medium, which misrepresents and blackens his whole character. It is not enough, that he is robbed of every right, and loaded with every wrong, he must also be so BELIED, AS TO INHERIT THE DISGUST OF THE WORLD. True, there are some words freely, disgustingly used, as "breed." But how have they always heard it used? So, do some English, use the word "delivered" in the same way. Yet it is no lack of refinement in them. Then, their dress, too, is often but the nether garment, and skirt. But, by most scrupulous care only the poor arms are exposed, while a waist, of all manner of mendings, saves the form, effectually. Invariably these women assert that they have no gown; sometimes they show you a lawn, or something equally tender, which has been given them by "the Association," and which they are "'bliged to save fo' Sunday."

Further, not a word, or indication of low conversation, can be drawn, or beguiled out of them. Not a low sensuous laugh is known! Never! It is as evident, in every way, that their converse in little circles is chaste, as that the sun shines, and it is only the intensity of their sufferings, that ever leads one to speak the least plainly to Missus.

CHAPTER XL.

NORTHERN CHIVALRY.

For 'tis a sight that angel ones above
   May stoop to gaze on, from the bowers of bliss;
When innocence upon the breast of love,
   Is cradled in a sinful world like this.
                        Mrs. Welby.

WHAT opinion can Northern pro-slavery men have of Southern ladies? Can they think them delicate, high-principled, virtuous? or do they think they nestle, with all possible satisfaction, in the foul nest of slavery? Are their own tastes, or associations, such, as that they think ladies, after all, care little for virtue? Or, do they pretend to doubt the vitiating nature of slavery? Do they presume, that universal testimony, even that of slave-holders themselves, is untrue, and that the mass, there, live chastely? Such ignorance cannot be supposed, for an instant. Then, there can be but one other conclusion, or rather two: first, that they believe the Southern ladies care nothing for it, or, in other words, are not virtuous; or, second, that they themselves care not what those ladies suffer. But the true fact is, that THOSE WELL INFORMED AND PRO-SLAVERY as a class, care little for any one, or anything, beyond certain plans, interests, pride of success, fleeting influence, or mean dollars, of their own. For, they know, that there are thousands of homes made utterly wretched, and desolate, by the awful curse, slavery. Perhaps they would say, "These ladies ought not to be made wretched by it." That shows the standard of their own virtue, and extends most dubious compliments to their Companions, and associates. In short they show the man. But the anti-slavery part of the North, with ourself, have a far better opinion of the Southern ladies. We believe they are, as a whole, genuinely refined, truly virtuous, and, of course, made as unhappy by vice, as any living.

To the chivalrous, of the North, we appeal in their behalf! Is there not a nobility, a manliness, a Christianity, in the North, that can, and will help them? that will extend a strong hand, and now, WHILE IT HAS THE POWER, will pluck slavery away

True, they would not own, that they suffer awfully, from its ruinous effects upon fathers, brothers, sons, husbands. What lady would? willingly? But is a wound concealed, a wound too deep for words, the less dangerous, or deadly, in its blight? Is there less probability of its terminating fatally? Such a wound must be quickly healed or so terminate. So it often does. You cannot converse with them, or their reliable servants, without seeing it. Yea more, you cannot use common sense even a very little, without seeing it, provided you believe, universal testimony, respecting the morals of most men there.

Now, what were it to be killed, instantly, to being tortured to the very extreme of endurance, daily, and hourly, for long weary years after years; to pray and pray for death, and yet it never come?

This is no fancy, no coloring, no attempt to make out a case against slaveholders; we have not words to paint up to the life. We speak from facts, and dare not hope, to make the impression they demand. Could we do that, we might move some, yes, even Congressmen, to raise the right hand, and solemnly vow that slavery should be no more, by their consent.

But do any doubt that the most utter debasement prevails, in slavedom? And can it exist in a family, without the chaste part, being wretched? Can all, all! be concealed from that pure, virtuous wife? Can it be concealed from those indulged, and proud daughters? over all whose beauty, and happiness, is coming a dire blight? Can it escape the searching glance of that pure little girl, of ten, or twelve? who is just opening her sad eyes to the knowledge, of what is in the world, of what pa is? Oh, have you the feelings of a man, and will you not seize that insane father, and pluck the instrument of torture,—slavery, from his furious grasp? Would you not pluck the power of being intemperate from your own brother? and is not slavery a vice, equally benumbing, and blinding? That man were noble, were a husband, a father, without the vice of "oppression, which maketh a wise man mad." Wrest slavery from him, and he will soon be reasonable. He will "return, to bless his household." He will bless you in heaven!

In our mission-house at Beaufort, was a poor maniac, once lovely, and cherished, the wife of a rebel well known there, made mad by oppression, by domestic tyranny. It was heart-rending to hear her dwell flightily upon the sweetness of the first few months of her married life, of her untiring, determined, efforts to win and woo back, that youthful husband. But the tide was too strong, though he often and bravely resisted it, and a mean pride, one of the progeny of slavery, at last came in, and drove away all restraint, and her reason with it. He often, and often, had whipped her, as she said, most severely, for being a woman. But, it was all forgiven, all borne, with scarcely a complaint, for the intense love, she bore him. She, in all these dark hours, said it was wine that mocked him, maddened him. Every effort to make home attractive was intensified, an hundred fold, if possible, and at intervals, she had hope. But every facility for debasement, was in his presence continually.

Overpowered, captive to sin, and pride, he drove her from the house, and revelled to his heart's content. It was slavery, in its influence upon him, his relatives, his associates, that did all this. It was slavery's facilities for all sin, that ruined him. And he is a type of a class of men, a large class, take the whole South, together. True, there are most noble exceptions, but will you throw, or rather, leave, your countrymen in such a current, because some can breast it? But, a man must have something to do, and he will, and if it be not good, must be evil. Father, would you put your fine young son, under the influence of slavery? for the best plantation of the South? yea, for him to inherit, with slavery's blights, the whole South? Not, if you deserve the sacred name of father.

See, the poor broken, bleeding-hearted wife, and mother, obliged to see her rival in a slave, and that for long, long, weary years. See her, a servant to that slave, for her children's sake, and all, because her husband is a brute. Did not the grave open for many, many, such, this land would be filled with lunatics. To pray for DEATH, is most common, FOR LADIES AT THE SOUTH. We were shocked to find it so common. Ah! there is a virtue even there, in womanhood, in spite of all the mists of ignorance, prejudice, and customs, of slavedom, that makes the cold grave a sweet refuge from its foulness. Ignorance and prejudice, we say, for those Southern ladies who do not travel North, know as little of what its people actually are, as of the inhabitants of the moon. Did they, and were they possessed, of the proper spirit, they would take that infant son, and seek a refuge in some Northern farmer's pure home, and there, toiling, if need be, they would bring him up to honor, purity, eternal life, instead of seeing him, become a drivelling, besotted brute.

What good mother, did she actually know all, delicate, unused to toil as she may be, would not do it, to save his body from ruin by slavery, and his soul from eternal death?

There are thousands who would break away, but ignorance enchains them. No free pulpit, have they, or pastor. No press, or mail, is free. No kind, able, hand is outstretched, that is permitted to reach them. Do you say, "Would they leave their husbands?" Those husbands have left them, in all that is sacred. Are we too severe? Read the following: "WE SOUTHERN LADIES ARE CALLED WIVES, BUT WE ARE ONLY MISTRESSES OF SERAGLIOS," said a sister of President Madison to the Rev. George Bourne, then a Presbyterian minister in Virginia.* Now, one who would prefer that post, to being an assistant in a Northern farmer's family, IS NOT VIRTUOUS—THAT IS EVIDENT.

Temptation comes over one, sometimes, that men, voters, Congressmen, think that there is actually no such thing as virtue, deep, real virtue, and chastity, and of necessity where it is outraged, no heart-breaking, in woman. There are those who would lead them to feel so, especially, 'tis said, at Washington. But those men know, that yonder among their precious babes, is one, who if they should become vicious, would die. She might not reproach, she might not weep, as mortal knew, but that vile worm, would cut the stem of life, and the sweet grave would soon close over her. Why? Because she has true virtue of soul. The world, yea, hundreds of worlds,

* Goodell's "American Slave Code."

would not compensate her heart, for that dear husband's virtue. All this, they know, and praise their Creator for. Then, why cannot they believe, and feel, too, that there are just such ladies at the South, and, who see their adored husbands, victims to slavery's temptations, whose poor hearts are made to stand still, with agony, then flutter as if to escape, day after day, night after night, until they stand still forever? Now, we have not a word to say to those whose unfortunate surroundings have convinced them, that virtue is a sham. But to those who believe it sits at the fount of life, in chaste woman, and holds its key, we ask, "What will you do for our sisters' agonies?" Rend! oh, rend away! the cause of them, and when their tyrants come to their right minds, and to see, and feel, correctly, they will bless you.

True, those women would sooner die than own that they believe their husbands vicious. But, does not this depth of concealed torture, appeal to your chivalrous aid all the more?

Some, we know, become devilish, pursuing the poor helpless, tempter, and dire victim of their lords, with every possible cruelty. Some few, become stoical, reckless of everything, yea, even of virtue itself in those around them. Is not that more awful than death? More to be dreaded than any other possible result? More to be opposed, by your manly efforts? Will you not rise in your might, manhood, chivalry, religion, and say, "This shall not be?" And for how short a time God shall give you the power, so to say, no mortal knoweth.

But, you ask, "Would you have us thrust the power of government between those wives, and their husbands, and to protect the one from the other?" Certainly. Precisely as you would, and do, thrust your power between, to shield wives in this city from the vice of intemperance in their lords. Precisely so. For what exists government, if not to protect the weak? And where is there a case of equal clearness, urgency, and appeal?

Now, it must be, that Congress labors under one of three delusions—1st. THAT ALL TESTIMONY RESPECTING THE VISCIOUS LIVES of most Southerners, or rather slaveholders, IS FALSE ; or, 2d. THAT THERE IS NOT IN THE HEARTS OF SOUTHERN WOMEN THE VIRTUE to suffer excruciatingly from it, even to heart-breaking, and death ; or, 3d. THAT THEY ARE INDIFFERENT TO WHAT THEY SUFFER, since they do not wrest the maddening cause away, when they have the full power and right to do so. One of these conclusions, is INEVITABLE.

ONE OF THESE THINGS IS TRUE of the present Congress. Which is it? Or, do they claim to be adhering to a line of policy? Lines of policy, alas! have guided our Ship of State to where it now is. The only true policy is righteousness. True, it was policy, self-preservation, that led England to emancipate. Yet it was an enlightened, clear-eyed, Christian policy. She could not have done it without the aid of holy, philanthropic men. No man, or nation, CAN TAKE A SELF-PRESERVING COURSE, merely because IT IS BEST. He MUST ALSO HAVE MORAL POWER to do it. That power is now offered Congress, and its members individually know, that they cannot look the final judgment in the face! and deny it, quibble as they may. It is a military necessity, and any Congress of able generals would declare it such, and it would doubtless be used as such, but for the same cringing to slavery that has nearly ruined us.

Whether this power will be offered, or available soon again, no mortal can know. It would have been of little use for Pharaoh to have proclaimed emancipation at the bottom of the Red Sea. So, this may be the only moment, the only lucid interval, in which all must be done.

How did difficulties seem to multiply, in the way of England's emancipating, until the very moment that she passed the act. Then, how soon light dawned, and they all rolled away. Satan always struggles, rends, in being cast out. But the struggling, rending, scares timid operators, and all the promised benefits are lost, and he remains, to torment the victim at his leisure.

Not content with debasing, by every power they can command, the poor dark victims, they THEN MALIGN THEM BY EVERY LIE THAT CAN BE INVENTED. How mean! How utterly contemptible! But, not only so; they make their wife, the mother of their children! equally odious, by representing that she does not care; and this they reiterate and reiterate in so many sly and accidental ways that the foul lie comes to seem as truth, even to themselves; and their meaner Northern advocate wipes his mouth, and says, "Oh, those Southern women do not care!" Poor victims to every insult that can be invented, and then not even left alone to suffer, but must entertain company of the very same grade, of their tyrant husbands, to beguile time and keep away reflection. They must, too, know, and that often, that the Northern youth is taking his first lessons in crime under their roof. Yet they are powerless, and pride, compels them to conceal all.

How can those Congressmen return to their pure, quiet homes, and leave the bondage and the bane resting upon other ladies just as pure, upon other babes born with equal claims? but who, under slavery, have not a right, not one, unimpaired. No! not even the right to their parents. Father is a beast. Mother is a withered fading flower, lovely, in the withering, but powerless, for the needs of the poor child. Home is a slave-driving pest

School, the comfort, joy, honor, of the oppressed Northern child, exists not. Society, of any variety, is out of the question. What can the poor child do, but find what pleasure, in sensual and idle pursuits, he may? and, with unlimited power over all the Colored, how certain is his ruin. But is there not a Chivalry in the North, that will arise in its might, and manliness, and say, "This shall not be! Women South shall not be so oppressed?"

True, there are those, who come only to look at the fancied profits, and forget all other considerations. But them we call not women, though they stand in her sacred place. Real womanhood would say, "Let us have poverty, if need be, with purity." And, this, even if all these theories of money-making were correct, which however are not. Will God permit a people to enrich themselves, by selling innocent children? See Virginia, with her yearly export of $12,000,000 in fathers, mothers, and babies. How utterly blasted with poverty. How totally behind all the free States around her, that have nothing of her age, and natural advantages. Yet, when, ever, existed a more energetically-proud and competent people, a people better prepared to make slavery profitable at every sacrifice, if it could be made so? So that all argument in favor of slavery from pecuniary advantage, falls totally and forever.

But the foulest slander upon the ladies, is, THAT THEY CARE NOT FOR ALL THIS, impurity. And to show the most utter meanness of enslavers, this slander comes from their own husbands, who have sunk so incredibly low, that they can glory in saying, "My wife doesn't care." "She's willing enough." Incredible! that such baseness can exist. It is never seen, out of slavedom. But even the swearing, gutter-drunkard, is at once erect in indignation at the least slur cast upon his wife's virtue.

We would not defile our pen, or page, with repelling this foul slander, were it not for this one fact; and, that by the persistent misrepresentation of their husbands, the belief is actually caused in the North, that the wives and mothers of the South care little or nothing, for all this utter debasement. And in all this, their false apostles help on, and reap its rewards.

Now, it is in the power of Congress to wrest away with one noble act, the whole cause. It is! do we say? It was. Perhaps the power is even now departing. It will depart, if not used. THIS IS THE INFLEXIBLE ORDER OF GOD, in all his moral realm.

The time was, when all those slaveholders could see, and hate slavery. They can no more do either now, than the inebriate can hate his cups.

"But," one says, "have you not licentiousness in the North?" Alas! we have, but not under our care! Not, in our houses! The Northern lady is not involved in the guilt, knows it not, usually, has not to see it, hourly, to feed, clothe, nurse, in sickness, the poor, hated, but most deeply wronged victim; feeling awfully, that she ought not to suffer it, ought to leave the roof, if no other protest will answer. But with eyes blinded, powers enfeebled, energies withered, she remains, "keeper of a seraglio," as the poor sister of President Madison said, "we Southern women are." But what moments of agony must a woman undergo, before she can make this charge in company, yea, this admission, to herself. What one refinement of cruelty, is wanting to the horrid system, of slavery? and shall we sit quietly by its side and foster it? when we have power to crush it, and call ourselves civilized?

And this, too, when it is proven by even Southern statistics over and over, past all mistake, as in Helper's "Impending Crisis," that it brings blasting poverty?

Why then can it not be put away forever? The North would be a unit in that work. We heard an able reliable minister of this city say he would himself go into the ranks, as a common soldier, under an act of emancipation. So would thousands of just such noble men. But we need not say, "put away slavery forever." For the poor victims once free, from its power, would not go under it again.

As Sewell, affirms, over, and over, the planters of the West Indies declare, "that free labor is preferable on every account." Even Henry Clay, convinced of this, in his speech before the Colonization Society, in 1829, said:

"It is believed that NOWHERE, in the farming portion of the United States, would slave labor be generally employed, if the proprietor were not tempted to RAISE slaves, by the HIGH PRICE of the SOUTHERN MARKET which keeps it up in his own.

Then, what possible plea, unless it intends, to stoop to that detestable meanness, can be found for not declaring emancipation, at once, by this chivalrous government?

Now, Congressmen, do you believe that most Southern ladies are virtuous? Certainly, you say. Then do you believe that such a woman in such circumstances, must either fail, sicken, pine away, die, or become a fury, or a stone? You know, one of these, must be the case, inevitably. Will you then rescue these noble women? Will you prevent those lovely ones, coming upon the stage, from suffering the same? Yea, will you save those men, and their sons?—for we are told by those who know, that few live past middle age. Their vices, and night carousals, and drink, kill them. Remember, too, that of the actual fruits of Southern life we have hitherto known little, just what determined pro-slaveryists have revealed.

Nor yet are these poor masters, beside domestic woes, without their dire heart agonies. As illustration:

The "Florida slaveholder" before mentioned, with his princely fortune, his educated and accomplished heirs, the children of his parental affection, HIS ONLY ones, but—under the "persecuting" ban of the "Colonization Society," "the pulpit"—Northern and Southern—and the "legislation" approved by them—outcasts, unable to testify in a Court, against a white man; liable to be colonized to Liberia under force of "flagellations" and untold "enormities;" or even to be kidnapped and enslaved!—the Florida slaveholder, we say, with such a family around his board, presents *another* specimen of the liberty and human rights enjoyed by the slaveholder! to say nothing of happiness.

Another slaveholder of fortune, lived with a quadroon woman, without marriage, of course, for the laws would not permit it. His daughters were elegant, beautiful, and nearly white. They were free, as was also their mother; but they were subject to the vexations that harass "*free* people of color." The father sought for them respectable connections in life, and nothing but the laws forbidding such marriages stood in the way; for they were much admired, members of the Methodist Episcopal Church, and *one* of them was loved and wooed by a *white* member of the *same* church, and a slaveholder; but the *law* stood in the way of their marriage!

What pain, shame, remorse, must such parents ever feel in the presence of those children. How small the pain of poverty in comparison, or of losses, or even loss of friends, or of life. NOTHING BUT GUILT CAN BRING SUCH ANGUISH. Well might Washington say, "the first wish of his heart, was to see slavery abolished."

CHAPTER XLI.

THE TASKMASTERS.

There walks Judas, he who sold
Yesterday his Lord for gold;
Sold God's presence in his heart
For a proud step in the mart.

J. R. LOWELL.

ALL the disgusting assumption of power, by the pretended slave-owner, who blasphemously claims God to be altogether such an one as himself, since he is asserted by God-defying D.D.'s to be the author of the lovely system —may be delegated to any one, or any number, of sub-demons, to the basest of all men, the overseers and even to his children, who each, for the time, has unlimited power, not only over his services, but his life, any one of whom can clear himself of any legal punishment, by his own oath! Was such folly and madness ever enacted out of a country where slavery reigned? Did it ever fail of being enacted in it? For instance.

"In South Carolina and Louisiana there are enactments, that '*Whereas many cruelties may be committed on slaves because no white person may be present to give evidence of the same, unless some method be provided for the better discovery of the offence,*' etc. '*Be it enacted,*' etc. The only remedy provided is, that 'when no *white* person shall be present,' or, being present, shall refuse to testify, 'the owner or other person having charge of such slave [who shall have 'suffered in LIFE, limb, member,' etc.] shall be deemed guilty and punished,' 'UNLESS such owner or other person, etc., can make the contrary appear by good and sufficient evidence, OR SHALL, BY HIS OWN OATH, CLEAR AND EXCULPATE HIMSELF;' and the Court may administer the oath and 'ACQUIT THE OFFENDER, if clear proof of the offence be not made by *two* witnesses at least.'"*

"Judge Stroud considers this 'a modification of the former law, not for the protection of the slave, BUT FOR THE ESPECIAL BENEFIT OF A CRUEL MASTER OR OVERSEER."†

One who had evidently drank deep into the cup of sorrow said:

"We couldn't tell how we suffer all dese long years, but God knows; he sees all tings. We leave all 'at wid him."

How tamely do these words read! Yet how thrilling were they as spoken! We try, in all cases, to give their exact words, and the facts are invariably corroborated by other testimony.

"When we see Massah comin'—wish we could die, but couldn't till Jesus call. We all cry, and cry to God; he hear, he make a way for freedom."

One said, and several others taken separately confirmed it:

"My brother was whipped four hundred and fifty lashes. Oberseer give three hundred; couldn't do no more; Massah give the rest; and when taken into 'at cabin, dere, he hab convulsions so 'at he shake de whole cabin;—sick fou' months."

"What did he do?"

"He hab care ob milk; Mistress put it in baby's tea, and it sour and curdle, and when Massah talk, he say 'he didn't put it in de tea.'"

* Brevard's "Dig.," p. 242.   † Stroud's "Sketches," etc., p. 76.

"What did you do when he was being whipped?" we asked, knowing that it is harder to be absent, and know that something awful is suffered by a friend, than to look on, hard as that is.

"Why, I stan' in dat cabin do' and hol' my head so," pressing her poor hands upon each side of her head. "But," she continued, " you mus' smile when Massah see you, else you get just same; and when eber you whipped, you untied, you must look right up in Massah's face and smile; and when white men come roun' you must smile and say, 'You happy!' and 'Massah so good,' else you get whipt so awful, so awful!"*

"Sometimes," said another, "dinner not cook good. We gone 'way to get a mouthful of corn-cake cook for self; driver come, say, 'You must go up and be whipped!' Have to go; didn't want to live, but couldn't

---

* As proof of the multifarious forms of cruelty to the slaves, as well as degradation it has brought on the whites, we give an extract of a letter addressed to Rev. Mr. French by a very distinguished gentleman, who was both a large slaveholder and planter, in South Carolina:

"————, S. C., March 23, 1858.

"There is an abiding prejudice in South Carolina against enlightening the minds of colored people, and against free people of color, living in the State. It seems to be believed, that the more ignorant the slave is, the better he is satisfied; therefore the Legislature has been endeavoring ever since 1800, to prevent the liberation of slaves in the State, and to prevent their being educated. Hence the law is, that no slave shall be set free, except by Act of the Legislature; and if otherwise, it is liable to be seized by any person, even a stranger, and made their own property; and if any person shall teach a slave to read or write, upon conviction thereof, they shall be heavily fined and imprisoned, and receive fifty lashes on their bare back; and that if any free person of color shall enter this State, they shall be taken up, and sold, and turned into bondage. So that you can see the policy of the State, that it is in opposition to enlightening the colored mind. ————"

die! We all nothin' to put in ou' head, but a little corn —no salt, nor nothin.'"

Scarcely an ex-slave has come under close observation here, who has not scars, welts, brands, and tales of woe too awful to be written. We went with some to their mill, where for long weary years all the grinding had been done, and with two, turning at their utmost speed, it required five minutes to get a teacup full of meal. They were never allowed to grind after light in the morning, so the hundred and more slaves had to take their turn, and grind in the evening, and then cook sufficient to last till the next evening.

"Too tired, ma'am, sometimes for cook it; den hab to go widout all next day, or fall sleep so tired; corn burn all up. Must go by light into fiel', beg mouthful here and dere; couldn't sometimes."

On another plantation, a pious woman, the precision and circumstantiality alone, of whose remarks were full proof of their truth, but which were corroborated, said, "We had to go to fiel' 'fore day, to get to work by light. Corn in basket, couldn't cook it, couldn't get it ready. Hab to go to pond, drink wid mules and alligators. Leave corn cookin' in 'e morning, sometimes burned up, sometimes raw, sometimes cook'd—couldn't stop. Had to fulfill tasks, or be cut up; had to fill our poor mother's basket too, to keep weight, so, she not be whipt and chil'ns too sometimes."

One said, "Massah gib task mo' 'an can do. You whipt. To-morrow finish 'at task, and do de oder for de day. If not done, whip' g'in. I Baptist minister, an' follow de people, doin' good, thirty-three years. My broder not get task done. Massah hab weight tied to his foot, iron, fourteen pounds! Den he hab to hoe one acre rice in day, with 'at weight on, all eat in! Den no food, 'fraid to offer spoonful hominy—'fraid not 'nough for self;—hard to 'fuse; but hab to, so tired—go to sleep, water dry out, corn all burn up! Now so peaceful, work in peace; so happy! DE LORD IS TRYIN' US TO SEE WHAT WE WILL DO, WID FREEDOM. We works, its de calc'lation. Work, ordinance ob God. Can't be Christian widout it. Now work quicker, better, so peaceful, so comfortable! Not 'bliged to cut ou' wood on Sunday, now Massah gone!"

"What could you do upon a plantation?" said we, to a woman of eighty.

"Oh, I min' de chil'n."

"You! How many did you mind?"

"Thirty, ma'am."

"Why I could not take care of two!"

"Oh, dey gits no care only so's to grow, dat's all, and big ones takes care little ones." It seems if a child is two years older than another, he is considered "big," at whatever age.

Poor mothers among field-hands, and in many other cases, never have the privilege of attending their children, till in the utter exhaustion of evening.

One physician, an aristocrat, of Beaufort, said to a slaveholder, "Why do not you go out upon your plantations, and see how those Negroes died? You know they are dead, why not inquire?"

"I have an energetic, good overseer," he replied, "and he states the case. It will not do, you know, to interfere."

"Ought you not to know of what they died yourself?"

"How can I be running all the time over my plantations."

"Well, I tell you as a friend, and as a physician, they

were whipped to death, and the smell was such, one could hardly go into the room before they died."

"I do wish men would mind their own business! Now you have got a piece of my mind."

"I do! It is my business; and I warn you, and I cite you to a day of testing. It will come to you, even in this world. You will repent of this, before you die." That man's house is now occupied by anti-slavery laborers. Oh, could the ministry, Congress, editors, but see and hear these things from the glowing lips of witnesses, how would they labor for freedom! The book of slavery is open, why is it not read by workers, and philosophers?

From Weld's able work, "Slavery as it is," take a few specimens. On page 47 are four cases, related by Rev. William T. Allan, son of a slaveholding D.D. in Alabama. (1.) "A man near Courtland, Ala., of the name of Thompson, recently shot a negro *woman* through the head, and put the pistol so close that her hair was singed. He did it in consequence of some difficulty in his dealings with her as a concubine." (2.) "Two men, of the name of Wilson, FOUND A FINE-LOOKING NEGRO man at Dandridge's Quarter, WITHOUT A PASS, and flogged him so that HE DIED in a short time. They were not punished." (3.) "Col. Blocker's overseer attempted to flog a negro. He refused to be flogged, whereupon the overseer seized an axe, and cleft his skull. The COLONEL JUSTIFIED IT." (4.) "One Jones whipped a woman to death! for grabbing a potatoe hill."

Compare these four cases with the slave laws already cited. The second and fourth, being deaths by whipping, would pass, probably, as cases of "death under moderate correction." The third, Col. Blocker's overseer, would be justified by a Court of law as readily as by the

Colonel. The slave was "resisting" or "offering to resist" the overseer, and was therefore an outlaw. The first case is not quite as clear. If the concubine "resisted" or "offered to resist" Mr. Thompson's advances, whether revengeful or lustful, she came, plainly, into the same legal predicament, and was LAWFULLY KILLED! For "the legal relation" must be maintained! Others, being in search of runaway negroes, surprised them in their camp, and fired their guns toward them as they were running away, to induce them to stop. One of the negroes was, however, killed by a random shot. Decision: "The firing of the defendant in the manner stated was rash and incautious." Slave hunts, with muskets and bloodhounds, are too horribly frequent, by the testimony of the Southern journals, to admit of any doubt on this subject. And so are advertisements of runaway slaves by their owners, with offers of reward for them, "DEAD OR ALIVE!" or "FOR KILLING THEM," or for "EVIDENCE OF THEIR BEING KILLED!"* Of such slave hunts the inquirer may find ample details in Weld's "Slavery as it is," pp. 21, 97, 102, 108, 155, 160.

"IN VIRGINIA, BY THE REVISED CODE (of 1819), there are SEVENTY-ONE OFFENCES for which the penalty is DEATH

---

* But lest some may still doubt that in all Slavedom, a man is justified both by law and public sentiment, in PROCURING the MURDER of slaves, we give a few instances.

"About the 1st of March last, the negro man Ransom left me, *without the least provocation whatever.* I will give $20 for said negro, if taken, *dead or alive.*" BRYANT JOHNSON. *Macon Telegraph,* Georgia, May 28, 1838.

"Ranaway, my negro man Richard. A reward of $25 will be paid for his apprehension, *dead or alive.* Satisfactory proof will only be required of his having been *killed.*" DURANT H. RHODES. *Wilmington Advertiser,* July 13, 1838.

"$100 will be paid to any person who may apprehend a negro man named Alfred. The same reward will be paid for satisfactory evidence of his having *been killed.* He has one or more *scars* on one of his hands, caused by his *having been shot.*" The Citizens of Onslow. *Wilmington (N. C.) Advertiser,* July 13, 1838.

when committed by slaves, and imprisonment when committed by whites."*

The very word slavery should be inadmissible in good society. Like the odious word brothel, the same, in reality, it should be spoken only with most aversion, and by a stern compulsion, never justified, but by great necessity. Still, slavery is far the foulest word, for it holds the idea of the compulsion of most of a large class. Yea more, the COMPULSION OF THE WEAK, THE DEFENCELESS. Yea more, of the DEPENDENT, the possessed, or claimed, in a way to constitute in all honorable minds a claim to protection. Yet at the basest of calls, the oppressor, as a general fact, walks through all these, his obligations, as a foul swine, through beds of pure lilies.

How have we and others, wished that Congress could take one tour here. If expense were considered, it would be economy, for it would stop all debate. For if one could see what we have seen, and then advocate slavery, he would be as much meaner than the common slaveholder, as the calm looker-on is meaner than the drunken fighter that mauls his innocent victim. But it could not, would not be if slavery AS IT EXISTS HERE, were understood, its MEANNESS, CANNOT BE FULLY PICTURED.

* Jay's "Inquiry," p. 134.

CHAPTER XLII.

TRUTHFULNESS IN THE COLORED.

Will not God impart his light
To them that ask it? Freely; 'tis his joy,
His glory, and his nature to impart;
But to the proud, uncandid, insincere,
Or negligent inquirer, not a spark.
                                COWPER.

IN most cases in conversation with the Colored, the answer was the perfect opposite of what they knew we expected, and in all cases diverged, but with the utmost politeness. Speaking to an aged Colored woman, a house-servant of one of the amiable, serene Southern Congressmen, we said, "We all trust you are free, now, from the chains, and agonies of slavery." With a countenance in which was reflected the smile of heaven, she said, "My dear Missus, no one but the Lord, can do 'at good thing fo' we. Jesus, Jesus! is ou' whole trust, for all 'at, for everything."

"The rebels seem to have no heart to fight," said we.

"Oh, Missus, de prayers of de poo' Colored people, make um run as 'ey did. God say he will hear 'e poor. He do. We pray," raising her poor hands, " O, we pray fo' 'e dea' sogers to come! to prosper! We pray wid every vein of ou' heart. Oh, we prays all night 'at Jesus may conquer."

"The Lord is surely on the side of the oppressed," said we.

"De Lord he burst 'e chains, 'at we all live in love, and peace, work in peace, work de ordinance of God. Can't serve him widout work good, all works good here, all! not a lazy, good-for-nothing people, on 'is place! Not one."

"We all watch you, and feel so thankful, to hear your noble Superintendents speak so warmly of you, as being so faithful, and industrious."

"De Lord is trying us, Missus, to see what we will do, to improve 'is good time ob freedom. Gets ou' rights now, suffer none. Neber, neber, did see such good time! Didn't think it possible, eber!"

"How did you feel," we said to one, "when you heard of the North taking Hilton Head?"

"Hold up my poor hands, so, and say, 'Jesus done it! Jesus done it!' when I hear of de victory."

To an aged saint, whom all loved, and Superintendent highly praised, we said, "We wish we could do more, every way, for you all."

"Oh, Missus, Jesus will thank you, I can't 'nough! So glad, so glad, you come. Hope you come to bury me! Children all sold, all gone, broke my heart. Got nobody but Jesus! Can't do no mo' now but pray."

"How do you feel about this war?"

"Oh, I so affected when it commence. Grieve so, so many die. God speak to my soul 'at ' he 'bout to break 'e chain, and set his people free.' Thank him for dis chance! all who open 'is good door, God bless um!"

To one, we said, "You doubtless feel great hopes of freedom?"

"I just try to save my immortal soul; I let 'e things of 'is worl' go. I likes liberty, I want 'at. But I MUST HAVE ETERNAL HOME, FOR MY POO' SOUL. 'At is what I think of."

Another said, "I want when I get to heaben, not be a stranger 'ere. I wants to live for 'at, and all my chil'n, and chil'n's child'n."

The fact of their candid answers, being so often the opposite of what they see that you expect, seems a little trying to them. Their saying so quietly of their wrongs, which rouse your indignation, "I LEAVE ALL 'AT WITH GOD, MISSUS," WHOSE RIGHTEOUSNESS IN THEIR CASE, MUST YET BE VINDICATED, melts the soul. As instances of candid answers: Approaching a plantation house, where one of our Superintendents had been recently put in charge, a beautiful colored boy came out to conduct us in.

"Is this the plantation of which Mr. S—— has charge?"

"It is, Missus; but he is absent."

"Sorry he is not at home. He is a good man. You all like him, I presume."

"Oh, yes, Missus," said both, the boy and a Colored girl, now out upon the steps to greet us.

"Yes, we are very glad you have got so good a man to protect you."

"We are very glad, Missus," responded both voices.

Turning to the boy, who had been so ready in his praise, we said, "Mr. S—— is going to take excellent care of you, isn't he?"

"I can't tell 'at, ma'am."

This, was spoken in so manly and truthful, yet so wary and discriminating a manner, all tinged so deeply, with his consciousness, of the possibilities of his future, in the power of others, yet of an inner existence above, and apart, from all the outer, that we had to turn hastily to hide our emotion.

Indeed, talking with these dear people, has a wonderful tendency to make one look suddenly at book on the mantel, at some ancient article, or out of a window. It has been amusing to see some of our excellent, educated, efficient, New Yorkers, or Bostonians, with all their theories, and plans, and their up-and-energy airs, pass gradually under this softening and subduing influence. Sometimes they turn with a puzzled look, and eyes not parched, and say slily, "There is, after all, something very deep in these poor people;" or, "I do not see through them, entirely, after all;" or, "Did you ever hear such natural eloquence, and depth?" This, is particularly the case, with those whose piety inhabits only in the upper tier of their residence. They feel a respect unlooked for, and an interest to hear more, and more, from them, springs up, and it would not be a marvel, if many fine scholars find that a man, in his lowest outward estate, is, after all, greater than any book, and that when the Divine presence shines through every feature, and word, it must be mighty, and felt, though that feeling may be, with any possible shade of dislike, or of love. This influence may not be understood, but its ennobling power is there, and is recognized. And in exact proportion, to the lack of an answering experience, the discriminating beholder, is more, or less puzzled.

But this candor, in conversation, together with deep thought, or "studying out 'e thing," as they call it, and the enlightenment of the Spirit in the pious, all give to their answers a wonderful originality, and zest, which make ordinary, polite conversation, so termed, seem oppressively tame and vapid.

CHAPTER XLIII.

KNOWLEDGE OF THE COLORED.

Who made the heart, 'tis He alone
   Decidedly can try us :
He knows each chord—its various tone,
   Each spring—its various bias :
Then at the balance let's be mute,
   We never can adjust it :
What's done we partly may compute,
   But know not what's resisted.

BURNS.

WE aver that a man may live here for years and know nothing of slavery, nothing of the true Negro character as a whole. He, for instance, looks out upon a plantation; he sees stealing out and in those miserable huts equally miserable-looking beings, especially if seen at a distance. The sight is repulsive, and human nature hates ugly appearances. He beholds it, from month to month, the same. If, in the army, he sees the worst side, of the worst, of those poor people. Were he a Lord Bacon, he would go in, and converse with them, for the sake of reading this open book of primitive, undisguised, human mind. He would bring his theories to the proof, as the anatomist does his, with the unconscious human body. Had he the mind of a Newton, he would learn God, in his revelations to these men. But how much cultivation does it require to appreciate! Suppose one at a distance of a mile from New York city, with only cases of delinquency or criminality to attend to, what opinion would he have of our city? What military dictatorship would he not advise? But let him go in, and become acquainted, and how would his estimation of the city be changed? So, let one from a distant camp observe these people, have the mere toil of military rule of them, of providing for them, in masses, and he knows no more of them in one year, than in one day. Or, suppose he takes the representations of one, two, or three, from casual observation, we say he can never know the Negro character thus. Why does he not converse freely with the masses? call them out and know what is in them? How is he losing opportunities, for which sages have sighed in vain! If he have prejudices against them, such, as to prevent this converse with them, his narrow mind, of course, can never understand them. But to show the fact, that this utter ignorance of them exists, we give remarks of those of high qualities and positions. In reference to arming them, one says:

"They will never fight, they will throw down their guns, and run right into the arms of their Masters."

Another, of the same opportunities for observation, replies: "No, they will massacre every man of them."

One says, "They will never stand fire."

Another, "They will fight like tigers."

Yet these are all men of equal parts, and opportunities. But all are mistaken, as one week's familiar converse with them would prove to them, for all history of them proves it. They will fight, we aver—and we challenge disproof—like tigers, for the freedom of their children, their wives, themselves. They will scarcely take a life, from revenge. We could prove this by abundant illustrations.

They speak of having certain overseers, who they all say

have caused the deaths of scores of Negroes, whom they name and tell all particulars of—arrested, and their crimes proven, when a Colored man's oath can be taken; but they never, never! speak of revenge.

In the "Memoirs of La Croix," a French officer, and therefore not partial to them, it is said of the Colored soldiers under Toussaint L'Ouverture, "that it was remarkable to see the Africans, half naked, with musket and sabre, giving an example of the severest discipline. They went out for a campaign, with nothing to eat but maize, established themselves in towns, without touching anything, exposed for sale in the shops, nor pillaging the farmers who brought things to market. Supple and trembling before their officers, respectful to citizens, they seemed only to wish to obey the instinct for liberty, which was inspired in them by Toussaint."*

And never were greater or more frequent and constant feats of valor performed, in the whole history of nations, than in Hayti, under that most able general. Only conquered at last, by being immensely outnumbered, and confiding in the honor of the French. But the just history, of all that noble contest for liberty is yet to be written, and it will be. Still, the Negro is most adapted to peace and to agriculture, though it is the testimony of accurate observers that never did they see persons so delighted with handling tools, and the wonders of mechanism. One chaplain says, they would work steadily for that mere pleasure, for hours, so delighted were they with saws, planes, chisels, etc.

"They work well," says a Superintendent, and all reiterate the same. "Three cases of trouble I have had," said he. "They had difficulty among themselves, and came to me quite excited. I said to them, 'I cannot

* See La Croix's "Memoirs."

hear you until you are cool. Go away, and stay until you are.' In every case," continued he, "they settled it among themselves. One came, and said, 'Massah, I could not sleep last night, because I had spoke wrong. Will you forgive me for speaking wrong to the foreman ?'—driver formerly—I said 'This pleases me most of all. Now I know you will be good.'"

This is substantially the report we get from all plantations. Not a Superintendent scarcely but is in most excellent heart, hale and happy. Though some say that money would not induce them to stay in those desolate places, still, when they see the wrongs, and needs, and ambitions, of the Colored, they do it gladly for their sake.

One is living in a barn. He says his presence saved them from awful wrongs from some unprincipled soldiers. They plead for a white man, to guide and protect them, under their disabilities, the work of slavery. They are universally kind, giving them many presents, etc., etc., and obedient. They usually get their tasks done between three and four P. M., and are very ambitious then, to work in their gardens, and read.

BUT IT IS AMUSING TO WATCH THE EXPRESSIONS of the haters of the Negro race. They will run on, that "they will not work," "will not provide," "will not live decently," "will steal," etc., etc. But fear not, having been allowed to spin out this whole thread, they almost invariably add, "But I have a servant, or servants, that are exceptions to the whole of them—the best, absolutely, the best, most agreeable, most capable, most complete, servant I ever had, without an exception. I must get them North somehow, for I don't see how I shall ever live without them. I believe the majority of the blacks," he goes on, " will steal, but I can trust mine to any extent. I never look after anything." "And we can say the same, of some," we add.

Now this, given almost word for word, but spoken with deeper meaning, than can be put into words, is the testimony of almost every one, South, with whom we have conversed, among all civil and military officers, civilians, and their relatives, and they have been scores. This, too, nearly all accounts, from all camps, corroborate. Still, these same persons will go right on and say, "What can be done with them if they are suddenly made free?" If they are asked,

What can be done with yours?

"Oh, he is, or they are, exceptions."

So are ours, we say; so almost every one's servant, or servants, prove exceptions. And if all who want help North, and South, under freedom, get "exceptions," the rest will be easily provided for.

The fact is, when the Negro wants to do, he is of all most competent, and the INVARIABLE TESTIMONY is, that he always wants to do, if he gets pay for it. And the same genius that is fruitful in finding "onpossibilities," in the way, in slavery, is equally fruitful in finding expedients, when free, and paid. So, on one plantation, in Jamaica, according to Sewell and others, "93! free Colored men, worked a plantation that had always required 225! slaves, and produced from it 52 more hogsheads of sugar," and instances of the like increase, might be multiplied, to almost any extent. But, as to domestic qualities, only one Superintendent says, "The Negroes care little about their wives, and children." Most others say, "they love them equally with the Whites." Others say, "they love them far, far, better." So that no one's opinion should be taken alone. Take a person not genuinely anti-slavery, with a dislike to the

Colored, and such, we regret to say, there are among us, at Port Royal, and put him over a number, he having much power, and he will almost surely come to criticise them more, and more, and, of course, that becomes mutual. When, if he hired the same persons, and paid them weekly, he would prize them very highly, at least.

To illustrate. Let a man have one hundred working emigrants, or day laborers, of any city, out upon a plantation, and suppose they were accustomed to, and attached to it. Let him merely give them rations, miserable cabins, dubious, and unsatisfactory promises, respecting pay. Then let him treat them with the love that his conversation, with you, would lead you to expect, and how, think you, would he succeed, with them? But, on the other hand, let the same man hire them knowing that they could leave his employ any day, or moment, and, always speak to them, and treat with them, under that knowledge, and how totally different would be the result. Here is just the difference between any apprenticeship, or gradual emancipation, and free labor. And shall this noble nation actually ENSLAVE, FOR THE PRESENT, by EMANCIPATING GRADUALLY? Forbid it, ye noble voters! In you we confide, for true nobility. But in fact, the Colored, here, have had far less liberty to go and come, than under their former masters. For instance, most were permitted to go from one plantation to another, or into Beaufort, upon the Sabbath. This, is prohibited not only by military necessity, but also, usually, by Superintendents.

Poor race, there seems no end to their disabilities. But they submit, very cheerfully, in general, saying, "We must all 'spect to suffer, and to lose ou' privileges, during 'is confusion. It's all for ou' liberty and ou' country, and we must bear ebery ting for 'at."

But while one sees that the poor Colored are looked at

with prejudice, to say the least, by most, he must remember that this has ever invariably been the fate of an oppressed race. Witness our own ancestors, not ten centuries since, made by every surrounding people to seem tenfold worse heathen, than they actually were, and that, surely, was bad enough.

THE ENSLAVED BRITONS.

The Romans might have found an image of their own ancestors in the representation they have given of ours. And *we* may form not an imperfect idea what *our* ancestors were, at the time Julius Cæsar invaded Britain, by the present condition of some of the African tribes. In them we may perceive, as in a mirror, the features of our progenitors; and by our own history, we may learn the extent to which such tribes may be elevated by means favorable to their improvement.*

When the inhabitants of a free country are heard justifying the injuries inflicted upon the natives of Africa, or opposing the introduction of liberal institutions among any portion of them, on the vulgar ground that they are an inferior class of beings to themselves, it is but fair to remind them, that there was a period, when CICERO CONSIDERED THEIR OWN ANCESTORS AS UNFIT TO BE EMPLOYED EVEN AS SLAVES in the house of a Roman citizen.

"Seated one day in the house of a friend at Cape Town," says Dr. Philip, "with a bust of Cicero on my right hand, and one of Sir Isaac Newton on the left, I accidentally opened a book on the table at that passage in Cicero's letter to Atticus, in which the philosopher speaks so contemptuously of the natives of Great Bri-

* Dr. Philip.

ain.* Struck with the curious coincidence, arising from the circumstances in which I then found myself placed, pointing to the bust of Cicero, and then to that of Sir Isaac Newton, I could not help exclaiming, 'Hear what that man says of that man's country!'"

Were it not so indubitably recorded on the page of history, we should hardly be willing to believe that there was a time when our ancestors, the ancient Britons, went nearly without clothing, painted their bodies in fantastic fashion, offered up human victims to uncouth idols, and lived in hollow trees, or rude habitations, which we should now consider unfit for cattle. Making all due allowance for the different state of the world, it is much to be questioned whether they made more rapid advances than have been effected by many African nations, and that they were really sunk into the lowest degree of barbarism is unquestionable.

Cicero relates that the ugliest and most stupid slaves in Rome came from England! Moreover, he urges his friend Atticus "not to buy slaves from Britain, on account of their stupidity, and their inaptitude to learn music and other accomplishments."

With Cæsar's opinion of our ancestors, we are, perhaps, some of us not sufficiently acquainted. He describes the Britons generally, as a nation of very barbarous manners: "Most of the people of the interior," he says, "never sow corn, but live upon milk and flesh, and are clothed with skins." In another place he remarks, "In

---

* "Britannici belli exitus expectatur: constat enim aditus insulæ esse munitos mirificis molibus: etiam illud jam cognitum est, neque argenti scrupulum esse ullum in illa insula, neque ullam spem prædæ nisi ex mancipiis: ex quibus nullos puto, te literis aut musicis eruditos expectare."—*Epist. Ad. Atticum*, l. iv., Epist. 16.

their domestic and social habits, the Britons are as degraded as the most savage nations. They are clothed with skins; wear the hair of their heads unshaven and long, but shave the rest of their bodies, except their upper lip, and stain themselves a blue color with woad, which gives them a horrible aspect in battle."*

"Let *us* not then the Negro Slave despise,
Just such our sires appeared in Cæsar's eyes."

Should we not laugh at Tacitus or Pliny, if, from the circumstances thus related, they had condemned the British Islands to an eternity of Bœotian darkness—to be the officina of hereditary bondage and transmitted helplessness? Yet this is the sort of reasoning employed by the perpetrators and apologists of Negro slavery. Alas, for Christian guilt! can it be equalled by any Pagan crime?

"We think unmoved of millions of our race,
Swept from thy soil by cruelties prolonged;
Another clime then ravaged to replace
The wretched Indians;—Africa now wronged
To fill the void where millions lately thronged."

In an estimate formed by Dr. Johnson of what mankind have lost or gained by European conquest, having adverted to the cruelties which have been committed,

* Quoted by Dr. Prichard, who also, after much research, imagines "the ancient Britons were nearly on a level with the New Zealanders or Tahitians of the present day, or perhaps not very superior to the Australians."—*Researches*, III., 182. At page 187 of the same volume, Dr. Prichard also remarks, "Of all Pagan nations the Gauls and Britons appear to have had the most sanguinary rites. They may well be compared in this respect with the Ashanti, Dahomehs, and other nations of Western Africa."

and the manner in which the laws of religion have been outrageously violated, he adds, "Europeans have scarcely visited any coast, but to gratify avarice and extend corruption; to arrogate dominion without right, and practise cruelty without incentive;" and he then gives it as his opinion, that "it would have been happy for the oppressed, and still more happy for the invaders, that their designs had slept in their own bosoms."

The direst study of mankind is man.

The system of oppression under which the African race suffer so grievously, renders it imperative on their oppressors to allege some reasons, as plausible as they are able, in their own defence. That slave merchants, who traffic in human flesh, and Negro drivers, who use their fellow-creatures worse than cattle, should attempt to justify their conduct by depressing the African to a level with the brute, is what MIGHT REASONABLY BE EXPECTED. Thus do the oppressors of their fellow-men satisfy their consciences by pretending to believe that the unfortunate Negro is a brute, or at best, only a connecting link between the brute creation and Man. They desire to degrade him below the standard of humanity, attempting to deface all title to the Divine image from his mind; thus do they reconcile the cruel hardships under which the victims of their oppression are still doomed to groan, maintaining that Negroes make a decided approach toward the native inferiority of the monkey tribe—that they are endowed by the Creator with the noble gift of reason in a very inferior degree, when compared with the more favored inhabitants of Europe. Two DESCRIPTIONS of men have come to this conclusion. The first are those who have had to contend with the passions and vices of the Negro in his purely Pagan state, and who have applied no other instrument to elicit the virtues they have demanded than the stimulus of the whip and the stern voice of authority. Who can wonder that they have failed? They have expected " to reap where they have not sown," and " to gather where nothing has been strewn." They have required moral ends, without the application of moral means; and their failure, therefore, leaves the question of the capacity of the Negro untouched, and proves nothing but their own folly. In the SECOND CLASS may be included our minute philosophers who take the gauge of intellectual capacity entirely in the support of slavery.

THAT VERY LITTLE IMPORTANCE CAN BE ATTACHED to the allegation of an external resemblance between the Negro and inferior animals, may be clearly inferred from the fact, that the same remark has been made, even by intelligent travellers, respecting particular people OF OTHER VARIETIES of the human race. Regnard concludes his description of the Laplanders with these words: " voilà la description de ce petit animal qu'on appelle Lapon, et l'on peut dire qu'il n'y en a point, après le singe, qui approche plus l'homme." An Esquimaux, who was brought to London by Cartwright, when he first saw a monkey, asked, " Is that an Esquimaux?" His companion adds, " I must confess, that both the color and contour of the animal's countenance had considerable resemblance to the people of their nation." N. del Techo calls the Caaiguas of South America, " tam simiis similes, quam hominibus;" and J. R. Forster, in the observations of his journey round the world, asserts, " the inhabitants of the island of Mallicollo, of all the people whom I have seen, have the nearest relationship to the monkeys."

Whether we investigate the physical or the moral nature of Man, we recognize at every step the limited extent of our knowledge. That the greatest ignorance has prevailed on this subject, even in modern times, and among men of reputed learning and acuteness, is evinced by the strange notion very strenuously asserted by Monboddo and Rosseau, and firmly believed by some, that Man and the monkey, or at least the ourang-outang, belong to the same species, and are not otherwise distinguished from each other, than by circumstances which can be accounted for, by the different physical and moral agencies to which they have been exposed. The former of these writers even supposes that the human race once possessed tails! and he says "the ourang-outangs are proved to be of our species, by marks of humanity that are incontestible;" a poor compliment to Man, indeed.

"The completely unsupported assertions of Monboddo and Rousseau," says Dr. Lawrence, "only show that they were equally unacquainted with the structure and functions of men and monkeys; not conversant with zoology and physiology, and therefore entirely destitute of the principles on which alone a sound judgment can be formed concerning the natural capabilities and destiny of animals, as well as the laws according to which certain changes of character, certain departures from the original stock, may take place."

"The peculiar characteristics of Man," continues the above writer, "appear to me so very strong, that I not only deem him a distinct species, but also put him into a separate order by himself. His physical and moral attributes place him at a much greater distance from all other orders of mammalia, than those are from each other respectively."

Sturge and Harvey state, that "a gentleman of great intelligence, long resident in Antigua, remarked to them, that the features of the Negroes had altered within his memory, which he attributed to their elevation by education and religious instruction." "Perhaps it is that the features become more agreeable, in proportion as people recede from the effects and influence of slavery."

As an illustration of the remarkable effects of education in altering the features of Man, and entirely changing the expression of his countenance, we have one circumstance on record which is very conclusive. I allude to the singular case of Kaspar Hauser, who was confined in a dungeon in a state of entire ignorance, till he was about eighteen years of age. His biographer, Anselm Von Fuerbach, President of the Bavarian Court of Appeal, whose authority may be strictly relied upon, relates, "that on Kaspar's being thrown adrift in the world, when he was first discovered by the inhabitants of Nuremburg, his face was very vulgar: when in a state of tranquillity, it was almost without any expression; and its lower features being somewhat prominent, gave him a brutish appearance. His weeping was only an ugly contortion of the mouth, and the staring look of his blue, but clear bright eyes, had also an expression of brutish obtuseness." Von Fuerbach expressed a wish at this period, that Kaspar's portrait might be taken by a skillful painter, because he felt assured that his features would soon alter. His wish was not gratified, but his prediction was soon fulfilled. The effect of education produced a wonderful alteration in his whole countenance; indeed, the formation of his face altered in a few months almost entirely; his countenance gained expression and animation, and the prominent lower features of his face receded more and more, so that his earlier physiognomy could scarcely any longer be recognized.*

* Life of Kaspar Hauser.

The alteration and improvement of the features, under the influence of the civilizing process, is elucidated by so many indubitable facts, that it is unnecessary to dwell longer upon this subject. If the operation of this influence could be applied more thoroughly and universally, it would cause a nearer approximation to each other, between the European and the African, and must tend, in a great measure, to obliterate those distinctions, on which the untenable theories of diversity of origin have been founded, and which have been adduced in favor of Negro Slavery. Dr. Philip, from the facts which have come under his observation, says, he has no hesitation in giving it as his opinion, that the complexion, the form of the countenance, and even the shape of the head, are much affected by the circumstances under which human beings are placed at an early age. In corroboration of the opinion here advanced, he says, "I have had the satisfaction to remark at our Missionary stations, what appeared to me an improvement, not only in the countenance, but even in the shape of the head, for three successive generations."

If, as travellers inform us, many Africans differ from Europeans in little else than color, the peculiar construction of the head, on the faith of which, some would class them as a distinct species, appears to be by no means a constant character. Dr. Knox, who has entered minutely into the study of Man, says, that in considering the lower specimens of humanity, too much importance has been attached to the cranium and the science of cranioscopy; *for it is not in the skull*, says he, but in the outer covering of the body or skeleton, that nature has placed the great marks of difference. "Strip off the integuments of Venus, and compare her with a Bush Woman, and the difference would be seen to be very slight." Dr. Knox, it may be observed, after considerable research, arrives at this important conclusion, "that there is an impassable gulf between the higher order of animals and the Negro."

I am not very partial to phrenology, but if quantity of brain and mental superiority have a connection with each other, we have a high authority, that of Dr. Tiedemah, an eminent German, for believing that no inferiority exists in this respect, for he asserts that in quantity of brain they equal the fair races. Dr. TIEDEMAN communicated a paper to the British Royal Society, detailing the comparative examination of the brains of a number of Negroes—size, weight, conformation, etc., demonstrating that no material difference exists, between them and the brains of the White races.

Professor BLUMENBACH, the great German physiologist, bestowed much labor and research on the question of Negro capacity. He collected a large number of skulls, and also a numerous library of the works of persons of African blood or descent. He is, perhaps, the greatest authority, in favor of the identity of species and equality of intellect of the Black and White races. It is to Blumenbach, that we are indebted for the most complete body of information on this subject, which he illustrated most successfully by his unrivalled collection of the craniæ of different nations from all parts of the globe. His admirable work "On the Varieties of the Human Species," contains a short sketch of the various formations of the skull in different nations; but he has treated the subject at greater length, and with more minute detail, in his "Decades Craniorum," in which the craniæ themselves are represented of their natural size.

From the results of the observations of Blumenbach and others, it appear, then, that there is no characteristic whatever in the organization of the skull or brain of the Negro which affords a presumption of inferior endowment either of the intellectual or moral faculties. If it be asserted that the African nations are inferior to the rest of mankind, from historical facts, because they may be thought not to have contributed their share to the advancement of human arts and science, the Mandingoes may be instanced as a people evidently susceptible of high mental culture and civilization. They have not, indeed, contributed much toward the advancement of human arts and science, but they have evinced themselves willing and able to profit by these advantages when introduced among them. The civilization of many African nations is much superior to that of the aborigines of Europe, during the ages which preceded the conquests made by the Goths and Swedes in the North, and by the Romans in the Southern part. The old Finnish inhabitants of Scandinavia had long, as it has been proved by the learned investigations of Rühs, the religion of fetishes, and a vocabulary as scanty as that of the most barbarous Africans. They had lived from ages immemorial without laws, or government, or social union; every individual in all things the supreme arbiter of his own actions; and they displayed as little capability of emerging from the squalid sloth of their rude and merely animal existence. When conquered by a people of Indo-German origin, who brought with them from the East the rudiments of mental culture, they emerged more slowly from their pristine barbarism than many of the native African nations have since done. Even at the present day, there are hordes in various parts of northern Asia, whose heads have the form belonging to the Tartars, to the Sclavonians, and other Europeans, but who are below many of the African tribes in civilization.

"The Christian philosopher," says Dr. CHALMERS, "sees in every man, a partaker of his own nature, and a brother of his own species. He contemplates the human mind in the generality of its great elements. He enters upon a wide field of benevolence, and disdains the geographical barriers by which little men would shut out one half of the species from the kind offices of the other. Let man's localities be what they may, it is enough for his large and noble heart, that he is bone of the same bone."

A powerful argument may yet be adduced, which appears to us conclusive of the whole question relating to man's unity of origin, and that is, the testimony of the sacred Scriptures, which ascribe one origin to the whole human family. Our Scriptures have not left us to determine the title of any tribe to the full honors of humanity by accidental circumstances. One passage affirms, that "God hath made of one blood all the nations of men, for to dwell on all the face of the earth;" that they are of one family, of one origin, of one common nature: the other, that our Savior became incarnate, "that he, by the grace of God, should taste death for every man."*

"Behold then," says the pious RICHARD WATSON, "the foundation of the fraternity of our race, however colored and however scattered. Essential distinctions of inferiority and superiority had been, in almost every part of the Gentile world, adopted as the palliation or the justification of the wrongs inflicted by man on man; but against this notion, Christianity, from its first promulgation, has lifted up its voice. God hath made the varied tribes of men 'of one blood.' Dost thou wrong a human being? He is thy brother. Art thou his murderer by war, private malice, or a wearing and exhausting oppression? 'The voice of thy brother's blood crieth to God

* "Tribute to the Negro."

from the ground.' Dost thou, because of some accidental circumstances of rank, opulence, and power on thy part, treat him with scorn and contempt? He is thy 'brother for whom Christ died ;' the incarnate Redeemer assumed his nature as well as thine; He came into the world to seek and to save him as well as thee; and it was in reference to him also that He went through the scenes of the garden and the cross. There is not, then, a man on earth who has not a Father in heaven, and to whom Christ is not an Advocate and Patron; nay, more, because of our common humanity, to whom he is not a Brother."

"WE HAVE NEVER HEARD AN OATH, among the Colored," is a general and so far as we know or have heard, a universal remark. But, if one will cast about him, he will recollect that profanity is comparatively unheard of among them, in the free States. Here, it seems to have been the prerogative of Massah. Still, it is a wonder that none caught it, that NONE are base enough to use it. Not one, many say, strange as that may seem.

Their REVERENCE FOR THE SABBATH, is great. Though from necessity many have labored even upon it, to be decent, still what their consciences do forbid they are strenuous in observing. On two plantations, they had prayer-meetings, nearly every evening among themselves, and quite a revival was going on. The devoted, seem to look for the salvation of souls, continually.

But docility, and reverence, seem their strong features. Last Sabbath as we passed to church, we saw some boys playing at ball. We said to one, "Do not play, boys, on this holy Sabbath." Running toward us with a low bow, and in full ivory, the lad said, "We will not do so any mo', Missus." But whether they kept this sincere intent is doubtful, for one says, "they are an exceedingly 'promising' race." This fact, or that they are "promising," we find, in many of our expedients for meetings, etc., all promising, most cordially, to TRY to come, and thanking Missus for calling to invite them, but generally, being missing at the hour, at least, often, absent altogether.

Still, all remark upon being surprised and disappointed, in regard to their truth, in assertions. Most say, "It is the very reverse of what they expected." "They are entirely reliable, in most cases, in assertions" especially among the pious. But probably "onpossibilities" occur in keeping promises.

IF THEY EXCEL IN ANY VIRTUE, it is perhaps in their CONSCIENTIOUSNESS, and high standard of Christianity. Still, some Superintendents say the pious ones will take things, for the needs of the body, and not seem condemned for it. We know it is as natural for a savage, to steal, as to drink when thirsty; and how far necessity has justified them, in past life, we leave to their Judge. Slavery is a system of robbery from top to bottom; and if a man should take your child and sell him, you would probably think little of taking a cup of his sugar.

But, when one is asked, "Are you a Christian?" the answer is:

"O! Is'e tryin', tryin'! to be, Missus. De gate straight. I tryin' to enter." Or, "Through 'e grace of ou' Lord Jesus Christ, I tryin' to be.

All their sayings, songs, and boatsongs, make it indeed like the camel, or cable, going through the eye of a needle to get into heaven. And what their conscience does require, they are exceedingly strenuous in observing.

Some ministers asked some slaves to sing "Dixie."

"We's members, we can't sing songs like 'at," was the answer.

We conversed with a driver, who called all around him to witness that he received "two hundred lashes, 'cause he wouldn't lie, wouldn't lie! wouldn't, sin so."

He said as his "Massah" talked to him before he whipped him, he "stood by railin'" on 'e porch, 'cause if Massah knock me down, fall ober de railin' and break neck and die; and wanted to die, but darsn't kill 'self. But 'e railin' was little too high, Missus," said he, "so when Massah hit me, couldn't fall over, couldn't die, but wouldn't lie, wouldn't! and didn't lie! so got two hundred lash. 'At ole Massah go horseback in fiel' and cut Nigger, ebery step while he working; seemed crazy sometimes. He whip ebery Nigger Monday morning, always, ebery one."

As to thieving, our experience proves that, with a given number of servants, the thieving is not one hundredth part what it is with ordinary emigrants, if it even equals that. We have two Colored servants that the ladies say "they would trust with uncounted money," after all the variety of tests to which they have been here put.

In fine, as to conscientiousness, they are very exact in doing what conscience does require, but that faculty needs the education of freedom, justice, honesty, in short, of free manhood, doubtless.

We! Christianize these Colored people! We rather learn the true, full spirit of Christianity from many of them. This is the testimony of most, in proportion to their candor, and access, either of officers, chaplains, privates, or civilians. While there is nothing abject or mean in their humility, it is as nearly perfect as possible. You are invariably reproved, just in proportion to your appreciation of real excellence, and of all relations. But the very features, which excite in one beholder, love, reverence, for their kindness, submission, piety, yea, for the "God in them," only lead another, a stupid person, to say, how stupid! But, to illustrate. In speaking of the injuries received, at the hands of their masters, there is in many, a dignity, a consciousness, of injured manhood, before which you, involved, with your country, stand as a culprit. You express indignation, which requires an answer. That answer reproves you; for instance, you say, "Was he not awfully wicked?"

"'At is all between him, or his soul, and de Lord, Missus."

Your pity for them, instead of sinking into contempt, rises into silent awe, of the majesty of God in man. The most wronged, and that, not, for one, or two, or more instances, which we visit so severely, even in friends, but for every moment of a long life—we say every moment, that includes his sleeping moments, for even in these he cannot have a bed, lest he be lazy, he cannot have even his poor rags, or blanket, alone. So that every moment, even in externals, he is wronged—every moment is he a sufferer, we say, but when you speak of the heart-breaking wrongs of his whole life, he says in the most touchingly plaintive manner, "I LEAVE ALL 'AT WID 'E LORD." And he does. It is nothing put on. But there is in that mute appeal to God, that casting of the whole case, upon him, a power, greater than dwells in armies, a power, that ca.. in the omnipotence of God, a power, that should make the slaveholder, the country, tremble. It is an appeal never, never! made to God in vain.

True, one may merely say, "I leave it to God," and not be avenged. But he cannot ACTUALLY in the centre of his soul, LEAVE IT TO GOD, and continue so to do, and not be avenged, speedily. Men fear those, who, with power threaten revenge. But that is nothing, to be feared in comparison with this mute leaving all to Omnipotent God, to whom "vengeance belongeth," as alas! this whole country is now finding. But why, why, should others, voters, Congressmen, incur this wrath, upon them and their innocent families, by needlessly becoming partakers of the slaveholders' sins, by justifying, or tardily, and feebly, opposing them, and thus receive of his plagues? For, in the Bible, invariably, the standing, and beholding, and consenting, or not interfering, is ever put on exact equality, with the crime.

CHAPTER XLIV.

SHALL THE BOND GO FREE?

Oh, Freedom ! thou art not a fair young girl
With light and delicate limbs : a bearded man,
Armed to the teeth, art thou ; one mailed hand
Grasps the broad shield, and one the sword ; thy brow,
Glorious in beauty though it be, is scarred
With tokens of old wars ; thy massive limbs
Are strong with struggling. Power at thee has launched
His bolts, and with his lightnings smitten thee :
They could not quench the life thou had'st from heaven.
BRYANT.

As to whether they are prepared for freedom, after conversing with scores who have the care of them here, together with all other evidences, we say unhesitatingly, they are. Besides, no man has a right to ask that question respecting another freeman. Of course, every man is prepared for freedom until he commits a crime, then he is prepared for a prison, and not before. The following we give as an illustration :

"Deacon Davis, of Hampton, Va., one of the class known as contrabands, was called to a platform. He delivered an address that claimed the earnest attention of the audience. He described the sufferings he had undergone as a slave—not of the body, but of the HEART and SOUL, in the sundering of domestic ties, the tearing of his wife and children from him—with a pathos not to be resisted. He said:

"'I had asked that I might be laid in my grave before I should see it, but God ordered otherwise, and I passed through the furnace, and, I hope, came out a better man. If you lose a son, you can bear it, for God has taken him home. But MAN tore my boys from me—and how much harder was the blow! Knowing these things, can anybody wonder that God has brought about this war? I believe that God will destroy either slavery or this Union.

"'And now it is asked, what was to be done with these sufferers? 'Will you turn all these people loose?' He would ask: 'Is you loose?' We don't want to be any looser than you. If Colored people need more law, then put us under more law. Others say: 'These people can't take care of themselves.' Well, let them go. Some White people can't take care of themselves. We don't want to be treated any better than White men. If a White man or a Black man is too lazy to work, let him take the consequence.* But he asked nobody to take care of him. He had been taking care of his mistress and himself, too.' He gave an amusing account of his escape, or rather, of her escape from him. He said that she went

---

* It was a general remark at Beaufort, that no class of whites could be found that would work so constantly and quietly, with so little encouragement, as Superintendents were authorized to give to the freedmen. And this is corroborated by official and other reports from every point where they have gained freedom. A deputation from the Baptist Missionary Society, London, Underhill and Brown, reported from Jamaica in 1861 that such was the industry of their negroes that "three-fifths of the cultivated land in Jamaica was the *bona fide* property of the blacks;" that the sum total of their property was £2,358,000, an estimate which he ventured to say was far below the mark. There were 53,000, or ONE-EIGHTH of the entire population communicants, and they raised every year, for religious purposes, £28,000. The people were orderly, affectionate, and well-behaved. Similar proofs of industry could be adduced from every place where they have had a fair trial.

away quite sanguine that Jeff. Davis would soon come back, and would do a great deal for her. Well, what has Jeff. done for her? 'She had a good house in Hampton, and that was in ashes; her servants were all gone away, and here—he said—is the best of them standing up here !'—[Exit, with tumultuous applause.]"

But it is well known, that all systems of apprenticeship, or partial liberation, have been failures, and must be, in the very nature of the case. For how can a man learn to act as a free man until he is free? Impossible! But these people are self-reliant, having always been obliged to be, for, in most cases, all they receive from "Massah" is one pair of shoes per year, and six yards of bare cloth for a man, and eight for a woman, and the weekly peck of corn. This leaves all trimmings, and all comforts to be purchased by the weary slave, and paid for by night work, or, by work beyond the regular amounts required.

Yet it is wonderful how they seize upon the least advantages. So sure as one has been house servant, been from home, as servant, waiter, boatman, or in any capacity, has had contact with men, it is instantly seen, for he adopts all possible improvements; and if he considers himself a little extra, who does not, for some, and perhaps not as good a reason?

We believe there is not a people upon earth at this day, who live so respectably and honorably, in comparison to their advantages, as this. Certainly there is not one who make so great efforts and sacrifices for "'spectability," comfort, and conscience.

They work from the smallest inducements—mere rations and long-deferred promises—cheerfully and well, not averaging two in one hundred who do not, and on many plantations not one in all. But they cannot be expected to work as freemen till they are made free.

To give one illustration, where multitudes might be adduced:

Barbadoes has doubled the price of her lands since emancipation. Says the candid, Sewell: "None are more ready than the planters to admit that the free laborer is a better, more cheerful and industrious worker than was ever the slave." But we give proof, and quote further from a published letter of Governor Hincks, January, 1858:

"As to the relative cost of slave and free labor in this colony, I can supply facts upon which the most implicit reliance can be placed. They have been furnished to me by the proprietor of an estate containing three hundred acres of land, and situated at a distance of about twelve miles from the shipping port. The estate referred to produced during slavery an annual average of 140 hogsheads of sugar of the present weight, and required 230 slaves. It is now worked by 90 free laborers: 60 adults, and 30 under 16 years of age. Its average product during the last seven years has been 194 hogsheads. The total cost of labor has been £770 16s., or £3 19s. 2d. per hogshead of 1,700 pounds. The average of pounds of sugar to each laborer during slavery was 1,043 pounds, and during freedom 3,660 pounds!! To estimate the cost of slave-labor, the value of 230 slaves must be ascertained; and I place them at what would have been a low average—£50 sterling each—which would make the entire stock amount to £11,500. This, at six per cent. interest, which on such property is much too low an estimate, would give £690; cost of clothing, food, and medical attendance, I estimate at £3 10s.; making £805. Total cost, £1,495, or £10 12s. per hogshead, while the cost of free labor on the same estate is under £4!"

In 1853, the French committee charged by the Governor of Martinique to visit the island, reported that "in an agricultural and manufacturing point of view the aspect of Barbadoes is dazzling."

In Trinidad or British Guiana the negroes were not obliged by competition to submit to the obnoxious tenure; and they soon found, where land was so cheap, that a path to independence lay open before them in working their own little properties. The planters became more stubborn and more rigid, and the result was, in many cases, the absolute abandonment of large estates for want of labor.

"The industry of the Barbadoes population is shown in the fact, that, out of the 106,000 acres of the island, 100,000 are under cultivation,* while the average price of land rises to the unprecedented height of five hundred dollars an acre."

"Notwithstanding the high price of land and the low rate of wages, the freed slaves have increased the number of small proprietors with less than five acres, from 1,100 to 3,537,† during the last fifteen years—an increase which alone testifies to the remarkable thrift of the emancipated Negro in Barbadoes."

Mr. Sewell has talked with all classes and conditions, and says, "none are more ready to admit than the planters that the free laborer is a better, more cheerful, and industrious workman than was ever the slave."

"The Colored mechanics and artisans of Barbadoes," says the same author, "are equal in general intelligence to the artisans and mechanics of any part of the world equally remote from the great centres of civilization. The peasantry will soon equal them, when education is more generally diffused."

If facts will convince men, surely these must do it, and

* Schomburg. † Governor Hincks.

equal facts might be given from every place where emancipation has been declared. But were they unfitted for freedom, what has done it? Slavery! and shall the cause be continued?

But the mass are not unfitted. They could easily dispense with the White man. They easily influence each other from their peculiar susceptibility to flattery, criticism, ridicule, their "oncommon hatred of tings dat 'pear bad," their love of money and comfort.

Many plantations were doing as well as " befo' Massah run away." All work good, subject to the driver, a slave like themselves. The reverse was true in some cases, but very few. Whites in this climate could not dispense with them. They could not cultivate and pick the cotton. The notables are all Colored. The "pilot whose keel never touches bottom" amid all these obstructions and sand bars, is Colored. The man who, on every plantation, knows how, when, where to do all desired work, is Colored. The guide is always Colored. The nurse, that rivals physicians here, is Colored, etc., etc. In short, in this climate, the Colored, is the ultimatum for advice in all practical matters pertaining to the country and climate.

Besides, he is on most intimate terms, with nature, seeming related to bird, insect, herb, flower, and perfectly familiar with their names, habits, uses. At least, they answered our many inquiries promptly, and with real fondness, for nature, as her youngest petted sons. Ah, she has taken them to her own heart, and amid their anguish she has opened to them her treasures of herbs, and roots, and healing leaves, to soothe their agonies. Yes, she even gives them a root, for soap, against the Master's avarice, or poverty. You seem to come into her real presence, and favor, more, while led by them.

CHAPTER XLV.

APPRECIATION OF ALL MEN.

> Give me to love my fellow, and in love,
>   If with none other grace to chant my strain,
> Sweet keynote of soft cadences above,
>   Sole star of solace in life's night of pain.
>   RALPH HOYT.

WHERE is the love of our neighbor, as ourself, manifested for the Colored? What writer, incidentally or spontaneously, shows it? He may plead for those mere rights, which, after all, it is little to accord to a man—it would be very little for your friends to accord to you, you would think, reader—he may even plead the excellence of his character, the absolute fact, that he is a child of God. But where is the writer, who alludes to the Colored, with the fondness, of true, Christian love? Fondness! you say, do you require fondness? What does the Word of God require? Have you not fondness toward yourself? and "thou shalt love thy neighbor as thyself!" Yes, we do say fondness, Christian fondness. And we further say, there is no writer who comes even up to the general, popular, Christian heart upon this point. Whereas many, alas! we must say, most, show a positive aversion, instead of love. Sometimes, this appears an effort to cater to the depravity of readers, or, to keep them assured of their candor, and freedom from bias, toward the Negro, or, in other words, freedom from pure Christian love toward him.

The South throws this, into our teeth, and justly, for, after all their base oppression, it is true as they assert, that there is an appreciation of the Negro South that is wanting North. This has grown out of actual knowledge of him, actual benefits derived from his mental powers and acquisitions, from his knowledge of nature practically, of herbs, and the forces and laws of life in animals, including man, of his sagacity, indomitable patience in pursuing an object, his devotion to the child, or family he loves; in short, to his adaptation to emergencies, his superior skill in devising, and executing, but above all, his actual wisdom, growing out of his almost invariable piety, and, consequently, his seeing light in the light of God, and his spiritual power with God, in great needs. For instance, the life of the child is given back to the fond mother, in answer to the prayers of the poor slave. Her own soul is sustained, or even converted, through obvious answers to his intercessions. In short, in all the prostration, and tending to weakness, to awful depression, yea to imbecility, produced by the system of slavery, he is the crutch, which the hand cannot hold, without leaning upon it, and, having done so, it has a knowledge of it, which inspires valuation, yea, demands the support of it, however it may wrong him, in his own person, or soul. So, that the Negro, actually comes to be virtual head of the house, in many instances, from his acknowledged power, and adaptation to the ever new wants, and emergencies, of families. And his occasional and barbarous floggings do not touch that power, for it is graven and grounded in *the experience*, of every member. His Master, this Negro often treats, as keepers do bears, avoiding adroitly his power, but actually governing, and leading him in many things by his superior skill, or superior knowledge, we might say, for this man knows most, of practical things, yes, his Master, better than that Master knows himself. Or, he can foresee what course he will take under given circumstances, better than he, and, in spite of promises, or threats. So, upon his actual qualities, and adaptation to the wants of all, the inequalities of all, his appreciation, of the whims, tastes, feelings of all, he is recognized, as the helper, yes, the sympathizer, the comforter, of all. In short, he is known as he is not at the North, and scarcely can be, and that he is appreciated, is owing simply to what he proves himself to be, and it would be far greater North, were he equally known there.

These writers are not, perhaps, to be censured. They have written under so strong an influence, an imperceptible spell cast upon the North, by slaveholders, that, to have expected more were unreasonable. It was not unreasonable to expect a largeness of mind, in Humboldt, Miller, Wesley; Watson, Edwards, Washington, Wilberforce, to estimate the Negro. But, to expect that largeness, from the common mind, were unreasonable, except, it be the product of grace, which, in actual appreciation of excellence, raises the commonest mind, above the philosopher. But where, out of the South, with all its faults, does actual, pure, Christian, love for the Colored show itself? We do not mean where is the pompous minister, that can work himself by the fire of his own eloquence into a heat that he actually mistakes for this love, and which we would not undervalue; but where is the incidental fondness ever leaking out like water from a full vat? We answer. It is in the military. Watch, scrutinize, the references, to the "contrabands" by nearly every one, who has come into actual contact, or acquaintance with them, or who has even stood aloof, upon the spot, and seen their capacity, skill, shrewdness, valor, or their patience, industry, fidelity. But this appreciation, though founded, at first, upon cold knowledge, becomes warm, and genuine, and permanent, and must continue more and more so, as time rolls on, and events develop true qualities.

As to the aversion, of many Christian writers, and speakers, for the Colored, we will, reader, you and I, "LEAVE ALL THAT WITH THE LORD," determined, by grace, NOT TO DISOBEY HIM, OR DAMAGE OUR OWN SOULS, BY JUDGING THEM. But, we will rejoice, that so many are coming near to the blessed Apostle Paul, in the spirit which he showed respecting the Colored Onesimus, when he said, "RECEIVE HIM AS MYSELF, and if he hath wronged thee, or oweth thee aught, set that to mine account." Increasing sensible, manly, scriptural, Christian; love for the Colored, is A GREAT FEATURE OF THE TIMES, and it must increase in proportion as knowledge of God, and of them, increases, inevitably.

And this knowledge of the Negro does, and will, increase. Every letter from the soldier in the South spreads it, and will, more and more, as the war deepens and the sickly season comes on. And many will know that THEIR LIVES ARE SAVED, through the care of these former slaves. We beseech all such, to be far more attentive to the dear soldier, they speak so much of, than they ever were to their old enemy of a master. Now, is a chance for them to show the army what they are, to raise a wave of gratitude, and appreciation, and love in all the Whites, that shall sweep away the prejudice created by the most persistent efforts of lying masters, and their tools, of mean Northerners.

And, permit us to say, let every soldier, while in health, get some Colored man under an obligation, or promise to see to him, when sick, and assure him of his wish that he shall do so, his expectation that he will. Next to our Heavenly Father, we leave ours, in that latitude, in the care of "Aunt Mary." We trust her next to him, and we know she will be faithful. They understand the care, the nursing, and bathing in tepid soap and water; the gentle stimulants of perspiration, far more important than medicine in those fevers. Their nursing will save many lives that strong medicines would destroy. A general in the South, seeing the good effects of "Composition," sent to New York for five pounds! and considers it a sure remedy, with bathing, for fevers there.

But, to return, speaking of affection for the Colored, let them, we beseech them as their friend, not fail to secure it, in every possible way. They are proverbially hospitable, and now, THE DEAR SOLDIER, whom they so love is THE STRANGER WITHIN THEIR GATES, whom the Lord commands them to care for. But as examples, as instances of Negro hospitality, also as illustrations of their native character, we give the following:

CHRISTIAN KINDNESS IN AN AFRICAN.

"In one of my early journeys," says Moffat, "with some of my companions, we came to a heathen village on the banks of the Orange River. We had travelled far, and were hungry, thirsty, and fatigued. From the fear of being exposed to lions, we preferred remaining at the village to proceeding during the night. The people at the village, rather roughly, directed us to halt at a distance. We asked water, but they would not supply it. I offered the three or four buttons which still remained on my jacket for a little milk; this also was refused. We had the prospect of another hungry night at a distance from water, though within sight of the river. We found it difficult to reconcile ourselves to our lot; for, in addition to repeated rebuffs, the manner of the villagers excited suspicion.

"When twilight drew on, a woman approached from the height, beyond which the village lay. She bore on her head a bundle of wood, and had a vessel of milk in her hand. The latter, without opening her lips, she handed to us, laid down the wood, and returned to the village. A second time she approached with a cooking vessel on her head, and a leg of mutton in one hand, and water in the other. She sat down, without saying a word, prepared the fire, and put on the meat. We asked her again and again who she was. She remained silent, till affectionately entreated to give us a reason for such unlooked-for kindness to strangers. The solitary tear stole down her sable cheek when she replied, 'I love Him whose servant you are; and surely it is my duty to give you a cup of cold water in his name. My heart is full; therefore I cannot speak the joy I feel to see you in this out-of-the-world place.'

"On learning a little of her history, and that she was a solitary light, burning in a dark place, I asked her how she kept up the life of God in her soul, in the entire absence of the communion of saints. She drew from her bosom a copy of the Dutch New Testament which she had received from Mr. Helme, when in his school some years previous, before she had been compelled by her connections to retire to her present seclusion. 'This,' she said, 'is the fountain whence I drink; this is the oil which makes my lamp burn.'

"I looked on the precious relic, printed by the British and Foreign Bible Society; and the reader may conceive how I felt, and my believing companions with me, when we met with this disciple, and mingled our sympathies and prayers together at the throne of our Heavenly Father."

THE HOSPITABLE NEGRO WOMAN.

The enterprising traveller, Mungo Park, was employed by the African Association, to explore the interior regions of Africa, in which he encountered many dangers and difficulties. His wants were often supplied, and his distresses alleviated, by the kindness and compassion of the Negroes. He gives the following interesting account of the hospitable treatment he received from a poor Negro woman:

"Being arrived at Sego, the capital of the kingdom of Bambarra, on the Niger, I wished to pass over to that part of the town in which the king resides. The people who crossed the river, carried information to Mansong, the king, that a White man was coming to see him. He immediately sent one of his chief men, who informed me that the king could not possibly see me, until he knew what had brought me into his country. He advised me to lodge for the night in a village to which he pointed. As there was no remedy, I set off for the village; where I found, to my great mortification, no person would admit me into his house. From prejudices infused into their minds, I was regarded with astonishment and fear; and was obliged to sit the whole day without victuals, in the shade of a tree.

"The night threatened to be very uncomfortable; the wind rose, and there was great appearance of a heavy rain. The wild beasts, too, were very numerous in the neighborhood, that I should have been under the necessity of climbing up the tree, and resting among the branches. About sun-set, however, as I was preparing to pass the night in this manner, and had turned my horse loose, that he might graze at liberty, a Negro woman, returning from the labors of the field, stopped to observe me; and perceiving that I was weary and dejected, inquired into my situation. I briefly explained it to her; after which, with looks of great compassion, she took up my saddle and bridle, and told me to follow her. Having conducted me into her hut, she lighted a lamp, spread a mat on the floor, and told me I might remain there for the night. Finding I was very hungry, she went out to procure me something to eat; and returned in a short time with a very fine fish, which, having caused to be half broiled upon some embers, she gave me for supper. The rights of hospitality being thus performed toward a stranger in distress, my worthy benefactress (pointing to the mat, and telling me I might sleep there without apprehension) called to the female part of her family, who had stood gazing on me all the while in astonishment, to resume their task of spinning cotton; in which they continued to employ themselves great part of the night.

"They lightened their labor by songs, one of which was composed extempore: for I was myself the subject of it. It was sung by one of the young women, the rest joining in a chorus. The air was sweet and plaintive, and the words literally translated, were these:—'The winds roared and the rain fell. The poor White man, faint and weary, came and sat under our tree. He has no mother to bring him milk—no wife to grind his corn.' *Chorus.* 'Let us pity the White man; no mother has he to bring him milk—no wife to grind his corn.'"

It were improper to speak of the new tenderness for the colored, in many of the most noble while living, but let the noble and dead Mitchell speak, who is now present with the Lamb who was slain for each personally of these dark brethren. We copy a few words from his letter to Sec. Chase, and one of his speeches to the people while in command at Port Royal:

"I have spoken to the *elite* of Boston—the solid, and the scientific, and the literary men of that learned city; I have spoken to the fashionable crowds of New-York in the Academy of Music; I have spoken to the rich and proud citizens of New-Orleans; I have spoken to multitudes in every State in the Union, but *I do not think I ever addressed any audience* WHOSE PRESENCE TOUCHED ME MORE DEEPLY *than the sable multitude to whom I endeavored to utter words of encouragement and hope yesterday.* And, my dear Governor, they are encouraged, and they do hope; and I feel that it is possible to convert the officers and soldiers from their UNJUST and UNGENEROUS PREJUDICES, and to make them the firm, fast, SYMPATHIZING FRIENDS of those unfortunate blacks. Already I find a very great change, and some of my thinking officers, who were most gloomy and most despondent when I first arrived, are now full of cheerful hope. With your past life I fully sympathise. I know and understand it all. I was reared in the midst of slavery, born in Kentucky, and know all about it.

"But it seems to me that there is a new time coming for you colored people; a better day is dawning for you oppressed and down-trodden blacks. You have in your hands the rescuing of those sufferers over whose sorrows you mourn continually. If you fail, what a dreadful responsibility it will be when you come to die, to feel that the only great opportunity you had for serving yourselves and your oppressed race was allowed to slip."

CHAPTER XLVI.

THE WASTE OF LIFE.

And what is life ? a weary pilgrimage,
Whose glory in one day doth fill the stage
With childhood, manhood and decrepit age.
QUARLES.

THIS waste of life is amazing, and can only be accounted for, even allowing for Southern lack of thrift, by the fact that the work of the plantation must be in the care of overseers, or drivers. The following description of "*overseers*" is from WILLIAM WIRT's Life of PATRICK HENRY: " LAST and LOWEST (*i. e.*, of the different classes of society in Virginia), a FECULUM of beings called *overseers;* the most abject, degraded, unprincipled race, always cap in hand to the Dons who employed them, and furnishing materials for the exercise of their pride, insolence, and spirit of domination." From this description we see in what hands human life is there. Besides, the infant is worth more to the Master, but the woman's work is usually worth more to the overseer or driver. This fact is recognized by the Master, often giving those dignitaries a PREMIUM, as is well known, for every LIVING CHILD. What volumes does this one fact speak, to him who can, and will think !

But the labor of the poor mother is worth, in the present, far more than the anticipated premium, the profits, being all that is considered, usually. This is illustrated by facts, collected by close scrutiny of twenty-five plantations.

One-third of the poor ex-slave women have lost one-half their children, two-thirds have lost one-third, and so on. Many have lost all.

Said we to one: " Have you no children ?"

" No, Missus, had to leab baby 'e in house all day while gone to work."

" Not alone ?"

" Yes, Missus, 'lone, couldn't help it, 'bliged to do it."

" Why how did you fix it ?"

" Hang it up dere in de basket, an' boil some flou' for it. It cry all day, an' I cry all day," said the mother, her eyes filling, and not hers only, " an' he die, 'cause he cry so. No nuss on dis plantation; all works." Now can a woman, a mother, read this, and not weep, with that poor mother, and not vow eternal vengeance upon slavery ? No surely, surely, not.

Another woman said:

" I los' tree ; got not one; fretted self almos' to deff."

" What disease had they ?"

" No disease, ma'am, only fretted to deff in 'e basket."

" In the basket ?"

" Yes, Missus ; when little, put um in basket an' take um to de fiel'. Dey cry all day, but you not stop, or be cut up. Sometimes, if driver not see you, you run wet it mouf a little ; make shade ober with some cloth, shade go off, sun make um sick. If he see you, you get lick."

Mother, sitting by your dear cradled one; Father, who amid all the bustle of business, sees, mentally, that beautiful wife and babe at home—pray stop reading, and imagine that equally tender mother, with breaking heart, and no, no, hope, toiling under a burning sun, upon scorching sands, fifteen hours per day, with the feeble wail of her famishing dying babe, in her car, or, faint and fainter in the distance, its little body, in all the agony of confinement in the basket, in the torrid sun, with burning thirst. Can you realize it? and that, when that poor mother had lost two, four, six, in the same way, precisely. Oh Blessed Jesus, who didst take little ones in thine arms, and bless them! Is there womanhood in woman? Is there tenderness in these mother's hearts? How then can one be silent? or even moderate, in opposing this awful sin? But slavery cannot exist without all this, never does, far South, and even then it does not pay, even in a pecuniary point of view. Oh, would the mothers of our land rise in their dignity! Will they not? Statesmen, editors, in some instances, have come down to put this awful system into political scales, obliged perhaps in some respects to do so, to refute its advocates. But all humanity, principle, manhood, religion, is wronged, when so sacred a question is put to such tests. We might as well discuss the propriety of killing all people at a certain age, from pecuniary considerations, as to discuss slavery, pecuniarily, or as if we would retain it, were it profitable. Oh, let noble men everywhere, let woman at the sacred home-table, hearth, altar, place and keep it upon the high noble grounds of eternal right. Noble ones are crushed under the awful scourge; we too. Will you help, or shall we die? We feel as we cannot live, if slavery be not put away.

"But I should think," said we, "if your Master had no mercy, he would rather raise the children, and sell them."

"Oh! yes, Missus, he want to do 'at, but den 'e work so tight, he not tink baby die, till gone, an' he drive we so hard. Massah make we go in fiel' an' work when baby dead in house. O! Massah hate us so."

But after all aspects of slavery here, the recklessness in regard to life is still the most astonishing feature. But the overseers are usually interested only in the present crop, not in the lives of slaves. The Master is away, mostly, or is too self-indulgent, of course, to see before light, who is able to work; besides it would break up all order, to allow that any are unable.

The general testimony is:

"Massah not let you speak to him." "Massah not let you speak to driver 'bout de chil'n; can't do nothing."

But the poor Master, under the pressure of all the difficulties and all the vices of the soul consequent upon his false relation to these poor laborers, pushes and pushes on the work, occasioning the deaths of many, to his own surprise, in many cases.

Calling yesterday, we found in one stall—for we can call many of the quarters in Beaufort nothing else—three women. After other conversation, we said to one woman: "How many children have you?"

"None, had fou', all dead." The other had lost all.

"Why, of what disease?"

"Hard work, strainin' so in fiel'."

"Awful! how long did they live?"

"None of them fou' weeks."

"Well you have got them in heaven, as you are a Christian."

"Oh, yes, Missus."

"But you Colored women do not seem to mourn so much for your children who die, though you are so very fond of those who live."

"No, Missus."

"I suppose you consider what a life of sorrow they escape, and what a joy they enter?"

"Some women frets awful, some frets self to death,

good many. But if it please de Lord to take um, don't mourn when dey gone."

"What do your masters say?"

"Some scolds and says dey kill um, 'cause so careless."

"Do you think they are careless?"

"No, Missus, de baby neber well, neber."

"Oh what a beautiful thought, that such a number of infant spirits are all the time going up from this hard land, to be

Forever with the Lord,

and to wait there, for their poor mothers, for nearly all these mothers are Christians, are they not?"

"Most all, Missus, couldn't live if wasn't."

"You! my poor woman," speaking to another, "not a Christian! and you have two there, and none here, and 'except you be converted, you cannot see the kingdom of God.'"

"It's very mean," said she, "not to be Christian and serve de Lord, when hab dis good time, dis liberty."

"Oh! if I could only show you how easy it is to come to Jesus, how he stands waiting for you to come!"

But alas, some who had been noble, and happy, sink to the level of their oppressors. O! womanhood, how robbed, despoiled, and worse, sometimes, degraded. But however it may sink under the influence of love, or deception, for a time, womanhood will assert itself, even when all that dignified it is gone. It will be a terrible thorn, where it cannot be a growth.

CHAPTER XLVII.

INGRATITUDE.

Since nothing is more odious to all than ingratitude, no effort has been spared by pro-slaveryists to brand the poor Negro with it. But the exact contrary is the fact. This all will aver who have dealt with them South. Their whole theme now is grateful recapitulation of their mercies. Indeed, if they err it is surely on the side of excess of showing gratitude. For one instance:

A poor woman said, "I so happy, now; work so peaceful; I have to drop courtesy as I go 'long in fiel', and raise hands so, and say, 'T'ank you, Lord! T'ank you, Jesus! for 'is good time of freedom.'"

Nothing could have made us so ashamed of our poor efforts for them, as to see their unbounded gratitude, expressed in prayers, for "dese dear, kind Massahs and Missusses, 'at came so far for teach we, lef' deir homes, and chil'n, and companions, and come to 'is poor heathen nation, to teach we, and care for we, and help we;" also their fervent prayers that we "may all be spared to reach home 'gin, and see dem all in peace and love, and we and dey suffer no damage for all 'ey do for we." In all their prayers, the first earthly blessing named is "dis liberty, 'is opportunity, 'ese kind teachers 'at suffer so much for we." And just in proportion as these teachers are filled with true discernment, wisdom, and piety to appreciate them, do they seem to perceive their true manliness, and worth, and piety. But their gratitude is active, and shown to the extent of their power.

For instance: A woman of 80 comes running to the carriage, as you leave a plantation and lifting her poor, bony hand, says, "Will Missus please 'cept dese fou' eggs, all I could get?"

We say, "My poor dear woman, you need them more than we."

"Oh, no, Missus, I neber eats um, neber. Please take um. Present, Missus, present!"

"Well, then, you must let me make you a present of this bit of silver."

"Oh, no, Missus! You so kind, come and care for we, when we so poor and so ignorant. Poor heathen nation. Don't know nothing. Nothing but Jesus. He all we got, nothing else. Chil'n all sold, gone. Ole man gone, neber see 'em no mo', neber! neber! in 'is worl'! But Jesus wid um dere. He see um all time. He eberywhere. He can save um. We trust him. O, we trusts HIS PROMISES, Missus! It's true what you say, we shall soon be home with God. But, poor ole Massah, O, Missus, WHAT DE LORD GWINE TO SAY TO HIM IN 'AT DAY 'bout what he done to we, all dese long years, all life, all whole life, Missus?"

Still the least kind act of either Massah or Missus is dwelt upon in a way that shows most touchingly how little they expected, and just as if it had not been for their own interest. None seem satisfied with words of gratitude, but must give something; and children unbidden run and pick beautiful bouquets, and present them most politely, and gratefully. Indeed, gratitude seems a specialty in their characters. As instances:

ANTHONY WILLIAM AMO,

The talented, the scholar, the filial, the grateful, was born in Guinea, was brought to Europe when very young; and the Princess of Brunswick took charge of his education. He pursued his studies at Halle, in Saxony, and at Wittemberg; and so distinguished himself by his talents and good conduct, that the Rector and Council of the University of the last mentioned town, gave a public testimony to them in a letter of congratulation.

Amo, skilled in the knowledge of the Latin and Greek languages, delivered with success, private lectures on philosophy, which are highly praised in the same letter. In an abstract, published by the Dean of the Philosophical Faculty, it is said of this learned Negro, that having examined the systems of the ancients and moderns, he selected and taught all that was best of them. Besides his knowledge of Latin and Greek, he spoke Hebrew, French, Dutch, and German, and was well versed in astronomy.

In 1774, Amo published dissertations on some subjects which obtained the approbation of the University of Wittemberg, and the degree of Doctor was conferred upon him. The title of one of these was "Dissertio inauguralis philosophica de humanæ mentis ΑΠΑΘΕΙΑ:" etc., etc.

Another was entitled "Disputatio philosophica," etc.

At the conclusion of these works are letters of approbation from the Rector of the University of Wittemberg, who, in speaking of one of them, says: "It underwent no change, because it was well executed; and indicates a mind exercised in reflection." In a letter addressed to him by the president, he styles Amo, "vir nobilissime et clarissime." Thus the University of Wittemberg has not evinced a belief in the absurd prejudice which exists against the Colored portion of mankind.

The COURT OF BERLIN conferred upon Amo the title of COUNSELLOR OF STATE, but after the death of his benefactress, the Princess of Brunswick, Amo *fell into a profound melancholy*, and resolved to leave Europe, in which he had resided for 30 years, and to return to the place of his birth at Axim, on the Gold Coast. There he received, in 1783, a visit from the intelligent traveller, David Henry Gallandat, who mentions him in the Memoirs of the Academy of Flessingue, of which he was a member. Amo, at that time about fifty years of age, *led the life of a recluse*. His father and a sister were living with him, and he had a brother who was a slave in Surinam. Some time after, it appears, he left Axim, and settled at Chama.

The Abbé Gregoire, from whose work the foregoing particulars are translated, says, that he made unavailing researches to ascertain whether Amo published any other works, or at what period he died.

Here we see this fine scholar, talented and caressed, become a recluse through excess of grief for his patron. Such instances, seldom adorn human records. Two other instances, must, where hundreds might be given:

GRATEFUL SLAVES.

"The more I have seen of the Negroes in Jamaica," writes Dr. Madden, "and observed their conduct, the more reason I have to think that they are naturally a good-humored, easily-contented, kind-hearted race, amply disposed to appreciate kind treatment and to be grateful for it. Of their disposition to appreciate benefits, even in the trifling way I have endeavored to be serviceable to them, by protecting them from injustice to the best of my poor ability, I have had proofs enough of their grateful feelings toward me. One poor fellow of the name of Cochrane came to me the other day to take leave of me: I had never rendered him the slightest service, but I had been civil to him, and he had been in the habit of coming to my house. He took leave of me with tears in his eyes: Dr. Chamberlaine was present: he took me aside and put a paper into my hand, which he said was a small present, which he hoped I would accept, to think of him when I was gone. I opened the paper, and to my surprise, I found it contained three Spanish doubloons (equal to £10 sterling). I cannot describe what I felt in assuring this poor Negro I did not need his gold to remember him and his race with kindly feelings. It was with difficulty I could prevail on him to take it back. He turned away abruptly from me, and that night I had a kid sent to me, which he sent me word he hoped might be of use to me on my voyage home.

"Two days ago, an old man, whom I had never seen before, entered the gate as I was going out, and addressed me in Arabic, he was a native of Africa, and he presented a pair of ducks, which he said he brought for me a long way, to make part of my sea stock. He SEEMED TO THINK I WAS A FRIEND TO HIS COUNTRYMEN, and he wished to prove to me THAT HE WAS GRATEFUL FOR IT. I accepted the old man's ducks, with more gratification than, perhaps, a European minister ever felt at receiving a diamond snuff-box from the Sultan. In short, for the last week, I have been receiving MORE PRESENTS of fruit and poultry than I know what to do with. In every instance in which I have been able to render any service to a Negro, I have found HIM MINDFUL OF IT, and FAR MORE GRATEFUL for it than I could have expected."

There is here, all the outgushing of woman's heart, in

gratitude, in all conversation. One was rapturously speaking of liberty, pure life, peace, the happiness of working in peace, with no fear of the lash, and of having comfortable food, and of "not being 'bliged for steal, no need for steal, etc." When the lady said: "Well, it is always against the law of God to steal. But, poor things, I suppose you know but little of the Bible." "O yes," said she, with all the true ambition of woman, "O yes, we does. Preacher teach us catechims. He teach us 'Thou shalt not steal,' 'Thou shalt not commit adulters,' 'Thou shalt not jump thy neighbor's fences, nor his gates.'"

But how will the heroes of this dire war, the work of slaveholders, be sung by Africa, through ages, with all her fervor, her vivid fancy and realization, her unutterable gratitude and love? That life is not lost, which so blesses a nation, which is yet to be, which is to introduce a higher, purer Christian love, and life, into the great mass. Africa is to administer, as a channel, the Christian graces to the world. The first fruits are appearing! the harvest will come! Will come, as sure as there is a God above us, when the little "one shall become a thousand," and the small one a strong nation.

But their unutterable gratitude, for those who fight, and die, in this holy war, which God hath assured their hearts, is for their liberation, their prayers, that every soul may be saved, are most touching, and are answered in the salvation of multitudes in their last moments assuredly; for these dear people speak to God, right from his bosom. And when the lone breaking heart, at home, feels resignation, love, bathing it, as sunlight the lily, in the lone dark dell, it is often in answer to them. Oh, how sad that such noble men sleep cold in death! upon the battle-field, while vile, traitorous self-servers live! But Jesus died. Herod, Pilate, wolfish high priests, lived.

CHAPTER XLVIII.

IS WOMAN WOMAN?

PERHAPS some may think, we now pen an unnecessary chapter. Perhaps there are none, or very few, who doubt, woman. But if there are a few such, should not their woes be assuaged? They are found in high life, so called, where leisure leaves the heart to chafe at feeding or emptiness. But, should such read this, should one, who exclaims in secret soul, "modesty is a lie," "love is a fable," "truth of soul is a dream," "political ambition, scheming and planning, low intrigue, slanderous gossip, concealed but active hatred, variance, wrath, strife, envyings, murders, of the dearer self, adulteries of the heart, at least, are the true realities."—if contact with the mere fashionable, of either sex, but especially woman, has given gigantic power to sore temptation to believe so; if that power has been intensified by disappointment, hollowness, rivalry; or anguish, by defeat in the war of social life, from those who used weapons in the contest, so mean and low, that you could not stoop to engage them, or even to ward them off; to all such we say take heart! Rejoice! Woman is woman yet. It is a fact. Rejoice! or if you are yet incredulous, come to South Carolina, rather than go to Springs, Mountains, Falls, or Sea sides. Here, you will see woman, uncultivated in some respects, it is true, but, she is woman. True she accords to the white man a power which, in some cases, is dishonored. True, from the intense capabilities of love of her heart, ever poor woman's first betrayer, she falls an easier victim, a more deeply duped victim. True, her love is such, in some cases, as in her fair sisters, as almost to deprive her of free agency, in treatment of the adored, simply because she cannot wound one, so dear, even though her soul pay the forfeit, which is the case with nine-tenths of the fallen—and O! were it realized, with how MUCH MORE TENDERNESS, and of course success, would they be treated,—still, admitting all this, woman is a thousand-fold more modest, pure, self-forgetful, loving, tender, true, devoted, in genuine love, than has ever, ever! been said or sung. We absolutely feel like one who has found a choice treasure. We shall ever, against all appearances and cavils, honor, and trust, and revere, woman, more, for observation and close investigation here.

The veil of artificialities is so thin, that all the soul shines out—self-sacrificing, loving, sacred, in short, with all her great nature, renewed by grace. In some cases they know that Massah, or Missus, is opposed to slavery, and is only a victim to it, with themselves, then, their devotion to them, is wonderful, and most resembles that of the tender parent for the suffering child. Could they be honorably hired by their former masters, there would be no bounds to their devotion, to their exertions, and successes, short of impossibilities. Oh, that the nation were wise! Oh, that it would fear God alone, stand with God alone, in relation to these, his peculiar people!

Yes, poor woman here, defeats her sorrow by patience, the life that now is, by realization of that which is to come, the wounds of oppression by the balm of divine Love. Oh woman! how lovely, where you see not the trappings, not the conventionalities, not the premeditated course of demeanor, but woman's naked, renewed heart. But their dwelling out of, above earth, while bearing its heaped up agonies, must be seen to be realized, and even then you feel that you see, but the surface. One such, at the close of preaching, walked so meekly up upon the porch, to be joined to him with whom she had long lived under a sham marriage. Her dress was of black, with white apron, kerchief, and turban. But what a countenance! She was there, yet not there. She saw the varied moods of those around her, yet saw nothing but the invisible. There was in her soul the depth of the Niagara but its stillness, volumes of feeling, but no expressed emotion—no dread of any bitterer cup, no shrinking from quaffing all—no censures, no regrets, no earthly anticipations, looking upon everything as if she looked through it, into God [we say it with utmost reverence]. But we will attempt no more such feeble description, which only shows that we attempt what we cannot explain; so sweet, gentle, pure, faithful! Ah the Christ in the mortal! She is forever clasped to our inner heart, in sincere admiration, and Christian love. Yet she, a field-hand, too, has been driven by those who could no more comprehend her, than an infant, Gabriel. Yes, the dust, agonizing heat, fatigue, dying spirit, and body, is only outward, though it rends our soul to realize them. Doubtless she has suffered scourging when task was not done. This is inevitable, for there is such a strife between masters, and overseers, who shall get most done in a given time with a given number of slaves, that the moment the poor toiler reaches one point, more is added; results are published, and all are dared to exceed if they can. In all these notices, slaves are spoken of as if they were inanimate. Oh ye jewels of my subjected to such barbarity. How he is just in case, mortal cannot see. But it shall appear more assembled worlds.

Her husband had the real tamed-lion appearance, of most burly men, who have excellent wives. One of our ladies attended the funeral of her child, and said, "I wept the whole time, to see that mother, so tender, but without a tear. It seemed as if the fount of tears was dry. Yes, she was past all weakness, past her grief, so chastened, so quiet." But lest any doubt that tasks are increased if performed, we give the following as proof:

Dr. Deming, a gentleman of high respectability, residing in Ashland, Richland county, Ohio, stated to Prof. Wright, at New York city:

"That during a recent tour at the South, while ascending the Ohio River on the steamboat Fame, he had an opportunity of conversing with a Mr. Dickinson, a resident of Pittsburg, in company with a number of cotton-planters and slave-dealers from Louisiana, Alabama, and Mississippi. Mr. Dickinson stated as a fact, that the sugar-planters upon the sugar coast in Louisiana had ascertained that, as it was usually necessary to employ about *twice* the amount of labor during the boiling season that was required during the season of raising, they could by *excessive driving*, day and night, during the boiling season, accomplish the whole labor *with one set of hands*. By pursuing this plan they *could afford to sacrifice one set of hands once in seven years!* He further stated, that this horrible system was now practised to a considerable extent. The correctness of this statement was substantially admitted by the slaveholders then on board." *

The late Mr. Samuel Blackwell, a highly respected citizen of Jersey City, opposite the city of New York, and a member of the Presbyterian Church, visited many of the sugar plantations in Louisiana, and says: "That

* Weld's "Slavery as it is," p. 39.

the planters *generally* declared to him that they were *obliged* so to overwork their slaves, during the sugar-making season (from eight to ten weeks), as to USE THEM UP *in seven or eight years*. For, said they, after the process is commenced, it must be pushed without cessation, night and day, and we cannot *afford* to keep a sufficient number of slaves to do the *extra* work at the time of sugar-making, as we could not *profitably* employ them the rest of the year."*

Rev. Dr. Reed, of London, who went through Kentucky, Virginia, and Maryland, in the summer of 1834, gives the following testimony.

"I was told, confidently, from *excellent authority*, that recently, at a meeting of planters in South Carolina, the question was seriously discussed whether the slave is more profitable to the owner, if well fed, well clothed, and worked lightly; or, if made the most of *at once*, and exhausted in some eight years. The DECISION WAS IN FAVOR OF THE LAST ALTERNATIVE. That decision will, perhaps, make many shudder. But to my mind, this is not the chief evil. The greater and principal evil is considering the slave *as property*. If he is only property, and *my* property, then I seem to have some right to ask how I may make that property *most available*."

Other testimony might be added. Southern newspapers have published the proceedings of Agricultural Societies, in which, after discussion, it had been agreed that the more profitable method was to "*use up*" a gang of Negroes once in seven or eight years, and then purchase a fresh supply of the dealers.

A terrible sacrifice of life arises from a change of

* Weld's "Slavery as it is," p. 39.

† "Visit to the American Churches," by Drs. Reed and Mattheson, Vol. II., p. 173.

climate. A writer in the New Orleans "Argus," of 1830, says: "The loss by death, in bringing slaves from a northern climate, which our planters are under the necessity of doing, is not less than *twenty-five per cent.*"

Does not this make every buyer, and seller, a murderer? Yea EVERY VOTER, WHO SUSTAINS SLAVERY?

But does any one find it difficult to realize the fact of a real life of every human soul above, and out of the body, or of an actual soul-life for which, or, its doings through the body, he is to be approved or condemned, in the great day of God, let him hold close converse with these dear people. Would we could describe it! But it speaks out in every look and word, of many of the devoted, most vividly. It then, becomes as evident, that Massah's— that this government's power is only over the body as that it is light, at mid-day. It is just as evident, we say, but it is indescribable. In speaking of what they have undergone, they do not dwell unnecessarily upon it. You wonder at the soul's triumph, as at that of a martyr. The deep impression remains to reprove every future moment of life, and to aid to lift you out of earth's sorrows, into the unseen.

But hear the moan prophetic of the present dire time of war, of Thomas Jefferson, himself a holder of slaves:

"When the measure of their *tears* is full; when their GROANS HAVE INVOLVED HEAVEN ITSELF IN DARKNESS, doubtless a God of JUSTICE will listen to their DISTRESS."

Ah! he doth listen, and will avenge them, in the day that shall burn as an oven. The "standing and beholding," "consenting," "partaking" the fruit, is the actual sin, and will appear so in God's inflexible eternal judgment. Slaveholders, those in this city, dear as friends, voters, all, with tears, in his dear name, and fear, and presence, we cite you to his bar as murderers, if you persist in fostering it.

CHAPTER XLIX.

ABSENTEES.

However hard the fate of the slave may in any case be, it is far harder for those, whose masters are habitually absent. Therefore those ladies, gentle, and apparently amiable, those placid and would-be dignified, men, North, who own slaves, are the true tyrants. For, however cruel the Master may be, he has some regard to life. The overseer often has none, or even enjoys the agonies, and death, of his hated victims, driving them often to desperate flights, resolved on liberty or death, as sung by Longfellow:

> "In the dark fens of the Dismal Swamp
>   The hunted negro lay;
> He saw the fire of the midnight camp,
> And heard at times the horse's tramp,
>   And a bloodhound's distant bay.
>
> "Where will-o'-the-wisps and glow-worms shine,
>   In bulrush and in brake;
> Where waving mosses shroud the pine,
> And the cedar grows, and the poisonous vine
>   Is spotted like the snake;
>
> "Where hardly a human foot could pass,
>   Or a human heart would dare,—
> On the quaking turf of the green morass
> He crouched in the rank and tangled grass,
>   Like a wild beast in his lair.
>
> "A poor old slave! infirm and lame,
>   Great scars deformed his face;
> On his forehead he bore the brand of shame,
> And the rags that hid his mangled frame
>   Were the livery of disgrace.

> "All things above were bright and fair,
>   All things were glad and free;
> Lithe squirrels darted here and there,
> And wild birds filled the echoing air
>   With songs of liberty!
>
> "On him alone was the doom of pain,
>   From the morning of his birth;
> On him alone the curse of Cain
> Fell like the flail on the garnered grain,
>   And struck him to the earth."

A noted D. D, resident of Baltimore, when told how his slaves had been worked, and suffered, threw himself into a chair, and wept convulsively. He could scarcely speak, or could not for a time, we cannot assert precisely, then he mourned, expostulated, plead, coaxed, was "willing to give up every slave if other members of his father's family would," entreated them to do so, but went North, again, leaving them, those poor members of Christ, for another year, in the same hands, as we are informed, by many witnesses, who all and separately, aver, that no slaves are treated more badly, for that is quite impossible! He, too, is a man before whom hundreds of his brethren cringe meanly, and bend the supple knee, and would not venture a prayer for the oppressed, in his presence, lest he be wounded, or offended! would far sooner quench the Holy Spirit, than his villainous hypocritical cant, and self-deception.

Beside it is impossible that these absentees, however kind, and determined, should actually know anything of the real case. For the poor Colored people know that he will soon be away, and that the lesser dignitaries will visit any complaints from them with tenfold vengeance.

One proof of this, has come to our knowledge. On a plantation where the bitterest tales were told us, the moment the Master, a Union man, came, the welkin was made to ring with his praises. Why? They were in his power, his irresponsible grasp, and had everything to fear.

Cotton, loved in freedom, is hated in slavery. Every appearance in speaking of it, shows that it was detested. How could it be otherwise? The more cotton the more anguish, the more deaths. Last year's experience, is all before the poor slave, its agonies, scourgings, deaths. The more it thrives, the more is to be picked. The only hope or help, is to dwarf it. And one who would not do it, were more or less than man. For however much there may be, not an extra hand will be provided. And how easy to dwarf it. For instance, now, in May, it is to be thinned, so as to leave two plants in a place. How easy to leave the poorest, and to slight and injure them, in cultivation. How else can the very great difference in plants, in the same soil, be accounted for? the wood of some, being variously large as a hen's egg, and small as a pipe-stem. Cotton, is the ever hated tyrant, of the South Carolina slave, his tormentor, his destroyer in the field and in the ginhouse. For in the latter place the toil ceases but about six hours, nightly, in hurrying seasons, on some plantations. The look of despair, with which women stood at the gin as at an instrument of torture, will never be effaced from our mind, and this, even when prospect of liberty, was bright. How astonishing that they should have been left to toil so hopelessly, so almost interminably, so excessively, wasted to a shadow. The only two, fleshy Negresses, we ever saw South, had each been made blind long years ago by the "foot cotton gin." Unwilling to leave masters! say some; such tales are totally unsustained by fact, as is everywhere proven. An illustration of this, is the case of the Virginian who was boasting that none of his slaves would leave him, and, to prove it, he called them into the presence of his guest, and said you are free and may go ! when lo ! every one expressed the greatest joy ! which soon changed his talk, to cursing them.

LOVED MASTERS.

The ex-slaves usually, speak kindly of their masters and mistresses. Often they dwell upon their various attractions. But by no slyness or innuendo, can they be led to say they want to see them. This is without one exception, so far as we can learn. True, pro-slavery persons assert that they have found some mourning for their masters, and wishing their return, or saying they were more comfortable with them. But, by all the skill we could use, we never found one. They express interest and tenderness, but push inquiry a little, and it will always be found, "it is for their good, for their souls."

In short, all the love they have, is a love that could not be conquered by hard usage, unrequited toil, for long, weary days, and years, by torture and worse, by contempt. It is Christian love, for no other could have endured this crucible, and that love is for the souls of masters, as much, and precisely, as for the soul of a heathen.

One, who was dwelling with apparent pride upon her master's family, was asked:

"You love them, don't you?"

"O, yes, Missus; but I hate deir ways. I prays for dem! O, I prays for dem!" lifting her poor, scarred arms, and hands, disfigured by severe labor. "I want deir souls sabed, but I neber want to see 'em, no mo', no mo'."

The idea of bondage seems so identified with their masters, that while they bear, in some cases, a personal affection for them, still all exclaim with horror, at the thought of their coming back.

Many say, "Massah would kill me;" "Massah would shoot me;" "Massah would hab me flogged to death!"

Should they know they were coming, under present circumstances, there would doubtless be hundreds of suicides among them. They never, never speak of injuring "Massah;" never, that we can learn, show any interest in understanding, or possessing, implements of death. Indeed, we have never heard the least allusion to them, or seen manifested a desire for them, although they speak very freely at times with, and before, us. But that they would "go to de bottom ob de riber," "would hang self," "would drown self," "might better drown self, than be whip' to deaff," "couldn't live to be slave again, couldn't!" are common and almost involuntary remarks.

Oh, as we see what our nation has done! what extremities these patient people have been driven to! we, and all here, wonder daily, more and more, that the land has not sunk, that judgments, fire, or flood, have not swept the oppressor from this land.

CHAPTER L.

THE BITTERNESS OF SLAVERY.

> Though with tardy step
> Celestial justice come, that step is sure :
> Unerring is her bolt, and where it falls
> Eternal will the ruin be.

SLAVEHOLDERS, of the Border States, will you candidly read and weigh this feeble plea, by a fellow-sinner, who ever gives most of you the credit of doing better under the system than most Northerners could?

Slaveholder, slavegrower, apologist for this system which Channing pronounced to be "every vice heightened by every meanness," we have no cause against you, no question, political or personal, to carry, no point to make against you. We have, and do look at slavery through the eyes of love to you, to your true, best interest, your present and future good. We were prepared to love slavery more if we could, or to see more palliation for it, if palliation existed. We are trying to befriend you, and yours, our country! as well as the slave. But as "right is right, since God is God," slavery *cannot* prosper, *cannot* produce prosperity. Many would do anything, suffer anything, for your benefit and salvation, of soul and body, whom you have long considered enemies. But only by putting away this sin can you prosper.

How many thousands have determined, as you now are tempted to do, to make slavery better. But what has resulted? Some few individuals, during one short lifetime, have been relieved, and that but little—since the soul so longs for liberty—but the great tide of misery has rolled on, and the best, are responsible, as they do most to keep it rolling. The best, among you, have testified against it. God has testified against it, even under less light than you now have, by REQUIRING his people to give it up, BEFORE THEY COULD DIE IN PEACE. The early annals of Methodism in the South, are full of such instances, and so are others, more or less. And does God change? Will you go into eternity, defying him? No, my dear brother, my sister, you will not.

All these stern, mighty influences, from infancy up, render it all but impossible for the slaveholder to look, rightly, at the question. Perhaps true divine grace only, can enable any one to do it.

Would you love to remember in heaven, that here you were a slaveholder? True, you might have been kind, but in upholding the system, you become responsible; for every crime of capture, middle passage, of slave-dealers, overseers, drivers, all! all! are upon you! for he that offendeth in one point is guilty of all. The law of God is exceeding broad, and neither you, nor I, can narrow it. Neither will the opinion of the whole world, change it; or its never, never ending penalty, or our award of eternal death, or life. And can our hearts endure, or our hands be strong, when God arises to judge the earth? We are not in heaven yet, whatever are our hopes. Where will you, and I, be in fifty years? How weak are words—how awful, eternity, coming on to meet us, inevitably, *interminable* in its bliss or UTTER WOE.

SLAVERY DOOMED.

WE plead not with the slaveholder from apprehension that this system will exist any great length of time. It is reeling to its death. But if it is wrested from you, it leaves you with all the guilt of transmitting it to all future ages, for that was your effort.

If you are prepared to care for slaves, are all so? Will you support a system that throws helpless women, girls, and infants, into the irresponsible hands of those awful slavedealers, and you know they are a part of the system, and must exist while it exists?

Now, you, for one, must do this, or refuse. You cannot escape. You live! you live, act, now! must die! must be judged! and taken to the bosom of God, or of devils. Oh burst away from surrounding influences! Act for yourself, as alone, with God, as YOU ACTUALLY DO. Oh! forget this inch of time, think of eternity, and eternal obligations to others. Are you too proud to change? in the face of friends, foes, the world? Behold, the day of the Lord cometh, that shall burn as an oven, and all the PROUD, yea, and all that do wickedly, shall be stubble, and the day that cometh, shall burn them up, it shall leave them neither root nor branch, saith the Lord of Hosts.

Never till now, have we imagined the awful bitterness of slavery. All the eloquence, of all the orators that ever existed, would not suffice to draw distinctly one of its features, as they actually exist. But while hatred for the system is intensified greatly by contact with it here, in every case we have known, without a single exception, yet sincere commiseration for the slaveholder is also heightened.

Pray think what an evil it must be, to be bound under that system, and trained to its support, by all the influences of early impressions and education; to believe in it during all the simplicity of unsuspecting childhood, the entire impressibility, and the strong biases of youth, to hear, from their earliest years, revered men of great talent defend and extol the system, as divine in its origin, Christianizing in its operation, and beneficent in its results, bringing to their aid all the self-justifying pleas of ages, from forum, press, and pulpit, led on by the arch-deceiver, in the guise of an angel of light—what wonder that multitudes on multitudes, in meekly following such influences, have not yet detected their mistake. A deceived heart hath turned them aside—a heart deceived as to principles, opinions, tastes, and interests, and delivered over to the rule of passions, and ere reason began her reign, pledged for slavery with all its fiery nature; in all loves, hatreds, fancies, and appetites, all intensified by the dogmas of a power-giving, because perverted, religion. Was ever Prometheus more bound to his rock? They are blinded by every influence that talented, learned and desperate energies, and determinations, by all possible sophistry through ages, could bring to bear;*for prejudices and judgments are handed down in slavedom, as they cannot be in a state of society, where free speech, and free light, help to correct all biases. Cases meet you on every hand where mere boys were unrestrained! yea, led to cause

---

* "Contrasting the condition of *white slaves* in New-England with our slaves in the South, is like comparing Egyptian bondage with millennial glory."—Rev. J. C. POSTELL, of South Carolina.

"Under this relation of master and slave, the two races have long lived in peace and prosperity."—Hon. J. C. CALHOUN, of South Carolina, U. S. Senate. 1836.

"Slavery is with us a parental relation."—Charleston Courier, S. C.

ILLUSTRATION OF THIS SWEET "PARENTAL RELATION."

"In case any person shall wilfully cut out the tongue, put out the eye, cruelly scald, burn, or deprive any slave of any limb, or member, or shall inflict any other cruel punishment, *otherwise than by whipping, or beating, with a horsewhip, cowskin, switch, or small stick, or by putting on irons, or confining, or imprisoning such slave,* every such person, for every such offence shall forfeit one hundred pounds, current money."—Law of South Carolina."

all manner of tortures, to train them, and to break the spirit of slave children, it is supposed. Oh! one must be HERE, to see the prints of the chains which have bound, from the very birth, these poor fellow-sinners.

What could have induced you, reader, had choice been possible, to have been born and reared under such influences?—no restraint, in many cases, upon a single passion or action—what? The wealth of the whole world? Certainly not; for were it possible for once to avoid sin and debasement in such circumstances, yet such a man must be miserable by an immutable law of our being.

Said an officer, "I opposed slavery, when I came here, on account of the blacks. Now I oppose it almost entirely on account of its awful effects upon the Whites."

"Yes," said we, "how awful, every way, and for them to use every measure, and constant, intense effort, and influence to put poor Whites below Negroes, and teach their slaves to show that they despise them by every means. How awfully mean that is."

"Well, all that is very true; yet those are not the grounds upon which I now most oppose it. It is because it so imbrutes the masters. They, as a mass, are SATISFIED with merely domineering, and glorying over the Negroes, and care not for improvement. Few, comparatively, in their whole army can write. In a case of a large number of soldiers, all, or nearly every one, had to make their mark. Then there is not a respect in which the system does not paralyze ambition, and debase them. Yes, I oppose the system now, solely from what I see of its effects upon Whites."

Not always that the "White trash" is poor, but that he has no one to domineer over, puts him down. So IT EVER IS, MUST, AND WILL BE, UNDER SLAVERY.

How awful, to see a man, master of a house, head of a

family, raving around, a madman. Yet this is the spectacle often presented. No wonder that in the East Indies, not a slaveholder can be found who wishes the return of the system, much as they clung to it. We do apologize for the slaveholder very much, all who can appreciate his real case, do. But is that a reason why he should still be placed in power? Because I lost my right hand, in not the most guilty manner, is that a reason why I should be put to labor, absolutely requiring it? The present race of slaveholders can never, never, be put to legislate in a republic, while slavery remains. Never! It has been thought that their courses and manners in Congress, were owing to peculiar circumstances. Well, there would always be circumstances leading to the same exhibitions, while they are what they are. They have never learned subordination to rightful authority. No human being can teach it to them. With deep sorrow we say these things. It is the slave system, not them, we blame. But they are what they are, insubordinate, headstrong, traitorous. Then their children's, their country's good, requires that they be restrained. Yet it is for a few thousands of such blustering tyrants, that this immense loss of noble lives in our army, is sustained; that the rights of four million Colored people must be sacrificed. For these eighteen thousand traitors, must everything pure in government be stained? What guilt, must rest upon those who could, and do not, do away with it. What judgments upon their posterity to "the third and fourth generations."

But, to go through life, subject to such a tyranny as slavery imposes. For a master, as to kindness, honor, truth, and all nobleness, must do just, and only! as slavery will let him!! to wear away youth, middle life, age, amid such passions, prejudices; variances with the great majority of the good, disgusting fellowship of the bad; the pangs of disdain, suspicion, criticism, guilt; the fear to break the chains which bind to slavery, even when it is most ardently desired; the stealthy, inevitable approach of the general judgment; the knowledge that " by thy works thou shalt be justified, and by thy works thou shalt be condemned;" the awful certainty that your doom will then be irreversibly fixed for all, all! eternity! —to bear all this, year after year, through a life, thus slowly and painfully, yet surely and forever, slipping away, leaving eternal retribution—oh, it is awful! awful! awful!

CHAPTER LI.

UNSANCTIFIED INDIGNATION.

The smallest pebble in the well of truth
Has its peculiar meaning, and will stand
When man's best monuments have passed away.
                                    WILLIS.

How weak is unsanctified indignation! True, the many, despise thieving, adultery, abusing helplessness, murder, evident soul destruction. But when all these are combined in their worst aspects in a system, called slavery, they stand aghast, at condemning it out and out. But the great fortress of slavery is anger. Into this, it ever runs, for not an advocate of slavery but will get angry at free speech against it. It seems to be the one magnet around which clusters all the imbecility, personal and political, of the nation. It is inadvertently treated as a sort of frenzy, as it is. The damage it has been to the morals, conscience, religion of the nation, CAN NEVER BE ESTIMATED. Would that the pages that must record it could be forever blotted out. But no, the dire facts must exist, forever! They may be forgiven. They can never, never be undone.

Why shall another day be stained with this guilt?

Darkness visible enshrouds all government action upon the awful sin of slavery. Every step toward, the less liberty of the poor bondmen, is acquiesced in, in silence. Every step, toward greater freedom, must be retraced. Tyranny is everywhere rampant, outspoken, overbearing; Liberty is cringing into silent corners, ashamed of the holiest and best principles, yea, of the law of love.

How silent, too, is the pulpit, respecting the duty of the people, to see that we have a righteous government! Some of the most decided in private conversation, use no influence in the pulpit against it whatever. One could not detect what were their sentiments. O, my Master, how art thou betrayed in the person of thy little ones! by false, or fearful prophets.

And where abettors of slavery might hate them, for clear speaking of truth, they only despise them for cowardice. If a principle is not right, pray give it up; if it is, with pure heart, and as acceptable manner as possible, express it.

We may have eminent precedents for all this; but so have we precedents for everything that is wrong somewhere. The public hungers for free speech, and no sooner does a minister begin to use it, than the multitude fly to him. Then he is called a sensation preacher, solely because the multitude, weary of platitudes, flock round him. Where is the cause of this war, of the deaths of all these noble men? There was principle, there was conscience, there was truth, there was light, but lest some one should curl the lip in scorn, they had to be hidden. Lest some influential member should be displeased and turned into an enemy, the minister, with most noble exceptions, had to be silent. Yet his whole audience, knowing his principles, and that he ought not to be ashamed of them, must despise him in heart, however they may flatter with their lips.

BLASTED MANHOOD.

But the direst evil slavery has brought upon the North net the thousands of millions it has, and will cost, not the suffering, not even the glorious deaths of noblest, bravest, dearest, officers and men. No. It is IN THE LOSS OF MANHOOD—of free, noble, honest out-speaking. This is the dire, dire loss. Mention slavery, for instance, at a promiscuous table. All is whist at once. Take those persons alone, and they will speak worthily of statesmen, of Christians; but it was not prudent, best, good policy to speak those noble sentiments there, at table; some one would have been displeased. Some Pecksniff would have stroked down his villainous beard and necktie, and said, "Hem!" and his adherents, male and female, would have looked scared, and Murdstone would have said, "Be calm, be calm; let those people be flayed alive, but be calm; do not get excited."

And this unmanly fear of speaking out, applies to all questions and subjects, so that conversations become nothing at all; disgusting cringings, giving birth to Child-wives, and Amazons. But it seems, from its present momentum, that the pendulum of national cringing has got to swing its full length in that direction, then, it will probably swing back.

Now, a person should not be uncourteous. But he should have a pure heart, and just principles, and then fear not to show them clearly, with all possible charity for those who differ. Whether our national manners will ever be in dignity, and manliness, and truth, what they would, had not the vile whiffet slavery, been ever ready to bark and fly in one's face, is yet to be seen. Would it not be a pity if this nation should at last subside into, or even die, of sneakishness?

There is no possible way of correcting these evils but to get rid of their parent—slavery. None! and that which actually benefits nothing, but blasts everything good, once and forever put away, there is no limit to the nation's rising in all that is wise, noble, and holy.

We defy the whole world, to point out one respect in which true patriotism does not cry out for the rending away of slavery, ere, in its anaconda folds, it crush us into one mass of putridity.

FEATURES OF THE TIMES.

WHEN HE MAKETH REQUISITION FOR BLOOD, HE FORGETTETH NOT THE CRY OF THE HUMBLE.

BUT of all the odious features of the times, the most odious, is, the self-admiring serenity with which many pharisees look upon the events of the day. What patterns of patience they are! since self is not imperilled. How self-complacently, can they say, "Providence"—almost blasphemed by their speaking of him—"is at work; in the course of years, or of a few generations, this system will be abolished, or, gradual emancipation inaugurated, or at least be in process, toward inauguration." Now these men, if actually realizing what slavery is, are as much meaner than the ignorant slaveholder, as can be imagined. If there is a class, in the world that ought to be driven fifteen hours, daily, or two, added to that, as is often the case, without food, because they were too exhausted, after the flogging of last evening, to grind, and cook it, and then, be permitted to sleep in thumb-screws, it is them. How long would they think the Christian world had better be, in liberating them? and how great had the comfort, and despicable quiet, of a pharisaic world better be in contemplating their torture?

But there is a long, never ending! Eternity! for adjustment, though it may be feared that if their meanness is actually known, in perdition, there will be a rebellion against it, even there, and Satan himself will protest against such mean company. He, of course, does all he can to get more into his anguish, but he does not say, "I will sit, and sing, in heaven, while you go down there." Neither does the true Christian. He goes weeping from house to house with holy Paul, dies with ancient, and. modern true apostles, and missionaries, does duties that otherwise had been impossible, as do thousands of ladies, for the sake of saving souls, or he dies with his Lord, in and by, perfect obedience.

Or, like John Brown, he does SOMETHING, for the enslaved. It may be wise or unwise, but it is the best his knowledge and "his circur nce allows."

And when gradual emancipation is spoken of, he feels as if it were his own children, or parent, or wife, in bonds, and in suspense. He would then say, "if you bring not up Joseph, you will bring down my grey hairs, with sorrow to the grave." Oh, is there beneath the sun anything so odious, as a false counterfeit religion, that the more one has of it, the more is he shut up in self-complacency, self-worship, and indifference to the sorrows, wants, and just claims of others!

But, can anything which comes down upon the soul of the philanthropic, the humanitarian, the Christian, part of our nation, as does THE REALIZATION, OF WHAT SLAVERY is, not be an evil, a mental incubus? Shall the Christian heart be pained, paralyzed, the Christian mind dwarfed, by it? We appeal to the Government for release, for rescue.

A Philadelphian said the subject of slavery has haunted my every waking moment for years. It is always in my mind. Who can measure this mental loss? Who imagine what strides this nation had made in mental greatness, had it not been for this one blight? which just in proportion as one has true, clear, mental and moral perception, is felt. We know there are hundreds, who can see nothing but expediency, with self in the foreground. They never lost a dinner over this, or any other humanitarian topic, as is evident at a glance, while another is absolutely wasted, almost to a skeleton, over it.

But the subject of oppression is now an encircling magnet. No line of living thought, but leads to it, in some direction. But many from surroundings relinquish the noble, manly, privilege, of freedom of speech, not touching or naming it. So back they spring into, and cramp themselves up in their shell of prudence, of nonentity, as to actual mental power, and true permanent influence, to say nothing of true excellence.

Mention a writer or speaker of any note, who never boldly cuts this circle. No one can do it. But thousands are minifying themselves for all time, yea, for all eternity, by a lack of bold manliness, in writing or speaking. Do not understand us to say, that by low cunning a writer or editor may not have a certain transient influence. But to live now, and show a large, deep, strong mind, and large, pure, loving heart, and leave, or slight, or defer, or contemn, this subject, is impossible, utterly so; and oblivion only awaits such efforts and writers.

But the whole subject of slavery is a constant irritant upon the Northern mind, a sort of blight, or worm at the root—an undermining, weakening influence. The soul wearily cries out, "I do wonder if I shall live to see this world rid of slavery?" A world or a nation without slavery! What a joy! a glory! a rest! a triumph! Yes, the good are worried, wearied, weakened, over this constant pressure, of so great, so mean, so shocking, an evil. The saying, "he is half crazed upon the subject of abolition," is not without foundation. True, it is not a fact; but that is owing, not to the horrible meanness of the irritant, or to any indifference in regard to it, but to "grace sufficient." Yet, the best minds of the nation are enchained, bound, retarded, by it. Yes, they are sickened, nauseated, enfeebled. True, all the powers of the man are aroused, at times, and his eloquence and depth are wonderful. But he settles back into that dire nauseated state, most antagonistic to great, free, deep, thought, so that, upon the whole, it effects a mental obstruction, if not partial paralysis.

Now, do not understand us to assert that all are so affected. No, there are men, editors, professed Christians, who have long been most serene over four millions suffering under our own flag, every loss, every indignity, oppression, brutality, that mean White men can inflict. And that serenity would be the same were there fifty millions. Yes, upon the whole, they say, "the sufferings of this class, are not lost, since they make us more grateful for our liberties." "Their toil," they continue, "is not quite lost, since it makes us realize our ease; the fact that they are not allowed to lie down when sick, makes our own couch, our pillow, softer, or, what is the same, in effect, gives us a realizing sense of it." "How good it is," say they, "to have a sense of our mercies, and how could we have it, if all had them." And these, who mistake themselves for men because they wear men's clothing, and Christians, because they belong to churches, stroke their sleek heads, smooth down their low foreheads, parrot's noses, thin lips, and smooth beards, and pretty white cravats, straighten down their vests over their one comprehensive department, brush a little dust off the nether garments, kick! at a—pebble, and say, "Yes, slavery is an evil, but it is not without its benefits." We will not describe the secular editor, or him who can afford but one head, and that secular; the Daily, but who rolls slavery under his tongue, as complacently as his quid, never failing to give his darling a good word, and a lift, or, what helps it more, a sneer. We say we will not describe him, for the words which should do it, have need to

"Come glowing from the lips of eldest hell."

Still, we will give him credit for not being a hypocrite, yes more, for not being ashamed of the lineaments and works, of his Father, or to be known, as on the best of terms with him, as a most dutiful satanic son.

Now, these men are far more slaveholders than those poor women and conscientious men South, who would sacrifice everything, had they the light, and energy, to be free from it; and who, if they knew the North, would be here in a trice. Yes, he is far more a slave-driver than those who seek death to get away from it, for his, is the mean despotism of the soul, not the dire rule and misfortune of birth, and legal oppression. Such, we say, are not injured, AS THEY CAN SEE, by slavery. And with what patronizing complacency do they say, "Pity he should be so excited;" "good man, but excitable," while it only increases my serenity, makes me more grateful and sensible of our mercies.

He could walk by the whole agonized, imploring four millions on his way to the holy sacrament, and it would not move one nerve, and only make the fount of tears dryer.

He can sit within hearing of this evil, and talk, and talk, of his enjoyments, his assurances that his soul is safe. He, were we about to say, not injured by slavery? He is dwarfed by it! For in some of his best moments there comes light, which, being rejected, he goes into actual darkness, though so gross, that he knows it not.

The North, as a whole, has so long yielded up for peace, principle, patriotism—or true patriotism, religion—or true, loving-neighbor-as-self religion, everything, that like a father that has demented himself in indulging, and then trying to manage, a petted child, it seems utterly impossible for it to rise to the manly defence of liberty. That damage to the whole man from cringing, is from a natural, inevitable law. No man can say, "I will be base to-day, and noble to-morrow." He cannot say, "I will cringe to-day, and stand erect to-morrow." If he take base mean policy, rather than suffer for the right, he must bear the eternal impress of it. So long has the nation bowed, for the sake of peace, to overbearing, blustering, sin, that its moral power to stand for the right seems gone. Too conscientious to take life, unless in actual battle, it sacrifices its own bravest sons. It cannot give up, even yet, that it cannot win over, by coaxing, the slaveholders. Oh, my Lord, who lovest the poor slave, where will all this end? How do the rebels despise us—guarding their property, returning to certain torture their panting slaves, showing ourselves weak and sneaking, they regard us as the mean spaniel, that loves you just in proportion as you abuse him. The North has got to make the South respect her. Oh, divine Master, how easily could she do that, if she would only stand by her principles, by her religion, the Bible.

Yea, she has got to maintain her own self-respect, which she is rapidly losing, while the South, by mere unity, and plotting is strengthening, in wickedness, is gaining.

The Congress of 1862 has done nobly at last, six months or a year too late. Now, it seems, its excellent acts are to be null, for want of Executive action. Slavery is a taint that it seems nothing will extricate. Let a man but be born on slave soil, and his preference seems forever fixed, unless in a few most noble and magnanimous souls.

But, hush, complaining heart, there will noble men arise, perhaps, in the border States. Here is fame to be achieved greater than

"Immortality in twenty worlds."

Who will be the Luther? the Washington? the Wellington of America? Some one that shall yet arise, and, from genuine inward worth, or some principle dearer than life, risk all, shall save all.

An EMANCIPATION SOCIETY ARISES in Maryland! the first formed in the South, at Cambridge, a place which gained, a few years ago, some notoriety as the meeting-place of a convention of SLAVEHOLDERS, WHO ATTEMPTED, but unsuccessfully, TO INITIATE THE PASSAGE OF LAWS FOR THE REËNSLAVING OF THE FREE NEGROES of the State! The county contained, in 1850, 14,595 whites and 4,282 slaves, and ranks among the counties of the State in which the slave population is large. Here an Emancipation Society has been lately formed, whose members have adopted the following platform:

"Believing the institution of slavery to be detrimental to the moral and material interests of Maryland, and a serious impediment to the growth and development of her resources, and that the emancipation of the slaves in the State, and their colonization to Hayti, Liberia, or some other tropical country, would prove fruitful of blessings to ourselves and our posterity, we therefore form and constitute ourselves into a society organized to further, by all proper and lawful means, the objects herein expressed, the owners of course to receive a fair compensation for their slaves."

The non-slaveholders of the State outnumber the slaveholders by an enormous majority. They are an intelligent and prosperous body of men, who carry on their operations by using the labor of free negroes. It is in the power of this class of the citizens of Maryland to effect emancipation themselves; but they would find coöperation in this work from intelligent slaveholders themselves.

The address to the "working men" assumes boldly that but for slavery there would have been no rebellion, and that in order to the pacification of the country, the slave system must come to an end. A sharp rebuke is given to the practice adopted of addressing all the arguments for emancipation to the slaveholders, the importance of the working men of the State being all the time quietly ignored. "Look," says the address, " at the course of the emancipation papers in this State. They all, with one or two exceptions, seem to labor under the impression that the non-slaveholders have no interest in the matter whatever. Their arguments and appeals are addressed solely to the sixteen thousand slaveholders, and they take especial pains to have it understood that they advocate emancipation exclusively for their benefit, whom they evidently think, or by their actions indicate, have a patent right to decide all questions of State polity, while the non-slaveholders, who are mostly working men, must quietly acquiesce in their decision. Surely it ought to be galling to our pride, and calculated to fire our hearts with burning indignation, to be thus treated with so little political consideration; but, nevertheless, we will have to 'grin and bear it' as long as we uphold the institution of slavery."

We have never seen the inequality of the operation of the slave laws better stated than in that address, in the following illustration :

"Suppose Jones and Smith were neighbors, Jones owns a very vicious ox, which meets Smith on the country road and gores him. One of Smith's slaves runs up with an axe and kills the ox. Jones' son happens along, and pitches into the negro for killing his father's ox, when the negro turns around and kills him, too. The negro is tried and convicted, and sentenced to be hung. Smith loses nothing, for the State pays him for his slave. But Jones, on the contrary, not only has to mourn the loss of a son, but his *property is actually taxed to help to pay Smith for the slave that murdered him;* and not only loses his ox, but is liable for damages for allowing him to run at large. And further, Jones was taxed the full value of his ox. Smith, on the contrary, although he valued his slave at $1,000, and received that sum for him from the County Commissioners, yet his assessable value was not over *four hundred dollars*, this being the highest sum fixed by law. What an admirable specimen of pro-slavery justice?"

Nor could the effect of slavery upon the value of lands be better put, than in this paragraph :

"According to the census of 1850, in the seven counties of Pennsylvania bordering on Maryland, there were 1,788,558 acres of improved land, valued at $100,-714,032, or $56 31 per acre; while in seven counties in Maryland bordering on Pennsylvania, there were 1,053,-142 acres of improved land, valued at $46,517,282 15, or only $44 17 per acre—a difference of $12 14 per acre, or a difference in the entire value of $12,785,143 88. In other words, it costs the farmers of those counties alone nearly THIRTEEN MILLIONS OF DOLLARS to uphold slavery in Maryland; for slavery is the sole cause of the great disproportion in prices in the two sections."

This is further MADE EVIDENT BY OTHER ILLUSTRATIONS. Doubtless this Society will be the precursor of many more. This is one excellent fruit of this dire war, this freedom of speech in Maryland. If the non-slaveholders will but assert the nobility of their former course and their cause fearlessly, and rise in their might, and in the dignity of freemen, patriots, and Christians, the work will be soon done, and those States will soon become rich. Then, they will no more than New York city, wish to colonize their Colored. See the result in every place that has emancipated, in Barbadoes, for instance, lands have nearly, or quite doubled their value.

Jay upon Colonization says:

"It certainly does not follow that a system must be bad, because bad men support it; but it does follow, that when mobs and infidels espouse a particular object, it is because that object is recommended to them by other than religious considerations. Yet colonizationists are fond of representing their Society as a *religious* institution; and the ministers of the Gospel are earnestly urged to preach annual sermons in its behalf.

That multitudes of religious men belong to the Society is not denied, but the participation of such men in an object, does not necessarily render it a religious object: otherwise the slave trade was a Christian commerce, because John Newton was a slave-trader; and free-masonry must be a holy fraternity, since it can boast the names of more good men than were ever enrolled in the ranks of colonization. But in what sense can the Society be termed a religious one? It is not professedly founded on any one principle of the Gospel of Christ. It exercises no one act of benevolence toward the free blacks in this country; and in transporting them to Africa, it is, by its own confession, removing nuisances. It takes no measures to Christianize Africa, but landing on its shores an ignorant and vicious population. It employs no missionary, it sends no Bible, and it cannot point to a single native, converted to the faith of Jesus through its instrumentality. On the contrary, may we not, in reference to the facts disclosed in this AFRICAN Colonization, affirm, without the imputation of bigotry or prejudice, that the general influence of the Society is decidedly anti-Christian? We have seen that it practically tends to the debasement and persecution of the free blacks; to the hardening of the consciences of the slaveholders, and to the indefinite continuance of slavery.

The objects of the Society, as stated in the declarations of its orators, are of such vast importance, and such god-like benevolence, that it is no wonder good men have been so dazzled by the gorgeous visions presented to their imaginations, as to have omitted to scrutinize the machinery by which these visions are to be realized.

But their visionary ideas respecting colonization cannot be better answered than in the words of Wilberforce:

"Our objections to it are briefly these; while we believe its pretext to be delusive, we are convinced that its *real* effects are of the most dangerous nature. It takes its root from a cruel prejudice and alienation in the Whites of America, against the Colored people, slave or free. This being its source, the effects are what might be expected—that it fosters and increases the spirit of caste, already so unhappily predominant—that it widens the breach between the two races—exposes the Colored people to great practical persecution, in order to *force* them to emigrate: and finally is calculated to swallow up and divert that feeling which America, as a Christian and a free country, cannot but entertain, that slavery is alike incompatible with the law of God, and the well-being of man, whether of the enslaver or the enslaved. We must be understood *utterly to repudiate the principles of the American Colonization Society.*"

Hear the present sentiments of the distinguished Z. Macauley, Esq., M.P.: "The unchristian prejudice of color, which alone has given birth to the Colonization Society, though varnished over with other more plausible pretences, and veiled under a profession of Christian regard for the temporal and spiritual interests of the Negro, which is belied by the whole course of its reasonings, and the spirit of its measures, is so detestable in itself, that I think it ought not to be tolerated; but on the contrary, ought to be denounced and opposed by all humane, and especially all pious persons in this country."—*Letter, 14th July, 1833, to Mr. Garrison.*

For a quarter of a century, William Allen, a London Quaker, has been prominent in every good work, and his name is familiar to all acquainted with the great catholic institutions of England. This eminent and zealous philanthropist thus writes: "Having heard thy exposition of the origin and main objects of the American Colonization Society, at the meeting on the 13th inst., at Exeter Hall, and *having read their own printed documents,* I scarcely know how adequately to express my surprise and indignation, that my correspondents in North America should not have informed me of the real principles of the said Society; and also that Elliott Cresson, knowing as he must have known the abominable sentiments it has printed and published, should have condescended to become its agent."—*Letter, 15th of 7th month,* 1833.

Mr. Buxton, the successor of Mr. Wilberforce as the parliamentary leader in the cause of abolition, thus expresses himself: "My views of the Colonization Society you are aware of. They do not fall far short of those expressed by my friend Mr. Cropper, when he termed its objects *diabolical.*"—*Letter of July* 12*th*, 1833.

Almost daily do we hear of colonizationists awaking, as from a dream, and expressing their astonishment and regret at the delusion into which they had fallen.

To the Christians we would now address ourselves, and ask, Have we not *proved* enough to induce you to pause, to examine, and to pray, before you longer lend your names, and contribute your funds to the purposes of colonization? Do no secret misgivings of conscience now trouble you? and are you perfectly sure that in supporting the Society, you are influenced by the precepts of the Gospel, and not by prejudice against an unhappy portion of the human family? If, on a full investigation of the subject, you discover that colonization is not what you believed and hoped it was, remember that it is your duty to obviate, as far as possible, by a frank and open declaration of your opinion, the evil your example has done. Be not ashamed, be not slow to follow Wilberforce in entering your protest against the Society. If that Society leads to the degradation and oppression of the poor Colored man—if it resists every effort to free the slave—if it misleads the conscience of the slaveholder, you are bound, your God requires you to oppose it, not in secret, but before the world. Soon will you stand at the judgment seat of Christ: there will you meet the free Negro, the slave, and the master,—take care lest they all appear as witnesses against you.*

But Hayti now opens her rich bosom with the noblest of governments, and invites the Colored. Many of the ambitious will seek her shores, will rise to eminence there. But to urge them away, is most unmanly, unchristian.

* Jay's Works.

A LATE REPORT TO PARLIAMENT FROM THE GOVERNOR OF JAMAICA SAYS:

"I look upon it as a settled point, that the great mass of the emancipated population and their descendants are betaking themselves to the cultivation of the soil on their own account, either as a source of profit, or as the mere means of subsistence." "There can be no doubt, in fact, that an independent, respectable, and, I believe, trustworthy, middle class is rapidly forming; and I assert my conviction, that if the real object of emancipation was to place the freeman in such a position that he might work out his own advancement in the social scale, and prove his capacity for the full and rational enjoyment of personal independence, secured by constitutional liberty, Jamaica will afford more instances of such gratifying results than any other land in which African slavery once existed."

"It would be difficult to conceive," says THE LONDON REVIEW, "a wider contrast between the condition of things as the planters imagined they would be—the idleness and debauchery, the ruin and desolation, they were sure would follow the emancipation of the slaves—and those features of RURAL INDUSTRY AND DOMESTIC COMFORT, IMPROVING AGRICULTURE AND GROWING OPULENCE, AWAKENED INTELLIGENCE AND MORAL PROGRESS, which are exhibited in the emancipated colonies. SLAVERY was the DESTROYER; EMANCIPATION is the RESTORER. The one tended invariably, through its whole history, to impoverishment and ruin; the other has awakened industry and confidence, and laid, broad and deep, the foundation of lasting prosperity and wealth."

But it is alleged that the emancipated Negroes are idle and unwilling to work. How, then, comes it, that among the people who are libelled as "squatters" on the land of others, there are 60,000! families all housed in their OWN COTTAGES; that they possess not less than 5,000 small sugar mills for manufacturing their own produce; that the accumulated property of the Negroes of Jamaica, since emancipation, amounts to £2,358,000! and three-fifths of all the cultivated land in that island is the *bonâ fide* property of the Colored people—bought and paid for by their own industry? Is it a mark of indolence and improvidence that the Negroes of Jamaica have nearly £50,000 in the savings bank, and of their apathy that they support their own religious institutions at an expenditure of many thousand pounds, besides contributing to the aid of foreign missions?

EMANCIPATION IN THE WEST INDIES.

In 1833 the act received the royal assent, which decreed that slavery should terminate throughout the British empire, but provided for its gradual cessation. From the first of August, 1834, there was to be an apprenticeship of six years for the prædial and four years for the non-prædial slaves, all under six years of age being declared entirely free on that day. And the change which transformed hundreds of thousands of slaves into apprenticed laborers was not only effected without bloodshed or disorder, but in all the colonies the behavior of the people was most exemplary. Two years after, there were such revelations of the violations of the new act, and the CRUELTIES PRACTISED BY THE PLANTERS, that the British public demanded, with one voice, that the apprenticeship system should be done away with. Parliament passed a bill for remedying the defects of existing laws, and providing increased protection for Negroes. But, happily, the LEGISLATURES OF THE SEVERAL ISLANDS resolved on immediate emancipation; and even Jamaica, which long held out, was obliged to follow the example of the other colonies. On the first of August, 1836, the Negroes of the West Indies became a free people. The great change was effected without the slightest difficulty or disturbance. Even in Jamaica, where the slaves had been most cruelly treated, the Governor refused to call out a single soldier, or employ even a policeman. " The influence of the RELIGIOUS TEACHERS, the MORAL RESTRAINTS, and the loyalty to the sovereign," he records, " sufficed to preserve perfect order in the midst of this great social revolution, *and 800,000 slaves became freemen without a single breach of the peace, or the slightest sign of disturbance.*"

The whole tone of reliable reports from the whole South has been the same. Nothing seems to exasperate the hater of the poor Negro more than their acknowledged amiability, energy, and ability in whatever place they are put, and their INVINCIBLE PATIENCE under every provocation. We give the following as a specimen:

A well-known citizen of New York, writes as follows, under date of Hilton Head, May 29th, of the Colored:

" Since I have come South, my views in reference to the Negroes have been very much modified. I am convinced that they are not afflicted with the disease of laziness more than their white brethren—only give them an object for which to labor. I am now visiting on a plantation where the few Negroes that are on it have had neither overseer nor master for the last three months; and they have planted as much corn, and potatoes, and rice as the same number of white men would have done with the same means; for, till lately, they had neither horse, mule, nor plough. All the first cultivation was done by hand, and with the hoe. They have now been furnished with a horse and a mule, I believe by the Government. They are working most faithfully day by day. No Northern farmers are at work earlier in the morning or later in the evening. I am an early riser, and when I first look out, I generally see the Colored men, women, and boys going out to the fields, or already there; and they do not come in till sundown, or even after. In view of their former habits and customs, this is not what I expected, short of twenty or thirty years— to see them labor with all the earnestness and steadiness of old Pennsylvania farmers. I am convinced there will be no difficulty in managing the Negroes in a state of freedom, only if the management be kind and judicious. This is the grand secret to make them useful to others and to themselves. The Negroes on this plantation have been peculiarly favored in the character of the soldiers encamped in the vicinity, who are mostly the sons of farmers in Central Pennsylvania. They have simply treated them kindly, reciprocating services and pleasant words, talking with them about the soil, its productions, cultivation, etc., and suggesting such Northern improvements as they could understand. The result is, that here is a company of Negroes as truthful, orderly, industrious, and kind as can be found of the same number of Whites anywhere. I wish I could say that all the Government agents were fit, by temper and principle, to discharge their duties properly, or even fairly, toward these people, but many are not."

CHAPTER LII.

HUNTER'S PROCLAMATION.

RIDING out to an appointment upon Sabbath morning in Beaufort, our carriage is stopped by a noted civilian, a millionaire, with " tell Mrs. French that General Hunter has declared emancipation in South Carolina, Georgia, and Florida." We clap hands, and praise the Lord, over and over. We say to our Colored coachman, " How do you feel?"

" Most beautiful, Missus; onspeakable!"

" But you don't say Hallelujah as I do."

" I am burning inward, madam."

Passing groups upon verandas and at corners, we exclaim, " You are free!" Clapping our hands, they clap in return.

" Now we will all serve the Lord better!"

" O, yes, Missus! must do 'at now!" and " no 'scuse now!" "time enough now!" "too bad if don't now!" " too mean if don't do well!"

How affecting it was to see the tears fall from manly faces, as the minister, in the most unexciting manner, told them of the fact, and to see the lips move in praises. One dear aged aunt, after the close of the meeting, raising her hands, cried: " Now Lord lettest thou thy servant depart in peace, for mine eyes have seen thy salvation, more'n I hoped to see, do I all'ays prayed for it. Now I ready to die! Praise Jesus!"

All rejoiced in the most warm and dignified manner, and one, too full to speak, when asked how he felt, straightened up, and dropping arms by his side, energetically said, "I feel like a man, like a man." Oh, it was a glorious sight!

It is Emancipation Day Sabbath eve. We are too glad, to read, or sing. Even one of Beecher's sermons will not do to-night. We must think and rejoice. We step out upon the upper veranda, broad and high, and extending around three sides of the house. We are nearer to nature since the proclamation, or she takes us into her secrets more, because man is going to be just to man. There! the sun knows it! See him gaze through that live-oak, all a-glow with golden red, yet so chastened, that we can look him full in the face; and the whole firmament is reddening with joy. And there, just above the oak, at the opposite corner, is the moon, full-faced, brighter than we ever saw her, or by daylight, her features clear, and all on a broad grin. The blackbirds carry on their family quarrels, as usual, in the live-oaks, but to-night they actually seem to have a good object. Never did the tide sweep up so merrily, and lap the very highest mark so joyfully, as it nearly touches our yard. We thought we would cool off a little, and sent for some of the rejoicingly advancing water, and took a sea-bath in our chamber. But no! our excitement is only intensified. "What a land this will be, under freedom!" is upon every lip, and those who, one month since, saw little in South Carolina, are entranced, and beginning to talk of living here. The hum of conversation rings from every part of the lower veranda. All are too joyous for reading, or even closet exercises. Yes, joy, thanksgiving, are the appropriate duties of this emancipation Sabbath. God bless General Hunter! is upon every lip, and Oh, how the Colored do bless and pray for him! And he needs it. This emancipation act is but the commencement of the war, IT IS OUR NATION'S DECLARATION OF INDEPENDENCE, and the victory will follow.

Oh! if every man would press around those who take these initiatory steps, as you tide-waves press against every elevation! But what is human sustainment or applause. To-morrow morn those waves will be gone, a dead waste of sand, only, will be there. But there is that, in old ocean's heart, that will send them up again rejoicingly. So in the hearts of these noble men, there is, and will be, a strength that shall overmaster all things, and make the low mud of pro and anti-slavery contention, one broad, smooth sea of freedom.

THE CHORISTERS OF FREEDOM.

Last evening, first, after the proclamation by General Hunter, riding past a marsh, one of these singers cried out, "Freedom! freedom! freedom!" Another with a deeper bass, cried out, "Let it abound! let it abound! let it abound!" And a little freedom shrieker, like ourself, a little afraid that there would be some catch in legislation, cried intensely, "Explicit! explicit! explicit!" While a little politician, scared, and hidden by bushes, cried, "Quit! quit! quit! quit!" as if he would overpower everything. This stirs up the poor, faithful, adversity bird, ever singing in the night, who now commences, "Quit who will! quit who will! quit who will!" The dark bird upon the tree-top cries, "Craw! craw! craw!" Yes, he would like compromise, or reconstruction, anything to get a fill of carrion, and provide for it, in future. But a sweet voice comes up from the meadow, "You can't deceive me! you can't deceive me!" While the most honest and loving of birds, cries up to the screaming politician, "No more quit! no more quit! no more quit!" But the politician goes on, as for the last century, "Quit! quit! quit!" anything but progress for him. As we return, the fife, bugle, drum, all seem inspired, and soldiers stand more erect, with more musical walk, and look a joy unwonted, for most of them are free to say that "every life is a sacrifice to slavery," that "it is the cause of all they suffer." Holy song rises from the African church, and reaching home, all is of a hum of joy. All nature joins the anthem. We know not how Hunter's proclamation may fare. But, it is a step that no human power can ever retract, in effect, at least.

Our own hearts say, "Glory be to God in the highest, on earth peace, good will toward men! all men!"

THIS LAND IS TRANSFORMED.

The President's proclamation brought dawn, the emancipation in the District, light, the prospects from glowing official utterances, and Hunter's proclamation, sunshine. Everything is renewed and illumined with the light which comes from Washington, freedom. The boughs of the splendid live-oaks and sycamores bow their joy gracefully to each other, every leaf sparkling with delight. You white sail on the river speaks mercy! not slavery, the waters ripple in gladness at the multitudes of barks that shall use, and adorn them, instead of now, very seldom a poor boat rowed by broken-hearted slaves. Soldiers and officers wear an exultant look, as if to say, "I know what we are about now." "We suffer for an end, worthy of death now." Multitudes are saying "I think my home will be in the South," where none said it two months ago. And what is remarkable, none of them feel that the

Colored people will be at all in their way, so agreeable, so necessary do they become in this climate. All say, "These plantations cut up smaller giving the Negroes homes of their own and land surrounding them, would employ and sustain twice the number of hands with proper management." One, a judge, says, "there is land enough wasted on every plantation to sustain ten families." Masses of timber are rotting. Live-oaks that ought to bring hundreds, lost. Oysters good, a part of the year swelling out of the water like reefs of coral. Lands cleared, lying for years covered with underbrush, saying to the beholder, "we are cursed." Ornamental buildings lost for want of paint; fruit trees running to shoots rather than fruit; roads travelled for 200 years, in which the poor animal draws a light load with incredible gasping, sweating and loss of strength, from the knee-deep sand which gives him no foothold and impedes his wheels, where free labor will put roads, of planks at least, in six months. Ladies, going blocks around to a crossing place, rather than plunge into deep sand to cross the streets. We are no financiers and see not hundreds of wastes that such would see, yet so much is obvious even to us. Then this land wants everything, everything to eat, drink, wear, use, even with its present inhabitants. What would it be with such a population as will soon be here? And it will want and have the Negro. The sun is life to him which is death to the White man. "The whole secret of health here," said a learned military officer long acclimated, South, "is to keep out of the sun. Do that on the healthy shores, and the evening air is innoxious."

The Colored, in freedom, will not hoard, but spend money. They will dress, and ride, in good style. The table and house, will be secondary, usually. Imagine the trade set in motion the moment they get wages. What brisk market for everything conceivable.

CHAPTER LIII.

CAPTURE AND PASSAGE.

Their speaking of homes and of their capture, in Africa, is heart rending. An aged grandmother said, "The White men came round, so kind, and sociable, so loving,

> "Hark! from the ship's dark bosom,
>   The very sounds of hell!
> The ringing clank of iron—
>   The maniac's short, sharp yell!
> The hoarse, low curse, throat-stifled—
>   The starving infant's moan—
> The horror of a breaking heart
>   Poured through a mother's groan!"
>   Whittier.

came in our houses, lounge around, praise us, see our dances, all pleasant, eat with us, invite us all on board their ship to have a feast and dance. We all go, so happy. Dey 'pear so kind, and so good. Dey get seven hundred on board, then while we dance, 'ey sail. Then, Oh! how we cry. . Dey git pistol, shoot some 'at would get over. Oh, Lord, how awful! Then all crowded in little place. Some cry self to deff. Awful sick. Most quarter die. Dey make us come up, jump and jump. Some dies up dere. See sister put ober, dead. God help me pray! So come to 'is hard country. See home no mo'."

Gustavus Vassa, under like circumstances, says:

"What tumultuous emotions agitated my soul, when the convoy got under sail, and I, a prisoner on board, now without a hope! I kept my eyes upon the land, in a state of unutterable grief, not knowing what to do, and despairing how to help myself. While my mind was in this situation, the fleet sailed on, and I lost sight of land. In the first expression of my grief, I reproached my fate, and wished I had never been born. I was ready to curse the tide that bore us, the gale that wafted my prison, and even the ship that conducted us; and I called on death to relieve me from the horrors I felt."

Oh, what a prelude is all this, to every loss, every sorrow, every agony. My country! what hast thou done? or suffered to be done? Is there repentance? or shall we, as a nation, forget our sin, and ask so selfishly, "what is for self's interest?" that God shall consider us not worth preserving? Some awfully grand, or gloomy, future is before us. We must glorify the grace, or the wrath of God, uncommonly. He hath not so exalted us for a common destiny. This nation cannot have two interests—one for the North, another for the South. Every feature of nature, of brotherhood, forbids it. The South hates with the dire hatred of a brother, not the cool aversion of a stranger. But in the prayers and exertions of the righteous, there is hope, through God.

STILL inevitable destiny seems to attend the conscientious to sneak at some time, to act, not openly and frankly, but politically, at some period, and the worst of it is, it is just when he is most needed. So when the whole nation was at a glowing heat, at the firing upon Fort Sumter, those who had despised that course, said, "Now let's whist," and "Let the anti-slavery sentiment grow." Just as if the smith's iron would grow into a chain.

No, they should have moulded the seething mass, not suffered it to cool into an impervious crust. There has never been such a moment since it, for moulding the public mind, the firing the public heart. And yet there have been moments, as when the noble Ellsworth fell, when Baker and Lyon, and when Winthrop and Perry fell, when it seemed that some who have a very high estimate of their being gigantic "oaks," in the literary world, might have thought the occasion sufficient for their great powers. And some beautiful sentences, yes, articles did flow forth, and some stanzas. But where is the mere literary man, that has followed up the subject, with stroke after stroke, to form and weld public sentiment? They ought to toil as hard, if need be, to do this, as those poor soldiers in the trenches, or upon the battle-field. True, magazines have contained some fine articles. But where is the Johnson of our anti-rebellion war? Our Hampdens and Sidneys we have. Our Sumners, Harlans, Lovejoys, Chandlers, etc. But where, in all colleges, is the Luther, that nails his great truths to the posts and doors? We have most noble editors—deep is the gratitude of the good for them. How have they fought. But the heart could weep when it feels how they have been permitted to stand alone. Most prize, but what magazine speaks nobly for them, in just, lengthy, able articles, honorable to them, liberty, and our nation? It is noble for a nation to love to exalt writers of the living present. England knows to do that. But America loves to show her acuteness by lowering hers.

Never did nobler men live than some who have graced our late Congress. Never were nobler sentiments uttered in a legislative body. Yet few magazines or reviews know it? Were it not wiser, than to go back and resuscitate some semi-savage, who, like many old philosophers, would not be tolerated now. Is a man that suffers mentally, all that mortal can, for a great truth, not to be delineated? May he be picked to a skeleton, by the meanest raven that ever said "craw," and whose weapons he will not stoop to use, and none regard it? What mere literary man will deserve mention, as a great aid, when the history of this rebellion is written? Editors there will be, lecturers, legislators, ministers of Christ, but what literary man is felt weekly, Whittier, excepted? And surely his muse ought to favor him, and us, oftener. Such men should toil as in the war, and see their influence, upon the public daily, renewed and deepened. There are others, whose rare articles just show what they might do.

Do WE GO TOO FAR IN PRAISE of the Colored in this work. Let facts speak. Take the city of New York. Where are your Colored beer gardens, theatres, free lunch, and free concert rooms, and gambling, drinking and other dens? Where? When do you see a policeman having one in custody? Old residents answer, never. Where do you see the Colored making themselves terrible to the timid as drivers, or in cars by untidiness? When strutting along, cigar in mouth, the very personification of sensuality, or begging? But visit their churches. You shall wonder that there are so many, and two-thirds of them throughout the whole country, are consistent church members. Visit their schools, you shall be amazed at the number, when you so very seldom, or never, see a Colored child at play in the streets.

How painful to close a volume, when so much remains to be said. But if the Holy Spirit deign to use it, little is effectual.

www.ingramcontent.com/pod-product-compliance
Lightning Source LLC
Chambersburg PA
CBHW031904220426
43663CB00006B/760